Four Legs :

Four Legs and a Tale

Alan Walker

Best Wishes

Alan

LIVE WIRE

Published in 2014 by

Live Wire Books,
The Orchard, School Lane,
Warmington, Banbury,
Oxfordshire OX17 1DE
www.livewirebooks.com

ISBN: 978-0-9553124-8-9

Printed and bound in Dubai by Oriental Press

Contents

Foreword   vii

Prologue   viii

1   A Family Tradition   1

2   To The Manor Borne   11

3   If At First You Don't Succeed …   26

4   On Yer Bike!   49

5   Walker & Son   63

6   An Inspector Calls   76

7   Horse Whisperer   89

8   'The Guv'nor'   101

9   'The Missus'   119

10   Extra Training   149

11   A Grand Tour   165

12   Conduct Unbecoming   181

13   Picking Up The Pieces   195

14   Olympic Games Maker   228

Epilogue   240

Appendix   242

Acknowledgements   246

Foreword

It was seven o'clock one morning when Alan Walker approached Gary's door. He was met with an icy glare, the eyes rolled upwards and quickly turned to dark crimson: "Oh sorry, Gary, it's nice to see you in your usual frame of mind," said Alan as he stepped back sharply from the door, while removing the brown smock coat he always wore when he was doing any veterinary work in my stable yard.

Garrison Savannah wasn't too keen on vets. If they were to enter into his space they had to abide by his rules: no brown smocks – and no spitting from the farrier, either, as he removed the last nail from between his teeth whilst tacking on Gary's shoes. A mutual respect between the vet and Gary was essential, or someone was going to end up in bandages.

It was amusing to watch Alan and Gary together. There was an unspoken "don't hurt me and I won't hurt you" kind of feel in the air.

Alan Walker has been a vet to my horses during the good times and the bad times. You understand the depth and qualities of such a man when he remains by your side as you steer through the storms. Alan Walker helped me navigate through those storms not only on a professional basis but also on a personal one.

My family and I have a huge respect for Alan. His kindness and treatment of my horses, much of which you won't find in a medical journal, enabled us to celebrate many successes that at times were totally unrealistic.

Thank you, Alan, for being there for us all.

Jenny Pitman
July 2014

Prologue: Judgement Day

"The committee has given careful consideration to the submissions made on Dr Walker's behalf: an oral statement given by Mrs Pitman, who attributed a lot of her success as a trainer to Dr Walker's veterinary skill over many years; and a letter from Dr Webbon, until recently Chief Executive of the Horse Racing Regulatory Authority, was also presented, testifying to Dr Walker's excellent clinical judgement and professionalism.

The Committee regards false certification on two separate and similar occasions as being an extremely serious matter and has considered the possible sanctions in ascending order of severity in this case. Therefore it has given anxious consideration to either a suspension or removal from the Register as being the most appropriate sanction.

The Committee acknowledges in his favour the frankness of Dr Walker in his admission of the facts, but also took into consideration that Dr Walker is well known in the racing world, holds a senior position in the Association of Racecourse Veterinary Surgeons, and ought to have known the significance of his actions. The Committee has decided that the only appropriate course is to instruct the Registrar to remove Dr Walker's name from the Register."

Struck off the Register! These are the words every professional person hopes they will never hear. For me, they were delivered by the Chairman of the Disciplinary Committee of the Royal College of Veterinary Surgeons (RCVS) at approximately 4.30pm on Tuesday, 30th January, 2007.

We were totally devastated. Words cannot express the depths of despair we felt as we adjourned once more to the small waiting room in silence. What little conversation there was between us was forced and hesitant. My barrister advised us to go home as there was nothing more to be done for the time being. So, with the words of sympathy and support from Jenny Pitman, her husband David Stait and my legal and professional advisors echoing in our ears, I and my wife, Diana, walked slowly and in numbed silence from Belgravia House, down Horseferry Road to the River Thames, along Millbank and past Westminster Abbey and the Houses of Parliament.

I felt a mixture of emotions. I was bewildered, confused, angry. I felt that the whole world already knew what had transpired and that people were looking at me, pointing their fingers, accusing me of being a disgrace. And then it seemed that my whole life was unfolding before my eyes in a series of flashbacks – my childhood, the rich and varied Walker family history of involvement with animals for over 300 years, my immediate family. How was I going to tell the children?

The frustration of having to wait and study for fifteen years before at last realising my lifelong ambition of qualifying as a Veterinary Surgeon; the building of a modern and highly successful veterinary practice with state-of-the-art facilities and fourteen full-time Veterinary Surgeons plus support staff; the interest I had developed in horse racing from a very early age, eventually going on to work professionally with some of the country's most successful trainers and to become actively involved in promoting the safety and welfare of racehorses through the Association of Racecourse Vets. All this reduced to nothing by those stinging words that still echo in my ears: "Remove Dr Walker's name from the Register."

My wife, always my rock, was at my side, a strong, calm, reassuring presence. "We'll get through this," she insisted. "We *will* get through this!" The journey back to Oxfordshire was long and painful. And yet I was about to discover, in the most extraordinary circumstances, the truth of the old saying that it is only in times of adversity that you find out who your true friends are.

1

A Family Tradition

"I can die a happy man knowing that you have got a son to carry on the family tradition." These were among the very last words spoken by my grandfather, William 'Doc' Walker, to my father, Jack, after being fatally injured in a road accident the day after Boxing Day, 1946. I had been born just a few months earlier, on July 18th, 1946.

The Walkers have been working with animals in the same rural area on the Oxfordshire/Warwickshire border for over three hundred years, first as farriers and then as cow doctors, castrators, veterinary practitioners and veterinary surgeons. It has been an almost uniquely unbroken father-to-son succession, stretching back at least nine generations and possibly even more. Sadly, it seems I am destined to be the last of this long line, as my son and daughter have both chosen very different career paths.

The surname Walker is thought to have derived from the fulling trade, fulling being a shrinking process that makes woven wool fabrics firmer and more compact and which used to be carried out in what was known as a 'walk' mill. At first this industry was confined mostly to the north and east of England and there are no records of Walkers in South Warwickshire before the 14th century. But as sheep farming and the woollen industry generally spread throughout the country over the next two hundred years or so, migrants of that name moved in.

The village of Long Compton, the family home from the time parish records began in the 17th century until my father moved just a mile or two up the road, lies in a valley at the southernmost tip of Warwickshire, close to the border with Oxfordshire, and is steeped in folklore and dark tales of witchcraft. Overlooking the village from the south are the Rollright Stones – the single King Stone, the King's Men stone circle and the Whispering Knights burial chamber, together dating back over 2,000 years. To the east is a narrow road known as Jacob's Ladder.

The village is situated on what used to be the main coach route from Oxford to Birmingham and includes three former lodges where passengers could rest while the horses were changed. There was therefore plenty of work for farriers and over the years some of them, including the Walkers, naturally acquired some basic veterinary skills and, in addition to merely shoeing horses, began to offer advice and treatments to local farmers for all their animals.

Towards the end of the 19th century the railway networks then developed, providing transport not only for people but for livestock as well. Sheep and cattle were regularly transported on the Great Western line from Wales to Moreton-in-Marsh before then being driven due east cross-country to the big cattle market in Banbury. The most direct route involved having to pass through a series of tollgates along the way, but some of these could be avoided by diverting through Long Compton and up Jacob's Ladder, so the village retained something of its strategic importance in the area. Not only could drovers avoid having to pay tolls – they could also drop in on the Walkers on their way through to pick up potions and to get treatment for any ailing stock.

By that time, the family's reputation as veterinary practitioners was already long established in the area. My great-great-great-great-great-great grandfather John (1674-1737) was the first Walker to be officially identified as a farrier, or 'horse doctor', in the earliest surviving Long Compton parish register. His son Joseph John (1708-71), grandson Frederick (1735-92) and great grandson John (1779-1832) all followed in his footsteps as farriers. His great-great grandson Joseph (1810-1884) then became the first to describe himself as a veterinary surgeon, although this was something of an anomaly as no formal training or qualification was required in those days.

However, another distant ancestor of mine, Bracy Clark – whose paternal grandmother, Margaret, was the sister of the John Joseph Walker mentioned above – had the great distinction of being one of the first students to enrol at the Veterinary College of London, now the Royal Veterinary College, when it opened in 1791. He is also said to have led the first horse into the infirmary when that was opened there the following year. The very first establishment of its kind in this country, the college had come into being thanks largely to the extraordinary success of one legendary racehorse. Eclipse, so called because there was a total eclipse of the sun on the day that he was born in 1764, swept all before him during the British racing seasons of 1769 and 1770 and retired to stud having never been beaten. RCVS research shows that eighty per cent of all modern thoroughbreds are descended from him.

Eclipse had become such a famous and important horse that when he eventually died in 1789 his owner and others in the racing establishment were keen to carry out a proper post-mortem in an effort to find out not only the exact cause of his death, but also whether there was anything in his physical make-up that could be identified as the secret of his phenomenal and unprecedented success on the racetrack. The only qualified veterinarian in the country at the time was a Frenchman, Charles Benoit Vial de St Bel, who already had it in his mind to start a veterinary school here. And following the eagerly-awaited publication of his Eclipse post mortem findings, his ideas for a school swiftly gained support, principally from the Odiham Agricultural Society, whose members had also recognised the need to encourage better understanding of animal husbandry and the treatment of disease.

Bracy Clark, who came from Chipping Norton, just down the road from Long Compton, studied under St Bel and then went on himself to become one of the country's leading equine vets, specialising in the care and treatment of horses' hooves. He wrote a series of books and pamphlets on the subject and in 1806, having concluded that the common shoeing practices of the day were causing damage to horses, patented a new type of shoe. With a practice in London, he soon established a world-wide reputation, becoming a Fellow of the Linnean Society – still the world's oldest biological and natural history society – and also a Member of the Institut de France and Ecole de Medecine, the Royal Societies of Berlin, Frankfurt, Copenhagen and Stuttgart and an Honorary Member of the Natural History Society of New York.

None of the Walkers managed to reach quite such exalted heights, but they did continue to serve the local community around Long Compton with distinction for generation after generation.

By the late 19th century, Joseph's son Alfred, my great grandfather, was one of around eight hundred vets practicing throughout the country, his own patch covering an area contained within a nine-mile radius of Long Compton. He lived there at Nightbell Cottage, so-named because there was a special bell outside the house that could be rung to summon him in an emergency by any client whose animals needed treatment during the night. Well respected locally for his veterinary skills and, in particular, for his extensive knowledge about traditional herbal treatments, he became even more widely famed for a time as the owner of the fastest trotting horse in the Four Shires of Warwickshire, Worcestershire, Gloucestershire and Oxford-shire. He had bought the horse from the Allen family, farmers and breeders from High Furze Farm at Tidmington, just outside Shipston-on-Stour. He managed to get it at a knock-down price on account of it being lame, but he had already diagnosed the cause of the problem as being a shoulder that was out of alignment, something he was able to sort out very successfully by taking the horse swimming. Restored to full fitness, the animal became his pride and joy, beating all opposition.

Alfred, however, was not an easy man to get along with by all accounts. Even his son William, my grandfather, found him difficult and almost impossible to work with, despite the fact that Alfred had provided him with all his early veterinary education, which included passing on all the secrets of his natural herbal remedies. From his father the young William learned how to make his own drenches and powders by boiling oak bark, was shown how poppy heads could be used for poultices and how ground ivy, agrimony, deadly nightshade, foxgloves, mallow and comfrey could be collected for use in various other herbal recipes, either taken from Alfred's own carefully guarded records, passed down through the family, or from other traditional sources. The only thing the old man wouldn't teach his son for some reason was how to castrate colts, so William took himself off to learn that particular skill from Ernest Taylor at Swell, going on to become officially registered as a Castrator.

Known affectionately to one and all as 'Doc', William was said to have "the gift of the veterinary". A striking figure in later life, with his grey bowler hat, cloth gaiters and elegant beard, he was a much easier-going and altogether more likeable character than his father, befriending his clients and becoming a central part of rural community life and a pillar of local society, respected far and wide. As soon as he married and started a family, William moved up the road from Nightbell Cottage to 50 Long Compton, where he set up his own veterinary practice.

Working as a country vet in late Victorian England was no easy business. Doing the rounds of remote farms and smallholdings by pony and trap, in all weathers and often along rough tracks that were sometimes almost impassable, could be physically demanding and not always financially rewarding. Times, generally, were hard, especially in rural areas. There was very little money about and farmers and horse owners were reluctant to pay anything but the very minimum, if even that, for the veterinary's services. Many of William's clients resorted to barter, paying him in kind with bacon, eggs, milk, butter, vegetables and any other spare produce they had available. Some simply couldn't afford to pay anything at all and had to ask for credit. 'Doc' was the kind of man who would never refuse to treat an animal in need, whatever the circumstances, and it was this community-spirited sense of understanding that helped to build his reputation and explained why he came to be held in such great esteem throughout the locality.

Communication in those days was not straightforward. Farmers or horse owners would often send their children on ponies or horses to deliver a message or collect drugs from the Walkers at Long Compton. Requests for a routine visit were frequently made by letter or in person when client and vet bumped into each other at a local market or fayre.

William had five children altogether, and his two sons – my father Joseph John, always known as 'Jack', and my uncle Alfred, 'Alf' to one and all – both started their veterinary education at a very young age, accompanying their father on his rounds during the school holidays. As already mentioned, transport then was by pony and trap, with a rubber coating put on the wheels to make for a more comfortable ride. William kept a selection of ponies, one for each day of the week, with a faster one in reserve for emergencies. Tommy, the brown pony, Kit, the little grey and the old mule were his favourites. On average he would travel twenty miles or more on his daily rounds – a considerable distance when relying on horsepower alone. When the boys first started going with him and were still very small, their job was simply to hop on and off to open and close the gates on the many gated roads and tracks across the fields, helping to speed up the journeys.

As they got older and were ready to start learning the ropes in preparation for carrying on the family business, they provided a source of cheap, not to say unpaid labour, employed as gofers to fetch and carry and generally make themselves useful. For instance, during the lamb-tailing season, when the lambs' tails would be docked using a hot iron (today the same task would be performed by the shepherd, using tight rubber rings) the boys would be responsible for making sure that the irons were kept at the correct temperature, while also helping to catch and hold the patients steady while they were being treated. They also acted as delivery boys, riding their ponies cross-country to clients with various drugs and potions.

There were no antibiotics then, of course, and no drugs wholesalers as such, so vets would make up all their own prescriptions, mostly from plants, herbs and other natural ingredients that they had collected from the fields and hedgerows. And there were no telephones, so Jack and Alf would also act as messenger boys, no doubt getting a great thrill out of galloping across the fields like the Wild West's Pony Express riders. Many of the farms were isolated and sometimes the farmers did not see any other people for long periods, so the arrival of the vet was eagerly anticipated as they knew he would have plenty of news and gossip to relay. In that way, the vet was a bit like their local newspaper.

Jack, in particular, was an accomplished horseman who rode everywhere, with nothing more than a hessian sack to serve as a saddle. With his best friend, Gig Shepherd, he would ride for many miles to take part in gymkhanas as far afield as Overbury, Tewkesbury and Stanway, excelling in show jumping and pony racing events despite the lack of a proper saddle. Wild, high-spirited and stubborn in his younger days, he was a constant source of concern for his father, always in trouble for some mischievous prank or other – things like tying an old tin can to a dog's tail and watching it run clattering down the road; putting a marble in a donkey's ear to see it gallop and buck; or suddenly blowing a hunting horn near horses that were pulling a cart and watching in delight as they charged off.

At the age of eleven he went to Bloxham School, first riding from Long Compton to Great Rollright, where he would then catch a local Banbury branch line train for the rest of the journey to Bloxham, leaving his pony to graze in a paddock until his return in the evening. Having left school at the earliest opportunity, he was sent by his father to work for an elderly local farmer friend named Tweedale, another pillar of the local community, who owned two farms – one at Long Compton and another about five miles away at Granby. The idea was that Jack would not only further his agricultural education and gain experience of working with animals, but might also learn to quieten down a bit under Mr Tweedale's stern and watchful eye. In respect of the latter aim, it didn't really seem to work too well at first.

Like Jack's father, Mr Tweedale was a God-fearing man, a leader of the local non-conformist congregation and a lay preacher. One Sunday evening, after preaching at Long Compton, he and Jack were on their way back to Granby in a horse-drawn trap when he handed Jack the reins and said: "You take over – I'm feeling a bit tired." He then proceeded to nod off, whereupon Jack started to encourage the horse to go faster and faster. Jolted awake with a sudden start, the old man exclaimed: "Jack, you are a veritable Jehu!", adding: "I don't suppose you have heard that name before?"

"Of course I have, " retorted Jack. "Jehu was Lord Roseberry's horse that won The Oaks."

Back at Granby, a Bible was produced and two hours later my father-to-be knew all about Jehu, son of Jehoshophat and a fearsomely warlike King of Israel in the 9th century BC, who was notorious among other things for driving his chariot "furiously" (2 Kings 9).

Overall Mr Tweedale did actually have a good influence on Jack, who found that he liked working on the farm and did eventually start to settle down. Meanwhile, however, his father had developed asthma, which meant he was no longer physically able to do some of the heavy veterinary work, so Jack returned home to help him out.

By now the pony and trap had been partly replaced by a Ford car, known affectionately as 'Tin Lizzie'. Jack taught himself to drive so that he could chauffeur his father on his daily rounds.

As well as the fetching and carrying that he had done as a young boy, he was now allowed to help with the examination of sick animals when no-one else was around. Then, on the way home, he and Doc would discuss the cases and suggested treatments. They found increasingly that they got on and worked well together. Unlike his own father, Doc taught Jack how to castrate colts while they were standing up, how to prepare the pegs and the anti-microbial dressings. He also sent him to Suffolk to learn about the latest techniques from Mr Bergen, a famous vet in that part of the country.

As time went on, Jack gradually found himself doing more and more and was especially proud when he managed, on his own, to calve a cow with quadruplets. "Son," said Doc, bursting with pride. "You have just calved a cow with four live calves, something your old dad has never done!"

The one thing Jack hated doing was docking the tails of foals. It was still common practice then, the foals heavily restrained while the tails were burned off, the hair then sold to the makers of rocking horses and to fairground operators to be used for the tails and manes of the Ginny horses on the carousels. Mercifully, this cruel and barbaric practice has long since been banned.

With the business thriving and Jack and Doc working ever more closely together, they became, to all intents and purposes, a fully-fledged partnership, advertising themselves in the local press and elsewhere as:

W.J. Walker and Son
Castrators
Long Compton, Shipston-on-Stour
Horses and Calves castrated without throwing
Operations carefully performed: ruptured colts a
speciality
Bulls rung: Distance no object
Infallible remedy for Scour in Calves

Although still confining himself mainly to the area around Long Compton and Shipston, Doc would occasionally venture as far afield as Oxford. The first time he had gone there, shortly after starting up his own practice, was to geld a colt and he charged the client one guinea. On his return to Long Compton his father, Alfred was outraged, insisting that it was a complete waste of time to travel so far for so little. However, the next time he went to Oxford he came back with fifty gold sovereigns, proudly explaining to Alfred that the main purpose of his initial trip had been to advertise himself to the horse owners and dealers there and to show them just what he could do in the hope of generating the new business that had now duly come his way.

One of the regular clients he picked up in this way was John Benson, a leading horse breeder and dealer, well-known throughout the Midlands and the South of England, who was based at Dunmore Farm in Abingdon. Over the years, Doc had often been accompanied on his visits to Abingdon by his sons, with what would turn out to be significant long-term consequences for the Walker family, me in particular. John Benson had a very large family, with no less than sixteen children of whom the youngest daughter, Kathleen, was an extremely attractive girl who soon caught the eye of young Jack. She went on to become his wife – and my mother.

2

To The Manor Borne

My parents, Jack and Kathleen, were married in 1937 and I was born nine years later, the youngest of their four children. Sadly, their firstborn, my older brother Joseph, died very shortly after a traumatic home birth that left my mother confined to a wheelchair and facing the possibility that she might never walk again, let alone have any more children. But Kathleen was a strong and extremely determined woman and was not only back on her feet within a matter of months, but went on to produce my older sisters Pat and Margaret and then me.

One of my earliest childhood memories is of riding with my sisters on the back of a flatbed trailer loaded with furniture and towed by an old-fashioned Allis Chalmers tractor that had been loaned to my parents by a local farmer friend, Joe Hirons, to help them move house. It was the spring of 1949. I was coming up to three years old, Pat was eight and Margaret five. As we were lifted onto the trailer we were told in no uncertain terms not to play around or jump up and down – and, most importantly, not to fall off.

The family was on the move from Mavis Croft, the house in Long Compton where we had been living since my father moved out of his parents' home at 50 Long Compton after getting married, to Burmington Manor, just three miles up the road. The move away from Long Compton was very much Kathleen's idea and did not meet with universal approval. Even my father was not initially convinced – the Walkers had been running their business from the village since time immemorial and his mother had warned him that he would never succeed outside Long Compton and would only bring shame on the family if he moved away. But Kathleen, who had never quite seen eye-to-eye with her mother-in-law, was quoted as telling her bluntly: "I married your son, not his family." She had set her heart on moving to the small manor house in Burmington, which dated back to the time of Oliver Cromwell and came with fourteen acres of land, and she managed to persuade Jack that it was the right thing to do. An old friend of hers, Eric Stratton, was duly sent along to the auction, where he secured the property for £3,000. This was an enormous amount of money in those days, certainly more than my parents could really afford, and they were forced to borrow in order to meet the cost. This further alarmed Jack, but merely galvanized Kathleen into action as she threw herself into restoring the beautiful but dilapidated old property.

Apart from a period during the war when it had been occupied by evacuees from Coventry, the rambling stone-built house had not been lived in for years and had become seriously run-down. The roof leaked, the paintwork was faded and flaking and the outbuildings had been reduced to little more than rubble. There was no running water or electricity and the only heating came from open fires, with the result that the whole place was cold, draughty and damp for much of the time, the wind whistling through ill-fitting window frames.

The facilities in the large kitchen, where we spent most of our time when we first moved in, consisted of little more than an ancient wood-burning Rayburn range cooker and a vast old Belfast sink, with a rough wooden bench serving as a draining board. However, there was a spacious pantry next door, in which the temperature remained constantly cool whatever the weather, and an exquisite flagstone floor. I can clearly remember my mother washing that floor down every day – and woe betide any of us who walked on it while it was still wet.

Like most small boys I was very adventurous and spent many hours happily exploring the grounds and buildings, oblivious to the lack of mod cons and other home comforts. Meanwhile, as a succession of builders very gradually helped to renovate the house and outbuildings, my parents worked overtime to make ends meet.

My mother set about creating a large vegetable garden that eventually extended to about a quarter of an acre, all of which she dug out and planted herself. It wasn't long before we were completely self-sufficient in fruit and vegetables. We also kept our own cows, pigs and chickens. We had three Jersey cows that my father milked by hand before and after work each day. He used to claim that it helped to keep his hands soft and supple for his veterinary work. We drank the rich, unpasteurized milk and my mother used the cream to make butter that she sold locally to help towards paying some of the household bills. She also sold eggs to the local packing station, a lorry calling each week to collect them, while walnuts from our two prized trees were sold mainly at Stratford-upon-Avon market in the lead-up to Christmas.

Once or twice a year, amidst great excitement mixed with a certain amount of tearful regret, a pig would be slaughtered and butchered on the premises. Every bit of the animal would be used, including the trotters and the ears. In those days nobody had freezers, so hams and bacon would have to be salted or smoked. Father always laid claim to the lard for use in his potions and ointments.

Running free in this wonderfully old-fashioned rural environment, I enjoyed a largely idyllic childhood, marred by only a couple of unhappy experiences. The first came when we had been at Burmington for about two years and my mother noticed that some bald patches had started to appear on my head, along with a rash of small blisters. Ringworm was diagnosed and I was whisked off to the John Radcliffe Infirmary in Oxford. I was admitted immediately and stayed in for two weeks, during which time I was miserable and homesick.

All my hair had to be shaved off and my skull was treated with ultra-violet light. My bed was by the window, looking out onto Walton Street, and while only parents were officially allowed to visit me, my two sisters would throw sweets in to me through the window. Needless to say, the matron caught us red-handed and we were severely reprimanded. She confiscated the sweets but, much worse, had my bed moved to the other side of the room, away from the window. With nothing to look out at, this made life even more intolerably boring. The ward was spotlessly clean and always smelled clinically fresh, but I missed my family, especially my sisters.

At the end of this little ordeal I was only too happy to get home to my adventure playground in Burmington, despite having to wear a woolly hat on my shaven head to keep me warm. Best of all, I was given a Golden Labrador puppy as a reward for being a brave soldier. I named her Amber. She was a wonderful dog and we became inseparable, except that she had to live outside in one of the sheds as my parents wouldn't let her in the house. Tragically, when she was five years old she was caught worrying sheep and was shot on the spot. I was obviously devastated and cried my eyes out, but was made to understand that sheep are completely defenceless when out in the fields and that dogs must never be allowed to worry them. It was nevertheless a hard lesson to learn for a small boy robbed of his constant and faithful four-legged friend. I thought the end of the world had come and although I understood the reasons, I vowed never to get as close to a dog again.

There was never a time that I can remember when I wasn't surrounded by animals – dogs, cats, chickens, pigs, sheep and cattle as well as horses and ponies that I learned to ride at a very early age. I loved them all, helping with the feeding and the mucking out and also holding them steady whenever my father needed to treat them for any reason. The little piglets had teeth as sharp as needles and had to have them clipped so that they wouldn't injure the mother's teats when they were suckling. We had to make sure the sow was locked securely away while we dealt with her babies, who would wriggle, squirm and squeal, especially when they were being given their iron injections. I had to hold on to them very tightly because I knew I would be in big trouble if I let one go. It was the same with the hens, which had to have their wings clipped to stop them flying away.

In the spring our cows would be moved from the paddocks at Burmington, where they had spent the winter months, and walked the three miles up the road to their summer pastures in Long Compton and, from a very early age, I would be allowed to help with this, too. Rope halters would be put on the gently lumbering beasts and I would then lead them along the grass verges and occasional footpaths that bordered the old A34, now the A44, giving them a tug every time they tried to stop and graze. Of course, the main road traffic in the early 1950s was nothing like it is today, but, even so, I was only six years old when I first started helping out with this mini cattle drive. And yet nobody thought anything of it at the time.

I remember being rather puzzled at first when I was very small by all the other animals, mostly horses, that people would regularly bring to the house and which would sometimes stay on for a while in our stables and paddocks. At the same time, I was also curious about what went on in the large, white-painted wooden building just outside the back door where my father and his frequent visitors spent so much time, but from which we children were banned. This, of course, was the surgery, as I soon discovered once I was old enough to understand the nature of my father's business and became more familiar with his daily work routine.

This would start at 6.00am with the feeding of the animals and the milking of the cows. The milk would be carried back to the kitchen in two metal pails and while my father then tucked into a hearty breakfast of eggs, bacon and fried bread that would set him up for the day, my mother would strain the milk through muslin cloth into large, flattish china bowls that would be placed on wooden tables in the pantry and left, undisturbed, for twenty-four hours, allowing the cream to separate and float to the top. This would then be scooped off and decanted into jars of varying sizes, some of it to be churned into butter, while the skimmed milk would be used in the house, with any surplus being fed to the pigs along with swill made from any food leftovers.

After breakfast, the calls would start coming in from clients requiring his services and my father would plan his rounds, logging appointments in the daybook that stood next to the phone in the sitting room. All these years later I can still clearly remember the number – Shipston-on-Stour 157. Anything urgent would always be fitted into that day's round, while routine treatments might have to wait until he was next going to be in the caller's area. Each appointment logged in the daybook had the client's telephone number next to it so that my mother would know where to contact her husband if a sudden emergency were to arise. In the days long before mobile phones, this was the only way of keeping in touch with Jack when he was out and about on his rounds. If my mother had to go out and be away from the phone, she would ring the ladies in the telephone exchange in Shipston-on-Stour to let them know where he was due to be at certain times so that they could put through any really urgent calls to him there.

By the time Jack went into practice on his own the days of the pony and trap were over and he always had cars – first inheriting his father's Model T Ford, 'Tin Lizzie', before moving on to a succession of various other Fords, Morrises and, later, Volvos and Fiats. He would set off each morning, after first dealing with any clients who had arranged to come to the surgery, and would then often be out all day.

I would occasionally peep into the open daybook, and on a busy day the list of entries, all noted down in ink in his remarkably neat handwriting, might include: lame horse; colt to cut; colic; cow with milk fever; calves to castrate; cows to dehorn; feet to trim; horse with cough; horse with warts; horse with swollen leg; drench; feet to trim. Sometimes he would be very late coming home and my mother would glance at the entries in the daybook and, noting which client was last on the list of visits, would suspect instantly that he was likely to have stayed on for a chinwag over a drink or two!

"I don't how he will manage to milk those poor cows," she would mutter impatiently. But, as I recall, he always did. He would certainly never get his supper until he had done so!

After he had eaten he would usually get down to the paper-work, booking the details of the various treatments he had carried out during the day and all the prescriptions he had dis-pensed. Sometimes, however, he would put off this chore for a day or two, or even, occasionally, for as long as a week. He didn't make notes as he went along, so it was all done from memory, which was fine unless he had been entertained a little too well by his pals somewhere along the line! In that case, the level of concentration required when the time eventually came for him to catch up was such that no noise at all would be tolerated in the house or he would fly off the handle.

My parents were both extremely hardworking and, together, they made a very good team. Mother was the driving force, run-ning the household, looking after me and my sisters, tending the large vegetable garden and taking responsibility for the chick-ens, the pigs and the rest of our menagerie, while my father was more than fully occupied with the business from dawn til dusk. He loved his work, was happy with his lifestyle and got on well with his clients, most of whom became his friends. And if he worked hard, it is true to say that he also played hard. A true country character, always highly thought of and still remem-bered with great respect by nearly all who knew him, he was an excellent raconteur – especially when primed with a few glasses of Scotch – and his tales of the countryside, of horses and hunt-ing and the great old farming and horse-racing families that he had got to know so well in his capacity as a vet were legendary, as was his repertoire of colourful case histories, in particular those relating to famous racehorses, their owners and trainers.

However, it has to be said that he wasn't always the easiest man to get on with. If he liked you, he would do anything for you. But if he didn't take to you, he could be very awkward. At the same time, rather surprisingly for someone who was notoriously short-tempered, he could be a very good and patient teacher as long as you were keen to learn.

My own elementary veterinary education began almost literally at his knee. From the time I was a toddler it had been obvious that I was very much at home with animals and having gradually become more and more involved in helping my father with the treatment of our own hens, pigs, horses and cows I was finally allowed to go with him into the surgery, which served mainly as the dispensary where he made up all his own medications – powders, ointments, drenches and so on.

My first venture inside what had always previously been a strictly enforced no-go area was a truly magical experience as far as I was concerned. As I stepped inside my nostrils were immediately assailed by strange clinical smells that I didn't recognize – camphor, iodine, aniseed and peppermint. Eyes out on stalks, I found myself looking at row upon row of brightly coloured bottles in all sorts of odd shapes and sizes, the contents of which were used in the preparation of some of his medications. There was a selection of corks to fit the various bottles and an implement that looked like a nutcracker, but which I soon discovered was used to compact the softened corks before they were inserted so as to ensure an airtight seal.

Some of the bottles had glass stoppers. It was explained to me that the liquids inside were extremely dangerous, so powerfully corrosive that they could eat through cork. The very names on the labels – Antimony Trichloride, Caustic Soda, Sulphuric Acid – conveyed a distinct air of menace and I listened wide-eyed as I was given grave warnings about what would happen if they were ever to get on your skin. I couldn't help wondering what would actually happen if you dipped your finger into the bottles. Would the flesh and bone just bubble and melt away amid a hiss of vapour? Fortunately, even as an extremely curious young boy, I was never tempted to experiment.

Alongside the shelves of bottles was an antique apothecary's cabinet containing a large number of deep wooden drawers about eight inches square, each with a little brass knob and a small brass frame into which was slotted a cardboard label identifying contents such as Potassium Nitrate, Nux Vomica, Glaubers, Epsom, Verdigris, Sulphur, Aloes, Poppy Seeds, Agrimony, Resin, Colophony and Belladonna.

Most intriguing of all to me at the time was a large locked cupboard at one end of the room, the door of which was adorned with a picture of a skull and crossbones and underneath, in large letters, the word POISON. I remember being both fascinated and mildly terrified by the thought of what might be hidden inside.

At first, I was allowed into the surgery only as an observer, watching in fascination as my father made up his medications. He was both methodical and meticulous. He would always start by donning one of the white coats that hung on pegs behind the door. There were always four coats hanging there – two white and two brown. The white ones – kept spotlessly clean by my mother, who changed them on a regular basis – were for use only in the surgery. The brown ones were for when he was working outside. But wherever he was working, inside or out, he always wore his flat cap.

There were no taps or running water in the surgery. Before he started work there, water would be heated over the open fire in the scullery and then poured into a tin bowl coated with enamel. This would then be carried out to the surgery and placed on the workbench along with a folded towel and a bar of Wrights coal tar soap. On the window sill there would always be an onion cut in half to nullify any harmful fumes. This would be changed as soon as the cut surfaces became mouldy, which, Dad explained, was a good sign, indicating that the onion was doing its job in cleaning the air.

If he was going to be making up potions and powders, he would have his own handwritten recipe book beside him, open at the relevant page, along with all the necessary ingredients, a set of scales and weights, a pestle and mortar, a sieve, some brown paper bags, string with which to tie them up, bottles and labels. His precious book, 'Walkers Wonder Cures', was filled with over a hundred different recipes for preparations to be used in the treatment of everything from wounds to warts, from mange to mud fever, from sore throats to saddle sores and from colic to cracked heels. Each ingredient would be carefully weighed out, ground up with a pestle and mortar if necessary and then sieved before being very carefully mixed together in a bucket. This was one of the jobs I was actually allowed to help with after a while, but I always struggled to get it right at first. I was told that his reputation depended on getting a perfectly even and consistent mix every time and I would have to keep on trying until it was done to his complete satisfaction. He would then tidy up again before going on to the next stage, which involved grating nutmeg, cinnamon or some other spice into the mixture. Different spices would be added to the various powders depending on what condition they were designed to treat, but this part of the process remained a secret that he wouldn't tell even me about, saying only that it was Walker's Special!

When it came to preparing liquid drenches, the main ingredients were taken from the rather sinister large brown bottles with the glass stoppers, known as Winchesters. The exact amount of each of the often different-coloured fluids required would be very carefully poured into a measuring cylinder before being mixed together in a large glass container with a lip on one side to facilitate the bottling of the resulting concoction.

What was known as Jack's Wound Lotion was particularly difficult to make up. The process had to be spread out over a period of three or four days because the syrupy sulphuric acid that was one of the ingredients would cause a violent chemical reaction if too much of it was added at once, the whole container shaking as the mixture bubbled, fizzed and steamed. Dad did seriously overdo it on one occasion, causing the container to break and the liquid to spill out all over the bench. Amid much cursing and swearing the mess had to be very carefully cleared up using sheets of newspaper and large quantities of cotton wool.

Ointments would be prepared using lard from the home-killed pig as a base, along with various wild herbs, flowers, seeds, leaves and berries gathered from the hedgerows, meadows and grass verges as well as from our own garden and stored in big earthenware pots sealed with large flat cork stoppers. Mallow, comfrey, rosemary, arrowroot, mandrake and sloes all had their place in father's apothecary. The lard would be heated up over the fire in the scullery and when it had liquefied the other natural ingredients, usually in dried and powdered form, would be added and the mixture then be left to solidify.

When each batch of medications had been completed, a sticky label printed with the words 'Medicine Supplied By Joseph J Walker (Veterinary Practitioner)' would be attached to the prescription bottle or paper bag, complete with my father's neatly handwritten directions on how it was to be administered. And the details of each batch, including the date when it was made up, would then be painstakingly entered in his office logbook.

Above his desk in one corner of the surgery there was a bookcase full of manuals such as The Cattle Doctor, Modern Farriery, The Anatomy of the Horse and Horace Hayes Veterinary Notes For Horse Owners, along with back numbers of magazines like Horse and Hound and The Farmer and Stockbreeder and catalogues from drug companies advertising their products. The latter included Evans Medical of Speke, White Rose Pharmaceuticals of York, Parkers of Reading, May & Baker of Dagenham, Harveys of Dublin and father's main local supplier, Wyllies of Coventry.

The Wyllies rep, a Mr Mottram, would come round every three or four months to take orders for powders, liquids and equipment which would then be delivered to Moreton-in-Marsh by rail and, at one time, collected from there by pony and trap. His visits were always treated as a very special occasion. A tall, studious man with glasses, he was regarded with great respect and would invariably be invited to stay for tea, the best china and cutlery having been laid out in advance.

I particularly remember the occasion when he somehow persuaded my father to splash out on a fancy electric sterilizer for his instruments. Billed as a state-of-the-art piece of kit at the time, this was basically a glorified kettle consisting of a large oblong metal box about nine inches deep inside which the instruments would be placed on a metal tray, with holes in it and a long handle at each end, and boiled for what seemed like hours on end, with steam belching out of the top. Up until then, dad had sterilised all his instruments very simply, just as effectively and much less expensively by boiling them for about twenty minutes in an open pot over the scullery fire.

As time went on, he prepared less and less of his own medicines, instead placing orders with wholesale chemists J.M. Loveridge & Son of Southampton, who would make them up and package them for him. Although this was undoubtedly a more cost-efficient way of doing things in most cases, there were still situations in which the old traditional methods seemed to work better. Today, new medicines are being developed all the time as the causes of more and more diseases are discovered. A whole range of antibiotics and vaccines now exist and the emphasis has very much moved away from the treatment of symptoms to health management and means of prevention.

I have happy and very vivid memories of that old surgery, what went on there and my boyhood fascination with the well-guarded secrets of some of my father's magic potions. One of the last mysteries to be revealed to me was that which surrounded the Poison cupboard. I had been desperate to get a peep inside but the opportunity never arose until one day when my father had to rush out in a hurry to deal with an emergency and, in his hurry, left the surgery unlocked. When I went in I saw immediately that he had also left the key to the cupboard in the lock.

This was temptation beyond endurance. With a mixture of fear and excitement I turned the key and opened the cupboard door, to be confronted by an array of big, brown and very threatening-looking bottles on which were written names that made me tremble. Chloroform Anaesthetic, Chloral Hydrate, Ether, Phenol, Butter of Antimony, Croton Oil, Vitriol, Arsenic, and Strychnine. I barely had time to take all this in before I heard my father's car pull up outside the house and had to make a very hasty exit.

One of the bottles in the forbidden cupboard that had particularly caught my eye was labelled Wart Paste. I learned much later that the recipe for this arsenic based paste had been passed down from my great-grandfather and had always remained a fiercely guarded family secret. I never saw my father make it up and he never talked about it until, one day, disaster struck.

Warts, angleberries and sarcoids are all types of growths that can appear on a horse's skin. They can be persistent and difficult to get rid of and tend to be a real bone of contention among the horse-owning community. Dad had been recommended to treat a horse called Household Cavalry that was at livery with Frank Slatter from Kingham and which had developed a wart on its ear. In his usual honest and straightforward way, father said that although he could certainly treat it the ear would probably be scarred as a result.

The owner, Charles Tomkinson from Tarpoley in Cheshire, accepted this and my father duly went ahead and treated the wart in the usual Walker way. A length of sisal twine was unravelled and some of the paste was spread on the fibres, which were then rewound and tied around the base of the wart. This was successful in removing the wart but did leave the horse somewhat disfigured with a hole in its ear. At this point, the owner decided to sue father for negligence. The case eventually went to the County Court in Rugby, where judgement went against father and he was ordered to pay damages of one hundred guineas, the presiding judge, His Honour Judge Hamilton, having decided that the horse had lost half its value of £200. Interestingly, Household Cavalry carried on racing after its ordeal and enjoyed a long and successful career.

As an 11-year-old, I knew nothing about all this until after the event. It was never talked about at home and the first I heard about it was when Mr Parsons, the headmaster of my prep school at Idlicote, called me into his office to break the news that my father had lost a court case and had been fined a lot of money, going on to assure me that even if my parents could not afford to pay the fees as a result of this financial setback I would be allowed to stay on at the school, where I was due to take my Common Entrance exam eighteen months later. This was an extremely generous gesture, although, thankfully, my parents never needed to take advantage of it.

I never saw the press report of the case at the time but several years later I spent hours in the Record Office at Warwick searching through the pages of the local Rugby Advertiser. I had somehow assumed that it must have been headline news, but when I eventually turned up the report in the edition of February 12th, 1957 I found to my surprise – and to my slight disappointment, I must admit – that it only rated a few lines, buried in the middle of the paper. Under the headline Treatment of a Horse, it reported simply that on the previous Friday, at Rugby County Court, before His Honour Judge A.M. Hamilton:

'Damages of £111.11s were awarded by His Honour to Charles Tomkinson of Willington Hall, Tarpoley, Cheshire in a case in which the Defendant was Joseph John Walker of Burmington Manor, Shipston-on-Stour.

His Honour decided that the binder twine arsenical paste system which Mr Walker, a registered Veterinary Practitioner, used for treating the Plaintiff's gelding, amounted to negligence. His Honour said the horse had lost half its value (£200) because of the method used for treating a wart in the gelding's ear. The ear, said His Honour, became mutilated, impaired and unsightly.

The Defendant denied negligence and said that for generations his family had used the paste successfully.'

Many years later, when I found myself facing my own nemesis, my father's story became all the more poignant.

At the time, he was shattered by this judgment, which he thought had very unfairly brought shame on the family and would be the ruination of his business. With his confidence in shreds, he wasn't even sure whether he wanted to carry on in practice. Characteristically, however, my mother would have none of that. She told him in no uncertain terms to pull himself together and show people what he was made of. And, as it turned out, the case soon proved to have totally unexpected consequences.

3

If At First You Don't Succeed ...

Far from destroying father's reputation and ruining his business overnight as he had feared it might do, the court case actually had exactly the opposite effect. In fact, it turned out to be the best publicity he could ever have wished for, attracting a lot of important new clients and opening up a whole new world for him.

One of the first people to seek him out was George Beeby, a highly successful trainer with nineteen Cheltenham Festival wins to his credit, including two Cheltenham Gold Cups. Having read about the case, Mr Beeby, who trained for leading owner Lord Bicester among others, summoned father to his Hamilton House yard at Compton, in Berkshire, to have a look at Ballyatom, a very good horse that was badly afflicted with warts to the extent that it could not be trained and was effectively out of action. Mr Beeby and his regular vet had tried everything they could think of to treat the condition, but nothing had worked.

Father was invited to try his method on a no-win-no-fee basis, with the assurance that there would be no repercussions, whatever the result. However, there was also a rather unusual but potentially very rewarding twist included in the deal should the treatment prove to be successful. In that case, Mr Beeby proposed to pay half the agreed fee in cash and to bet the rest, on father's behalf, on a horse named Arcandy that he was training for that year's Steward's Cup at Goodwood. It was a bit of a gamble all round, especially given that Arcandy was an unfancied runner in the race, but father was happy to go along with it, confident that his treatment would do the trick and rather suspecting that the trainer was equally confident in Arcandy's ability to spring a surprise on the bookies. He was right on both counts, Ballyatom being restored to full fitness so effectively that he went on to win the Cotswold Chase at Cheltenham later that same year while, at Goodwood, Arcandy, ridden by Tommy Gosling, romped home in the Steward's Cup at odds of 100-7.

At a stroke, the £200 court fine was covered and the next term's school fees paid, with a fair bit left over. More importantly, father regained his self-respect and all thoughts of retiring were banished. Word spread fast within the racing fraternity about his success with Ballyatom and suddenly he was in demand at top yards all over the country. Fred Winter, Atty Corbett, Major Bewick, Captain Foster, Atty Perse, Vernon Cross, Ken and Frank Cundell, Fulke Walwyn, Edward Courage – they all called him in at various times. But what was literally his crowning glory came when Her Majesty's Crown Equerry, Colonel Miller, invited him to treat warts on some of the carriage horses at the Royal Mews in London.

Colonel Miller lived not far away from us at Shotover Park, just outside Oxford, and father started going there quite regularly to meet with him. I occasionally went along with him, but was always instructed to sit in the car while he went in to talk business – and no doubt to enjoy a drink or two. I had been warned repeatedly that when it came to father's clients, especially the more important ones, I should only speak when spoken to. One day, the Colonel accompanied father back to the car to see him off the premises and when I was introduced to him he asked me whether I was going to be following in my father's footsteps.

Taken by surprise, I just stood there with my mouth working but no words coming forth. I was totally dumbfounded. I immediately got a lecture from father on the need to learn some good manners, but the Colonel kindly and sympathetically came to my defence, recalling that he himself had been very shy as a young man, finding it extremely difficult to talk to older people, especially if he didn't know them too well.

Father certainly wasn't shy in telling all and sundry about his newfound success and all the well-known clients he was working for, but at the same time he was never in the least bit snobbish about it. He had a wonderful knack of treating everybody in the same way, regardless of whether they were big name trainers, wealthy owners or simply stable lads. One of his many favourite little homespun sayings was: "Never forget – you work *for* the boss, but you work *with* the staff."

He himself had always had a keen interest in racing and regularly went to local steeplechase and point-to-point meetings with his friends, as well as making occasional visits to Cheltenham, Stratford and Warwick. I was always desperate to go with him but was considered too young. More and more horses were coming to Burmington as Jack Walker's reputation grew, and with them came owners and trainers, some to check on the progress of their animals or to pick up medications that they had ordered, others to visit during the evening to talk racing over a few wee drams of whisky – Johnnie Walker, of course! I was fascinated by the stories I overheard as I eavesdropped on these little get-togethers, which only made me even more determined to get to the races myself. However, when the opportunity eventually arose it ended in disaster – and tears.

Father had always dabbled in racing ownership, albeit in a very small way, and at this time he had a steeplechaser named Royal Abundance in training with Jimmy Brennan. A big, bright, friendly chestnut with a white face, he had been kept at home the previous year, along with our other horses and ponies, and had become a great favourite of mine. So, after much pleading, and as a special treat, I was at last taken to see him race at Bromford Bridge, in Birmingham, a course that no longer exists, having closed down in 1965.

I was twelve years old and in a state of high excitement on the day as we drove up to Birmingham. Although it was only a relatively small meeting at the eleven-furlong circuit near Castle Bromwich, the atmosphere was everything I had hoped it would be – the noisy, milling crowd spilling out of the bars and making their way to the little grandstand, the punters gathered around the bookies while the tic-tac men called the odds and the owners and trainers giving their jockeys last-minute briefings.

Ours was the third race of the day. Royal Abundance also seemed excited as he moved off towards the start, straining at the bit in anticipation, ears pricked, anxious to be off. However, the race had barely started when, coming to the first, he jumped badly, landed awkwardly and went down with a broken leg. Father realised instantly what the situation was as the stricken animal tried and failed to get back on his feet and, pulling me after him by the hand, hurried to the scene. By the time we got there the course vet was already in attendance. After briefly examining the leg, he reached into his bag with a sad shake of the head and took out what looked to me like a short metal tube about a foot long. He put something into one end of the tube and after gently positioning it against Royal Abundance's forehead, hit the other end with a small mallet. The horse slumped, instantly dead. I later became familiar with the piece of equipment with which he had been dispatched as a Bell's Pistol.

The shock I experienced that afternoon was, of course, absolutely devastating. The tears ran down my face as I leaned forward and tried to stroke the prostrate animal, but father led me away, telling me firmly not to cry because these things sometimes happened in racing and we just had to be thankful that Royal Abundance hadn't suffered for too long. I did my best not to show how upset I was, but the images loomed large in my mind for some time afterwards.

Meanwhile, that dreadful day got even worse when we arrived back home to find that my pony, Dolly, had suffered a bad cut to her front leg, the gash going right down to the bone. Father took a look at it and confirmed that it was very nasty and would need a lot of careful nursing, along with the regular application of some special wound lotion that he would need to make up. His recipe in this instance involved equal measures of chloride of lime and boracic acid dissolved in distilled water. I was told I would have to bathe the area thoroughly each day before soaking some gauze in the lotion and bandaging this around the wound. He explained how a deep-seated wound needed to heal from the bottom and I was warned that I would have to make sure I carried out the treatment exactly as directed every day until further notice. It terrified me to think that if I didn't do it properly then Goodman's, the knackers, would be sent for. Thankfully, Dolly was a wonderful patient and slowly but surely the wound healed.

I had been criticized so often for not making a good enough job of something or other that I was flabbergasted when praised for my efforts with Dolly. As a reward father said that he would let me have some of his special hair restorer to stimulate re-growth of her coat on the bald patches that had developed around the scar on her leg. He once again consulted his recipe book before preparing a mixture of chimney soot and hog's lard. The lard was melted over an open fire in a metal container and when the soot had then been very thoroughly mixed in with a spatula the mixture was left to set. The resulting ointment then had to be applied daily to the affected area. Over time this magic formula certainly seemed to have the desired effect on Dolly's leg and I've often wondered since whether it might also work on the human head!

Although Dolly recovered well, she was never thereafter completely sound. Despite this, father, who was normally fairly unsentimental about such things, was quite happy to let me keep her because she was so good at nurse-maiding clients' horses that came to stay at Burmington for treatment. This came as a huge relief to me and helped further to sow the seeds of determination that one day I would devote all my time to looking after horses.

It was not long after this that, with father keeping a close eye on me, I got to lamb my first ewe, who needed some help as there were two lambs slightly tangled up in the womb. This momentous step forward in my early practical veterinary education took place on Arthur Taylor's small farm at Sutton-under-Brailes, with father talking me through every stage of the process:

"First of all, wash your hands thoroughly with soap and water. Now feel inside the ewe. Can you feel a leg?"

"Yes."

"Good. Put a rope on it and follow the leg upwards. Can you feel a head?"

"Er, yes!"

"Is it attached to the same leg?"

"I think so."

"Well, now find the other leg and attach your second rope, feeling around to make absolutely sure that both legs belong to the same lamb. Have you done that?"

"Hang on a second – yes!"

"Right. Now, with both ropes held in your left hand, gently pull the legs while using your right hand to guide the lamb's head up towards her pelvis. Careful. Pull firmly and steadily, but not too hard. Once the head is through the pelvis, remove your right hand and complete the delivery."

Once the lamb had been successfully delivered I was instructed to clear all the mucous from its nose and mouth and then to stimulate breathing either by moving its front legs backwards and forwards or swinging it by its hind legs, head down, so that any remaining mucous would drain out. I was told that as a last resort, in cases where a newborn lamb didn't immediately start to breathe, you could insert a piece of straw into one of the nostrils to reach the back of the throat, the irritation helping to kick start the process of taking a first breath.

Both lambs were successfully delivered. With each of them in turn, I dipped their navels in antiseptic, as instructed, before laying them in a comfortable place where their mother instinctively started caring for them. I watched spellbound as, within minutes of being born, the tiny lambs staggered to their feet after a few failed attempts and then reached to suck from their mother.

Wow! What a feeling! For me it was like lighting the touch paper. I was proud of my achievement and ready for more. During that season I lambed quite a few more, but only the easy ones. My confidence was building until, inevitably, I had a failure. I couldn't find the head because the lamb was lying awkwardly and father had to step in and finish the job. But for once he was very reassuring, telling me that experience would soon teach me how to deal with such minor complications, adding: "You have big hands, so if you can get a hand into the womb you will always be able to get a lamb out."

I was next initiated into the regular springtime ritual of lamb tailing. Father would arrive at the farms with the necessary equipment, including a special bench, several tailing irons and a plentiful supply of his own green, home-made antiseptic ointment and other medications such as a tetanus antitoxin, packed into the back of the car. The farmer would already have prepared a campfire in advance and the irons would be placed into the glowing embers to be heated up. The bench would then be laid across a couple of five-gallon oil drums next to the pen where the lambs would be caught one-by-one and handed over the hurdle to whoever was going to be holding them while the procedure was carried out. They would be laid on their backs and the males would first be castrated before the tails were then burned off with a hot iron. The whole operation would take under a minute, carried out with such speed and expertise that the lambs experienced a minimum of distress. My job was to keep the fire stoked and to make sure that there was a steady supply of hot irons. I was always in trouble – the irons were either too hot or not hot enough, depending on the mood father was in on the day. And if I made the mistake of being too slow on the job he would touch my hand with the hot iron to liven me up and aid my concentration.

Although it was hard work for everyone concerned, these

tailing sessions were usually quite social occasions. Some farmers liked to keep the tails to eat, regarding them as a bit of a delicacy. This meant they had to be skinned. A pot of boiling water was kept over the fire and six or eight tails at a time would be tied together with string and immersed, using a stick. If you left them in too long they would scald so that when you went to skin them the flesh would be pulled out, but if they were not left in long enough the wool would stubbornly stay put. I soon became quite good at judging exactly how long to leave them in. Father would usually ask if he could have a few for himself and certain of his friends. In particular, he liked to be able to give some to Tom Taylor, a horse dealer from Broadwell who also happened to be a keen angler and would occasionally give him a fresh salmon in return – a rare treat in those days.

Father was especially renowned for his expertise in castrating colts, a procedure that he carried out with the horse standing up, rather than having it 'thrown', laid down and trussed up, effectively hog-tied. His way of doing things required a great deal more skill and finesse, but was much quicker and less traumatic for the 'patient'. He was therefore much in demand, travelling many miles around the region to carry out the procedure, and, to this day, his methods are still talked about in reverent terms.

Nowadays the procedure is carried out using a piece of handheld equipment known as an emasculator that cuts and seals in one go, with the colt both sedated and locally anaesthetised. However, neither that equipment nor the drugs were available in father's time. He simply used a sharp knife and special wooden pegs with which he would then isolate the exteriorized testicles prior to clamping and removing them.

The pegs, which he used to buy from the gypsies, were each about six inches long, pointed at the open end and with a notch at the other end in which to slot the piece of string that held the two halves together at the top. The outer edges were flat while the inner sides were slightly hollowed out. Before being used they had to be scraped and scrubbed thoroughly clean, after which they were put in an open wooden tray to dry. An anti-septic dressing was then made up in batches, consisting of 2lbs of corrosive sublimate, 4lbs of red percipity powder and double strength gum, mixed together with water to form a paste. Stored in earthenware jars until required, this would then be painted on to the hollowed out sides of the pegs and allowed to dry just before use.

A lot of the colts he operated on tended to be less accustomed to being handled and some had never been caught before. He would often deal with them several at a time and they would be rounded up and put in a small pen so that they couldn't run away. Father was an ace with a halter and completely fearless, prepared to challenge even the most aggressive colt. People used to insist with a respectful nod of the head: "No matter how wild, Walker would tackle it!"

He actually put this lack of fear down to two things. He always carried in his pocket a 'false tongue'. Known technically as a hippomane, this can be found in a mare's afterbirth fluids and is traditionally thought to confer good luck and protection. He also used a few drops of cumin and cinnamon oil on the palm of his hand, or on a red spotted handkerchief, which would help to calm them down.

Once a halter had been put on the colt, it would then be con-trolled by a twitch, a pole with a noose attached to it that is twisted around the horse's nose. Father's twitch had been inher-ited from his father and I still have it. Father always stressed the importance of having a good man on the twitch. If the colt still proved to be unmanageable it would either be lunged or worked with a series of ropes wound through the legs until it tired. The less excitable ones would be blindfolded. The thor-oughbred colts he gelded were mostly used to being handled, but thoroughbreds are not the most predictable and were always a challenge.

No scalpels were available in those days. Instead, father used a special folding knife that would be honed on a whetstone until razor sharp. Every year, a travelling knife sharpener would pay us a visit to put an edge on all his knives and the whetstone would then maintain them through the season. The testicles would be exteriorised, using the knife to make an incision in the scrotum, and the cord would then be clamped using the pegs, the open ends of which would be closed and tightened using a leather washer. The peg always had to be put on the cord at a point above the epididymis. "Wouldn't want to leave him proud, " father would say. "Shows you don't know your job!" The testicles would then be cut off below the peg. A return visit the next day would be required to remove the peg and tidy up the cord. One great advantage of this method was that the peg very effectively prevented any bleeding. As for the lack of anaesthetic, father used to say: " Speed is my anaesthetic." Even when having to deal with a powerful and excitable young colt, his skill was such that the whole operation would be over in minutes and the patients would then very quickly recover.

I had to wait a few years before I was allowed to watch, and eventually to help, as father castrated colts. Meanwhile, I had gained practical, hands-on experience of most other aspects of everyday veterinary practice.

It was shortly after helping out with lambing and lamb tailing that I first put my hand into a calving cow. That was on the Warriner estate at Weston, where we arrived to find a large, docile Hereford cross, red with a big white face, on the point of giving birth. I was told to wash my hands thoroughly and to clean around the birth opening so as to make sure that no infection was taken in. Having inserted my hand rather apprehensively, I was asked what I could feel. At first it was just a warm feeling, all mucous and warm fluids, but then I came into contact with something solid – the leg of the unborn calf. I was told to pinch it and it instantly moved away. At that point I was told to withdraw and my father took over, adjusted the calf inside and duly delivered it.

After that, it was then a matter of making sure that the airways were clear and that the calf was breathing. Calves are not as easy to deal with as lambs. Sometimes they need vigorous rubbing to get them started and in some cases it might be necessary to hang them over a gate, holding them by their hind legs, in order to let any remaining mucous drain away. As with lambs, the navel then has to be dipped in antiseptic to prevent infection creeping through the open cord. Once all that has been done the mother has to be checked to make sure there is not another calf inside her and that she has not suffered a tear during delivery.

For a twelve-year-old this was a steep learning curve and yet I was eager and enthusiastic. Unfortunately, my enthusiasm for this sort of fieldwork and my thirst for practical knowledge did not extend to the classroom and my academic studies. I was entering my final year at Idlicote House Preparatory School when the headmaster called my parents in to inform them that if I was really serious about becoming a vet then I would have to work a lot harder, play a little less sport and generally apply myself more diligently to my academic studies. It was agreed that I should be capable of passing the Common Entrance exam and that I would be entered for Epsom College, an expensive public school option that was made financially viable largely because of a generous three-terms-for-the-price-of-two discount for the sons and daughters of anyone involved in medicine, whether of the human or animal type. Offered the chance, I knuckled down, passed the exam and was duly accepted for Epsom, where I became a boarder.

Quite apart from its academic standing as a leading public school that had originally been founded by the medical establishment, specifically for the children of doctors and vets with ambitions to follow their parents into the medical professions, Epsom College also turned out to be an inspired choice as far as I was concerned for several other less worthy reasons. For one thing, it had a very strong sporting tradition and I spent many happy summer afternoons playing cricket for the 1st XI. For another, it was located at the very heart of British horse racing, just a stone's throw from Epsom racecourse, the home of The Derby. And I soon discovered that these two very appealing assets dovetailed rather conveniently.

The school cricket coach at the time was Arthur Wellard, the wonderful Somerset and England all-rounder, who, in his day, had been both a formidable fast-medium pace bowler and an occasional off-spinner as well as a legendary smiter of mighty sixes. Now Arthur loved to have a bet and he soon found out that, through my father's racing connections, I often had access to some good tips straight from the horse's mouth, as it were. And he obviously felt that having me in the team would enhance his betting returns, so my place in the 1st XI was fairly secure. At the same time, he introduced me to the discreet Tom Guntrips postal betting service, postal betting being the only way you could bet off-course in the days before the first betting shops were opened in 1961.

Before long I was running a small syndicate that included Arthur and a select group of three or four fellow pupils. There was a slight problem at first insofar as betting on the horses was strictly against the school rules and the porters very quickly sussed out what was going on when the identical plain brown envelopes in which Tom Guntrips would send back any winnings by recorded delivery started arriving, addressed to me at the boarding house. However, in return for me sharing some of my inside information with them, plus a small percentage of the winnings (they could always tell when we'd had a particularly good week because the envelope would be fatter!), they were prepared to turn a blind eye.

This was all happening in the late fifties and early sixties when Lester Piggott, Scobie Breasley, Ron Hutchinson, Joe Mercer and Jimmy Lindley were at their peak and we developed a system whereby we would back these top jockeys along with the odd dark horse that I would hear about through dad and the trainers he was working with back at Burmington. We would also get the occasional tip from the yards that operated near the school on Epsom Downs, among them those run by Walter Nightingale, Staff Ingham and the Smythe brothers, Tom, Ron and Monty. Sgt Harvey Raker, who was in charge of the school's cadet force, was a great mate of Monty's and would often pass on useful bits of information.

Making the most of all this, the syndicate enjoyed considerable success and showed a healthy profit most weeks, with the result that others soon wanted to join in. But Arthur advised caution and said we should keep it small and it became common knowledge around the school that it was harder to get into Walker's betting syndicate than it was to get into the 1st XI! Meanwhile, we had developed our own sort of tic-tac system so that when we were involved in a cricket match on a Saturday afternoon the scorer could keep us up to date with race results while we were fielding.

Derby Day was a big occasion locally, of course. It seemed that most of London would descend on Epsom Downs via Tattenham Corner by car, bus and train. The school boarders were allowed to go to the Derby Fair, which was held in the middle of the course during the weekend before the big race, which in those days was always run on the first Wednesday in June. It was a memorable experience, full of the noisy, colourful razzamatazz of the fairground rides, the boxing booths, the striptease tents and the food stalls, the air thick with the scent of candyfloss and toffee apples. We used to walk over the Downs to get to it and, of course, no visit was ever complete without also going to Tattenham Corner to find out which horses were being tipped by the gypsies. If we were lucky we might spot one of the famous tipsters like Michael Lynch, a small man with a club foot who walked with a limp and whose son, Kipper, was a jockey; or, most entertaining of all, Prince Monolulu, dressed in a Red Indian chief's headdress and performing a sort of war dance while repeatedly shouting out: "I gotta horse! I gotta horse!"

Derby Day itself was very special. We were not allowed out of school unless accompanied by our parents and there were

Generations of devotion: (from the top) Great grandfather Alfred
Walker, Alfred in his younger days with his pony and trap in
Long Compton, grandfather William John Walker ('Doc') and
my father Joseph John Walker ('Jack').

Portrait of my father in a familiar pose!

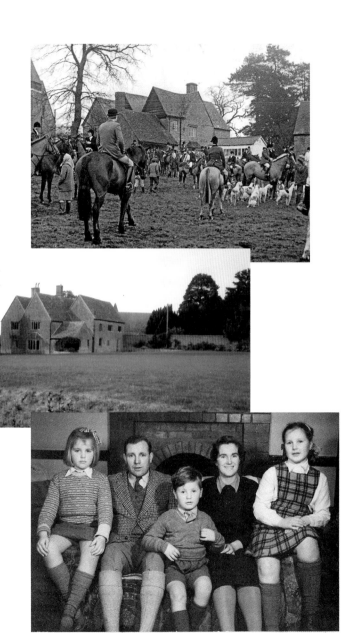

Burmington Manor (top and centre) and me pictured with my parents and sisters Margaret (left) and Pat when we were growing up there. Beyond the huntsmen you can just make out the white shed that served as father's surgery.

Father with me as a baby and (below) me getting to grips with
small animals, while sisters Pat and Margaret feed orphan lambs.

Father and assistants
swimming a horse in the
lock at Somerton, near
Deddington, in 1960
and (right) father with a
horse and foal.

A likely lad! Posing for a graduation day portrait at Sussex University – and a less formal pose with Diana.

(Opposite page) With mother and sisters on holiday in Blackpool, monkeying about as a teenager and with the 1st XI hockey team at Epsom College.

With Diana, fellow mature student Rob Pilsworth and his wife, Lynn, after returning to Cambridge to be awarded an MA degree two years after celebrating my BA graduation (below) with my parents, sister Pat and daughter Lucy.

frequent roll calls throughout the day to make sure that no-one had managed to abscond. The road leading up to the actual racecourse passed close to some of the classrooms and through the windows you would see a continuous stream of slow-moving traffic, including an array of Rolls Royces, Bentleys and Jaguars, many of them chauffeur-driven, along with every make of fancy sports car, with many of the gents wearing top hats and morning suits and the ladies all looking highly glamorous in their finery. And in amongst them would be smaller, more ordinary cars containing less well-heeled punters in everyday clothes, because The Derby has always been a great social leveller, appealing to people from all walks of life, from the toffs to the hoi polloi.

Needless to say, our syndicate would always have an interest in the race. Our best year was 1961 when, following our usual practice, we backed a couple of fancied runners while also venturing sixpence each way on a rank outsider. Psidium proceeded to upset all the odds, romping home at 66-1 and winning us nearly £8/10s, a small fortune as far as we were concerned at a time when we rarely bet more than half-a-crown on any horse.

I enjoyed my time at Epsom – in fact, the undeniable truth is that I enjoyed it a bit too much. The many outside distractions were a barrier to serious study. I spent too much time playing sport and following the horses and not enough time with my nose in a book. When I did go to the library it was to read the newspapers and, in particular, the back pages, poring over the form guides and assessing the runners and riders.

The letter that arrived in the mid-August following my final term imparted the news that I had not achieved a single A Level pass. Not surprisingly, this dismal performance didn't endear me to my parents. My father, especially, was furious.

"A complete waste of time and money."

"You're not stupid – you're just lazy."

"You're far too easily distracted".

"Why are you unable to concentrate on anything that matters?"

These were just a few of the printable barbs that were aimed in my direction.

Ordered to think seriously about what I was going to do next, I decided that the only sensible option would be to re-take my A Levels at Oxford Technical College in Gypsy Lane – now Oxford Brookes University. And in an effort to pay my own way, I would go out and find part time jobs as a gardener as well as helping out with the visiting horses at home.

Having duly signed up for the A Level courses at the college, I was pleasantly surprised to find that my services as a jobbing gardener were much in demand and I spent every available spare moment at weekends and in the vacations cutting grass, digging, weeding and clearing rough patches of ground. And, of course, I supplemented my modest earnings with some very selective and reasonably profitable betting investments, helped by the tips I managed to pick up from the trainers and other racing folk who regularly turned up at Burmington.

Everything seemed to be going very well until, just before my A Level exams were due to start, I went down with glandular fever. This notoriously debilitating illness hit me hard. I became so weak, tired and listless that I could barely walk the length of the drive at Burmington without having to stop for a rest. There was certainly no way I could possibly sit the exams. My mother was understanding and supportive, but I got scant sympathy from my father.

"Another year wasted, Alan. What now?"

I thought this was a little unfair as I obviously hadn't deliberately gone out and contracted the illness. But I bit my lip and simply said that I would try again the following year and that this time I would support myself fully, including picking up the bill for my digs in Kidlington, which father had previously paid for.

I signed up once again, confident that going over all the coursework a second time would help me to pass the exams at the end of the year with flying colours. But tragedy then struck my family quite out of the blue when Margaret, the younger of my two older sisters, who had been working as a nurse at Evesham Hospital, died of leukaemia after a very short illness. We were all devastated. My other sister Pat and I were completely shell-shocked, unable to comprehend the enormity of what had happened. Mother, being a devout Christian, took refuge in the thought that her kind, gentle, caring daughter had been too good for this world. Father was inconsolable.

We always used to say that Margaret was dad's favourite. She would wait on him hand, foot and finger and would never hear a word said against him. He used to act as a Special Constable and on one occasion he was out on duty all night. When he came home the next morning in his uniform we kids, who were still very young at the time, were most impressed and hailed him as a returning hero only for mother to deflate us by snorting cynically that his activities as a Special Constable were probably just an excuse for an all-night booze-up. Margaret, normally the most mild-mannered of all of us, exploded with anger, flew to his defence and really put mother in her place.

There seemed no great cause for concern when Margaret came home from work one day with a headache and complained of feeling generally under the weather. Everybody assumed that she was probably just going down with flu, but when the symptoms persisted she went to see our local GP who sent her to hospital for tests. Leukaemia was diagnosed and we then received the shattering news that the cancer was already so advanced that it was likely to prove terminal sooner rather than later. She was moved to a specialist unit at Stratford-upon-Avon where, after about five days, she suddenly rallied dramatically, raising our hopes. But forty-eight hours later she had a relapse and died very shortly after that.

My parents never really recovered from the terrible shock of her untimely death, made all the more tragic in retrospect because advances in cancer treatment since then have meant that the particular form of leukaemia from which she suffered can now be treated successfully in most cases. For me, too, the loss was almost unbearable. I vividly recall riding home from the hospital on my old Velocette motorcycle – a water-cooled ex-police 'Noddy' bike – with tears streaming down my face, amazed and somehow angry that the rest of the world was carrying on as normal despite the fact that Margaret was gone. The birds were still singing, animals grazing in the fields, people driving along the road and generally going about their business as usual and as I rode furiously down the road I found myself shouting at everyone in general and nobody in particular: "Don't you know my sister has died? How can you carry on as if nothing has happened? Show some respect!" Time, of course, is a great healer, but more than fifty years later I still miss Margaret.

The tragedy of her death diverted father's wrath away from my shortcomings, but I had meanwhile decided that I no longer wanted to carry on doing what I was doing, pursuing my A Level studies without a great deal of enthusiasm while struggling to support myself financially with menial odd jobs here and there. I resolved instead to quit college and get myself a full-time job and after making a number of applications I eventually succeeded in securing a position on a Management Trainee course with the worldwide meat production company W. Weddell & Co. Part of the Vestey Group, Weddell owned huge beef-producing cattle ranches in South America and a string of wholesale depots throughout the UK.

The trainee scheme was based in Oxford. I found that I really enjoyed the work and soon got to know all the ins and outs of the wholesale meat trade. After a while I was sent up to the old Smithfield market in London to learn about buying. Taken under the wing of the area supervisor, Mr Jarrett, I stayed there for two years. I had dreamed all along of being sent out to South America to work on the ranches out there instead of which I was offered the position of manager at a new depot in Slough. At that point, aged twenty-three, I came to the conclusion that this was not the way I wanted to go. The lure of being involved in the care of horses, and racehorses in particular, was too strong.

So I gave in my notice, having decided that I had to go back to college once again in an attempt to get those elusive A Levels.

This time I signed up for a night school course and started looking round for a day job, which I eventually found conveniently close to home. Butcher Peter Checketts was an old friend with whom I used to play cricket for the Long Compton village team. He had recently purchased 50 Main Street, the very property where my grandfather had once lived and had his surgery. Peter had set up an abattoir on the premises and wanted someone to develop the wholesale side of the business. It couldn't have been better. Not only did I have bags of experience of the wholesale meat trade through working with Weddell & Co, but the job also involved very early morning starts, which was ideal as far as I was concerned because it left the afternoons free for me to pop up the road and help out with the horses at Burmington before going off to Oxford Tech in the evenings.

At around the same time in 1969 my father kept talking about a horse he had seen while working at the Budgett family's world-famous Kirtlington Stud, an establishment that has, over the years, produced no less than fourteen Classic winners, including two Derby winners and a World Champion. The horse that had caught dad's eye was a colt named Blakeney – the groom felt that he was the best they had ever had up until then. When he was entered in that year's Derby I invested modestly at an ante post price of 50-1 and backed it several more times as the odds then shortened in the weeks before the race. When Ernie Johnson duly rode him to victory I collected £540, a substantial jackpot in those days.

My family and all my friends predicted that I would soon be giving it all back to the bookies, instead of which I splashed out on a brand new maroon Mini, registration LAC 140E. Taxed and insured, it cost me exactly £536. And, at the time, £1 would buy you four gallons of petrol. Happy days! My trusty old Velocette was meanwhile retired to the barn and later given away to the local police sergeant's son.

When the A Level results were announced in the August my grades were an improvement on my previous performance, but still not nearly good enough to even contemplate applying to any of the veterinary colleges. Given my poor exam record, I was advised to aim instead for a related science degree and in the autumn of 1969 I was accepted through the clearing system to read Biological Sciences at Aston University.

Despite being warned by the tutors that I would have to work flat out all the time in order to keep up with everybody else I actually took to the subject very quickly and never felt in any danger of falling behind. In fact, I had no difficulty staying comfortably on top of the work – so much so that I had plenty of time for sport and a fair bit of racing! There were frequent trips in the Mini to the Midlands tracks such as Warwick, Nottingham, Worcester, Leicester, Stratford, Uttoxeter and Wolverhampton.

I was only about fifty miles away from Burmington, so on those weekends when my sporting fixture list allowed, I would go home and help father with the horses, taking the opportunity while I was there to check his book to see who had been in, which horses had visited and what they had come in for. Most importantly, I was able to catch up on any gossip from the yards – which horses to look out for and any that were considered dead certs. Father told me: "Don't go filling your head with racing and betting – get down to your studies!"

I managed to do both and graduated in 1972 with a very respectable 2:1 Upper Second Class Honours degree, but, alas, this was still not good enough to open the door to veterinary college. Was it ever going to happen, I wondered? I was seriously beginning to doubt it.

As a last resort, I applied to the University of Sussex to read for a D.Phil in Membrane Biochemistry and was accepted, starting the three-year postgraduate course in September 1972 under the supervision of Dr. Ken Wheeler. The course involved difficult but rewarding work investigating the mechanics of the sodium potassium pump, which has to do with the function of enzymes found in human and animal cells. As at Aston, I found I had no problem getting to grips with the subject and my research project went very well indeed, once again leaving plenty of time for sport and other extra-curricula activities.

Sussex in the 1970s was a great place to be, with an extremely lively, modern campus environment and a reputation for radical student political protest. Coming, as I did, from a relatively conservative rural background, where things tended to be done fairly quietly and in moderation, it came as something of a culture shock to find myself pitched into a social and political whirl of wild parties and student militancy that included locking the Vice Chancellor, Asa Briggs, into his office and preventing US government adviser Samuel P. Huntington from making a speech as a protest against the Vietnam War. It was a vibrant scene and once I had overcome my initial surprise, I took to it like a duck to water.

I played a lot of sport, including cricket, rugby, hockey and squash and, needless to say, also found the time to acquaint myself with southern racecourses. Brighton, Lewes and Wye (both no longer in existence), Plumpton, Folkestone, Lingfield, Goodwood and Fontwell Park – all were conveniently located within easy striking distance of the university. Being so far from Burmington meant, of course, that I had less contact with home and the horses there, but I didn't miss that too much. In truth, I was enjoying my work and university life so much that my focus had shifted.

My wide-ranging university sports activities led to me being elected Chairman of the Sports Federation. This meant that I had a seat on the Inner Council of the Students' Union, which consisted of the President, Vice President, Treasurer and Secretary of the Union along with the Union Administrator. Our debates were often very heated, and mine was usually the lone voice counselling moderation rather than outright militancy and disobedience. However, I found the experience both very interesting and highly stimulating and it taught me a lot about the need always to listen to and respect other points of view, to be courteous and calm and yet also firm and sincere, and to be prepared to compromise. In its way, all that was to be as useful in the future as anything I learned in the lecture theatre or the laboratory.

Sussex was a momentous period in my life in many different ways. Most significantly, it was there that I met my wife-to-be, Diana, who was working as secretary to Sydney Shall, the Professor of Biochemistry. She was much fancied by the male students in the department and at the start of my second year in September 1973 somebody bet me that I couldn't get a kiss from her by Christmas! I won the bet – and a steady relationship soon developed

It was Diana who, when I told her how desperate I was to become a veterinary surgeon, eventually suggested that I speak to Professor Shall to see if he had any ideas about the best way forward. He advised me to apply as a mature student to Wolfson College, Cambridge, adding that I should also find a respected veterinary surgeon to act as a referee. I approached Captain McGhee, a vet from Kineton who knew my family well and who had acted as a witness and had provided a character reference for my father during his court case back in 1957. He was only too happy to do the same for me.

I completed my D.Phil thesis, entitled The Role of Phospholipids in a Membrane ATPase System, and started a three-year post-doctoral study on growth hormones. And in January 1976, after submitting applications to all six veterinary schools, I received a letter informing me that I had been accepted to read Veterinary Medicine at Wolfson College, Cambridge. I didn't even have to go for an interview. At last! At the age of thirty, twelve years after making my first application while still at Epsom, awaiting the results of my first ill-fated A Level attempt, I had finally achieved my ambition. I couldn't quite believe it at first and had to ask Di to read out the letter again and again to convince me that it was true. "If at first you don't succeed, try and try again," is what they say – and it had worked for me.

The offer of a place at the college was conditional on my having a financial guarantor for the duration of the course, a role that my father readily agreed to take on, delighted that I had finally made the grade and would, after all, be upholding the long-established family veterinary tradition. In fact, he very generously went much further than that. By this time Di and I had been together long enough to know that we wanted to get married. So, as part of his financial support, Dad said that if we could find a small house in Cambridge he would buy it for us rather than simply helping me out with rental payments. At the same time, he would expect the two of us to find ways of working to support ourselves.

We duly started house hunting during the summer months prior to me starting my first term in October 1976 and eventually found a rather dilapidated little two-up-two-down terraced property at 97 York Street that Dad purchased for £6,400, a knock-down price partly accounted for by the fact that the only loo was outside. With great excitement, and the help of a couple of local builders, we set about making the place habitable. At this point we had a great stroke of luck when the City Council declared the district around York Street to be an official Improvement Area, enabling us to claim a 60% grant towards essential repairs to the roof and the installation of an inside toilet.

Having settled in together at York Street, Di and I decided to go ahead and get married during the Easter vacation of the following year. The date we chose – April 9th – had a special significance for me as it had been my late sister Margaret's birthday. The wedding took place in the little village church at Burmington, with a self-catered reception at home in the garden of Burmington Manor, which was right next door. Given that we were living on a shoestring at the time and also because Di's father, Michael, had recently suffered a stroke, we decided on a low-key event, with a guest list that we restricted to family members and close friends. It was nevertheless a very happy day.

Back in Cambridge, making ends meet was inevitably going to be a bit of a struggle for the first few years of our married life during which I would have to concentrate on my studies. We would have to get by on what Di could earn, supplemented by the mature student grants I had managed to get from charitable organisations such as the Sir Richard Stapley Educational Trust, and whatever I might be able to earn from part-time work at weekends and during the vacations. We also took in lodgers, renting out our spare room to language students who came to Cambridge in the summer, and even managed to make a bit of extra money from baby-sitting. It was pretty much a hand-to-mouth existence, but we both went into it with our eyes open, looking to our long-term future together.

Di was fantastically supportive right from the word go. It was through her that I'd got the introduction that had helped me to gain my place at Wolfson and she was as determined as I was to see it through. And after the many years of frustration and disappointment during which it had sometimes seemed as if I might never achieve my great ambition of becoming a vet, nothing could detract from the joy and satisfaction I felt, knowing that the future I had always wanted for myself was now within my grasp.

4

On Yer Bike!

A few months into my course at Cambridge I found myself chatting to my tutor, Alan Wilson, and asked him casually why he thought it was that I had finally been accepted at Wolfson after all those years of applying to various other colleges in London, Edinburgh, Glasgow, Bristol and Cambridge without ever managing to progress even as far as getting an interview. I was hoping to hear him say something about how my dedication had shone through and how the college authorities had been impressed by my refusal to be put off by the earlier rejections. Instead of which he explained that he also happened to be the Admissions Tutor and that as such it was his job to process the three hundred or so applications that came in each year from mature students seeking one of the three or four places that were available. My application had stood out only because Captain McGhee, one of my referees, had been his Commanding Officer in the Veterinary Corps in India. Although he hadn't been in touch with the Captain since leaving the army many years before he had retained the greatest respect for him and had accepted me largely on the strength of his reference – a slice of luck that just goes to confirm that it's not so much *what* you know as *who* you know that counts.

I found the course hard going at first, especially as I was quite a bit older than most of my fellow students. During the first two years of pre-clinical studies the vets shared lectures with the medics and the biologists, a lot of whom were very bright little sparks who had come in with top grade 'A' levels and 'S' levels to their name, on top of which some of them were also arrogant, toffee-nosed prats! Keeping up with them could be stressful at times, but my delight at being there, along with the help and support I got from Di and others and my determination to make the most of the opportunity that I had been given, helped to get me through.

I soon adapted to the traditional ways of student life in Cambridge, which included going everywhere by bike, this being by far the easiest and most convenient way of getting around the city's congested streets. I had acquired an ancient Moulton de Luxe, one of those rather odd looking machines with small wheels and fat tyres that had become all the rage in the sixties. Mine had the advantage of being so old and clapped out that it never got stolen. Each morning I would set off from York Street and cycle to college in the middle of Cambridge via Mill Road, across Parker's Piece and then down Hills Road, often accompanied by my friend Rob Pilsworth, a fellow mature student who lived with his wife Lynn just round the corner from us in Ross Street.

Students were not allowed to have cars in their first two years at college, but this ruling did not affect Di, who had managed to get herself a secretarial job, so we did also have a little bright yellow Fiat 500, affectionately known as Fifi.

The university terms were short, each lasting just eight weeks, but the work schedule on the two-year pre-clinical part of the course was fairly intense and left little time for extra-curricula pursuits. As it happened, injury had anyway forced me to give up playing rugby, but I did manage to do a fair bit of refereeing, which helped to keep me fit. Having taken over from my great friend David Wippell as Secretary of the College Rugby Referees Society, I regularly officiated not only at mid-week college games but also at club games in the area. The highlight of my refereeing career came when I took charge in the annual match between the Blues XV and Edinburgh University.

The long vacations gave me the opportunity to earn some

extra, much-needed income with a variety of part-time jobs that included working as a bacon packer in Cherry Hinton, a vegetable sales assistant at Tesco in Bar Hill and – best of all – as a council dustman. Early starts would find me walking the streets of Cambridge from 6.00 am, emptying bins into the dustcart. Occasionally, I would be asked to drive the 'Specials Vehicle', which was used for house clearances and the collection of large, bulky items such as armchairs and sofas. The regulars who accompanied me on these missions were a canny lot who knew exactly how and where to dispose of any items that were still worth a few bob!

The other great advantage of the dustman's job was that it left the afternoons free, allowing me to hitch a lift over to Newmarket two or three times a week to work as an unpaid volunteer in the equine hospital run by the legendary Mr Bob Crowhurst, where Di had managed to get herself a job as a laboratory technician rather than as a secretary or personal assistant. With an eye to the future, as ever, her idea was to get as much veterinary experience as possible so that she would be able to help me out when I eventually set up in practice in my own right. At the same time, she was able to put in the word that opened the door for me to go in and help out in what was one of Newmarket's top specialist equine veterinary practices.

Bob Crowhurst was God in the racing world in those days. All the smart owners and trainers went to him, including Lady Beaverbrook, a leading owner at the time. His services were also much in demand from the Arab owners when they first started becoming heavily involved in British racing. It has to be said that he was a gruff character who could actually be quite difficult at times, but for some reason he took to me. I started off simply by doing the chores – sweeping the yard, helping out in the stables and generally fetching and carrying, anything just to be involved – but he and the other partners gradually allowed me to get more and more hands on, to the point where I got to go out on calls with Mr Crowhurst himself.

The first time this happened was when he took me with him to examine a pony belonging to the daughter of one of his friends. He listened to the pony's heart and then, out of the blue, handed me the stethoscope and said: "Tell me what you hear." I listened intently but could hear absolutely nothing. I started to panic slightly, not wanting to look stupid and wondering what I should say to him.

"Come on, we haven't got all day," he muttered impatiently. I hesitated for a moment before admitting rather sheepishly: "I'm sorry, but I can't hear anything at all."

"No, nor can I, " he snapped. "The pony's too fat. That's all that's wrong with it."

On the return journey he told me: "'I deliberately set you up a bit back there. I suspected that you would be thrown when you found that you were unable to hear anything through the stethoscope and wanted to see how you would react. I'm glad you were honest, it's the only way to be." Thereafter, I was regularly invited to accompany him on calls.

Of the other partners, Mr Simpson, Richard Greenwood and David Ellis were all very helpful, understanding and patiently tolerant of my incessant questions. David Ellis, in particular, was a brilliant teacher. One of the many useful little tips he gave me concerned the best way to go about learning how to age a horse accurately. He said that I should go to the sales yards, look in a few horses' mouths and note down my estimates of how old they were. I should then go back to the practice and look them up in the sale catalogue to discover their exact ages and how close I had been to getting them right. "Don't cheat because then you won't learn, " he warned.

The experience I gained there was a huge bonus and the other students on the course were green with envy. In particular, it gave me a great head start over the rest of them when it came to 'Seeing Practice' – a key part of the final three years clinical study that involved spending a minimum of twenty-eight weeks working with a selection of different veterinary practices throughout the UK. We could choose where we went, but there was a structured framework that meant you had to divide your time between large and small animals, Ministry work and meat inspection. Also, you could only spend two weeks at any one practice. And yet I had already been working on and off at the Crowhurst practice for months, albeit only on my spare holiday afternoons. It was time very well spent.

My 'Seeing Practice' stints took me from Stratford upon Avon to Suffolk and from Norfolk to Devon and all the vets I worked with in the various and very different practices were helpful and welcoming.

In Stratford I spent valuable time with Brian Needham and Derek Knottenbelt. I already knew Derek well as he had worked with many of my father's clients over the years, testing their animals in his capacity as a Local Veterinary Inspector for what was then still the Ministry of Agriculture. And I saw a lot of small animal practice with John Grieve, who, as a student, had seen practice with my father many years previously, before eventually setting up his own practice in Cherry Hinton Road, Cambridge and who, as a result, was more than happy to return the favour.

As part of my Seeing Practice requirement I also spent a very informative couple of weeks with a father-and-son practice in Crediton, Devon that I was especially keen to see in action because the set-up was similar to what was likely to be in store for me if and when I eventually went into business with my father. Rather like Bob Crowhurst, Roy Wood, was not an easy man to get on with but, again, he seemed to take to me for some reason. His son, Jonathan, with whom I have remained good friends ever since, was still very much under the old man's thumb in those days, but was gradually beginning to establish himself. However, as I myself was to be reminded time and time again when I started working with my father, a lot of old farmers tend to become so devoted to their regular vet over the years that nobody else will do and even a son is likely to be treated with suspicion, not to say to say downright contempt, when he first starts taking over from his dad. You have to get used to being told when doing anything slightly differently or when treatments don't immediately produce the desired effect: "Well, you know nothing!" This happened to me so many times early on after I joined my father in practice that I quickly developed a thick skin and acquired a complete immunity to such slights. I just kept quiet and got on with the job, confident that I would win the doubters over in time.

From the moment I had been accepted at Wolfson, father had always taken it for granted that I would be joining the family business and as he became more and more incapacitated by the arthritis in his hips he was impatient for me to come home and start helping him out as soon as I qualified. I, meanwhile, felt increasingly drawn to Newmarket. I loved all the history, the tradition, the horses, the characters and the general buzz that existed at the very heart of the British horseracing scene. Although the Crowhurst practice had never taken on graduates fresh out of veterinary college there was a vague suggestion that they might be prepared to consider making an exception in my case, because of all the experience I had already had there, and I knew that if this were the case then I would be very tempted, even if I only went there for a few years.

When I first mentioned this to my father during a discussion about my future plans about halfway through the course my time at Cambridge he was devastated. He had assumed that I would jump at the opportunity to join him as soon as possible. Already hobbling about on two sticks by this time, he was physically incapable of carrying out some procedures. He was just about managing to keep the business ticking over, promising his clients that everything would be back to normal once 'his boy' came home and started helping him out. As partners, we would be a great team, he told them. And the clients remained very loyal, agreeing to stick with him, a testament to the goodwill he had built up over the years.

In my heart of hearts I knew that I couldn't disappoint him, that I had always been destined to return to my roots and my heritage at some point. And given his rapidly deteriorating state of health, I eventually came to realise that I would probably have to do so sooner rather than later. However, I felt that I needed to make a point and put down some markers, so I rather pompously announced that I would agree to join the practice as soon as I left college on two conditions: firstly that the accountant, whom I didn't trust, was sacked and, secondly, that I would take over the organization and day-to-day running of the practice.

Not surprisingly, the old man went ballistic at this point. Who the hell did I think I was, he demanded? No way was he ever going to be dictated to in that way or bound by any such conditions. And how dare I speak to him like that when he had supported me right through veterinary college! The angry confrontation ended with him ordering me out of the house and warning me, in time-honoured fashion, never to darken his doorstep again. However, the seeds had been sown and when I did venture home again a few months later, shortly before I started my final year, he had calmed down and his attitude had changed completely.

"I've been thinking for some time that we should change our accountant, " he remarked casually, almost as if our previous conversation had never taken place and that this was all his own idea. "Also, I'm starting to feel rather tired these days and I'm in a lot of pain, so I guess it would make sense for you basically to run the practice and pay me to work for you, as and when required. That way, you will be free to get on with things and I can take it a bit easier." And so it was that the matter was settled. All I had to do now was make sure I passed my finals.

By this time, I had become a father myself, daughter Lucy Margaret having been born on December 27th, 1979. Di had left the Crowhurst practice the previous year, largely because of the time and expense involved in commuting daily from Cambridge to Newmarket. Instead, she got a job as a secretary to the consultants at Mill Road Maternity Hospital in Cambridge, which was just a few minutes walk away from our house. There was a standing joke there that those who sat in the Secretary's chair would soon become pregnant and Di was no exception.

Lucy was a wonderfully smiley, bubbly baby right from the start. I became totally besotted with her and loved taking her for walks in her pram. As she got a bit older I would take her along with me to watch the rugby and the rest of the boys adored her, a baby on the touchline with a father who was a fellow student being something of a novelty. The fact that Di had had to give up work to look after her did make a bit of a dent in our finances, but, as far as my studies were concerned, having Lucy around was no problem – quite the opposite, if anything. When it came to revision she was actually a great help. It was always a bit difficult to get her to sleep so instead of reading her stories I would recite extracts from my notes and text books – the symptoms of this and that, the make-up of the cranial nerve and so on. She would gurgle away quite happily in her cot and would eventually fall asleep, at which point I'd be quite relieved that I could take a break. Then she would wake up again and I'd have to repeat the exercise. In that way, I'm sure she helped to get me through because she made me do so much extra revision!

At the same time, there were plenty of other distractions adding to the pressure in the months leading up to finals as we started looking around for a house for ourselves in the Burmington area while also making plans in advance for the re-organisation, modernisation and expansion of father's practice.

Once he had accepted the idea in principle that I was going to be taking over and doing things my way, the old man was happy to step back and let me get on with things. He first of all agreed to the purchase of a smart new Portakabin, complete with running water, electricity and all other necessary mod cons, to replace the old surgery in the shed at Burmington. Next, I set about getting it properly equipped. I had heard that Pat Dorrell, former radiographer and founder of Veterinary X-rays, the first British company to specialise in providing this sort of equipment to vets, sold second-hand as well as new X-ray machines, plus a whole range of other instruments, both new and used. Pat was very helpful and knew what I needed far better than I did. I took father along with me to Seer Green in Buckinghamshire, where the business was based, warning him that we were going shopping, so he would need to bring his cheque book with him. The journey from Burmington to Seer Green seemed to take an age, with Dad complaining non-stop: "All you ever want is money! I can't go on spending like this – it will break me."

When we finally arrived Mr Dorrell himself came out to greet us and, watching in a concerned way as father struggled out of the car with his walking sticks, turned to me and said sympathetically: "Would the old gentleman care for a drink?" It was like pressing a magic switch! Accepting the offer with enthusiasm, Dad settled into a seat in the office and, nursing a large scotch, announced: "I want my boy to have the best – I'll leave you to get him sorted out." He had taken instantly to Pat Dorrell and all thoughts of over-spending suddenly evaporated.

As I looked around what was an Aladdin's Cave, my order was soon made up and included a second-hand X-ray machine, plates and film, surgery tables and instruments of all types. I was also advised to buy a brand new 'Little Sister' autoclave. The total bill came to around £600 – still quite a lot of money in 1980 – but father didn't bat an eyelid. In fact, he wanted to write a cheque there and then, but Mr Dorrell insisted that he wouldn't take any money until he had delivered the goods to Burmington and had set up the X-ray machine.

Meanwhile, Di and I were busy house hunting. Ideally, what we were after was somewhere that was close to Burmington, but not too close. It needed to have a garage or outbuilding of some sort that could be converted into a surgery; and it had to be located in a village large enough to support the small animal practice that I wanted to develop. With this in mind, we searched around in Little Compton, Shipston-on-Stour, Tysoe and Moreton-in-Marsh before eventually finding a non-estate, semi-detached property in Hook Norton that fitted the bill, with an integral up-and-over garage at the front that could just about be turned into a small consulting room.

The house was on the market for £27,000. In those days the mortgage rules were very strict. You were only allowed to borrow three times your annual salary and you had to put down a deposit of at least 10%. As my father stood to make a decent profit on the Cambridge house he'd bought for us, he was happy to help us out with the deposit, but that still left us with the problem of how to secure a mortgage of nearly £25,000 when I had no current income and when any future income was entirely dependent on passing my final exams. On top of all that, I had no true idea of predicted figures and no real business plan. Talk about the potential for toxic debt! I was extremely fortunate to find a sympathetic manager at the Alliance & Leicester Building Society in Cambridge who was intrigued by the proposition. He agreed to lend me the money provided that I passed my exams and on condition that I could find a financial guarantor. Once again, father agreed to take on that role.

I sat my final exams in May 1981. On the day that the results were posted I was in such a state of nerves that I couldn't bring myself to go up to the Senate House to look at the lists and sent Di in my place. She was thus the first to know that I had passed. In a state of euphoria, I then rang my parents with the good news before cycling straight round to the Alliance & Leicester to let them know. The staff all stood and clapped and the manager congratulated me and confirmed that our mortgage agreement would be honoured.

Graduates were not allowed to practice until they had been admitted to the Royal College of Veterinary Surgeons at a graduation ceremony about a month after the exam results were published. This allowed me time for a few days of celebration before we got down to the business of moving house and putting the finishing touches to the new practice facilities at Hook Norton and Burmington.

My very proud parents attended the graduation ceremony, after which I took them along to visit the National Stud at New-market. This was not normally open to the general public, but through Mr Simpson, one of the partners in Bob Crowhurst's practice, I had been able to arrange a special tour of the facilities during which we were able to see some of the stallions. Dad felt extremely privileged to be allowed behind the scenes, saying ecstatically: "I feel like the King of England!"

Before finally moving to Hook Norton and opening up my own small animal practice at the house I remained in Cambridge for a further six weeks to work as a locum for John Grieve, with whom I had earlier spent time 'Seeing Practice'. It was John's custom to hire a new graduate as relief cover during the summer holiday period and I was delighted to be offered the chance to gain more invaluable experience.

In a veterinary context, small animals basically means pets rather than farm animals and horses and this, along with the fact that you find yourself dealing face-to-face with everyday members of the general public rather than farmers, breeders and trainers, ensures a far greater variety of both animal patients and human owners. And this means you have to be prepared for all manner of unexpected eventualities, as I soon discovered while working with John Grieve.

On my very first day on duty a King Charles Spaniel was brought into the surgery for his annual vaccination jabs. This was straightforward enough in itself, except that he arrived in the arms of a very attractive, very suntanned, very well-endowed blonde wearing a revealingly low-cut blouse. Despite the obvious distractions I did my best to keep my mind on the job in hand and, purely by way of making conversation, remarked casually at one point: "That's a lovely suntan you've got – have you just come back from somewhere nice."

She fixed me with a steely glare and snapped: "You're meant to be looking at the dog!" Talk about being put in my place!

And then there were the two gay guys who came in carrying

a box from which they produced a two-foot-long Indian Corn Snake, explaining that he was feeling poorly and that they suspected he was suffering from pneumonia. As it happens, I'm not too good with snakes, but they insisted that I should examine the creature. "He won't hurt you," they assured me. "Just hold him with confidence." Easier said than done! As soon as I rather reluctantly took the snake from them it slithered over and around my forearms and then reared up alarmingly and looked me straight in the eye. "Oooh! He likes you," purred his owners in unison.

I had to admit that I hadn't got a clue what to look for and so they proceeded very confidently to give me not just their own diagnosis but also a suggested course of treatment. They pointed to a puffy area under the jaws that they said was a definite indication of pneumonia, in which case, they continued, what was needed was the injection of the antibiotic oxytetracycline three times at regular intervals over a set period. Clearly having encountered the same problem before, they went on to explain that the tip of the needle needed to be inserted at a point between the scales and the antibiotic injected into the underlying muscle. When the needle was withdrawn you needed to keep your thumb pressed over the site otherwise the muscles would contract and squeeze the dose out. I did exactly what I was told, repeated the procedure as directed and all was well. I'm pleased to say that it was the only time I have had to treat a snake of any sort. And it was also the only time that a pet's owner has had to show me exactly what to do.

I learned another useful lesson during my time with John when, in the middle of a busy morning surgery, a man came in with two healthy and very lively young Golden Retrievers and told me that they would unfortunately have to be put to sleep because he and his wife were moving to a small flat where pets were not permitted. I protested that it seemed a dreadful shame to destroy two lovely dogs in the prime of life and suggested that we might even be able to re-home them, but he remained adamant that they had to be put down. Did he want to be present? No, he was already late for work. Still not sure how I was going to handle this very upsetting situation, I got him to go through the process of signing the consent form. Fortunately, I was then saved from having to do anything straightaway by the sudden arrival of an emergency case resulting from a road accident. I told the man that I would have to deal with the dogs later and, as he left, I got the nurse to put them in a holding pen while I helped with the emergency.

About an hour later, the man's very distressed wife burst into the surgery in hysterics, causing a terrible scene in the crowded waiting room as she demanded to know which 'bastard' had killed her beautiful dogs. I was summoned by the nervous receptionist and tried, unsuccessfully at first, to get the distraught woman to calm down, eventually managing to usher her into the consulting room where I assured her that the dogs were fine and still very much alive. You can imagine her relief when she was then re-united with them. I explained what had happened and showed her the signed consent form and it turned out that she and her husband had had an argument as a result of which she had kicked him out of the house, only for him to sneak back and take the dogs while she was out, intent on having them put down out of pure spite. He had then rung her to tell her what he had done, assuming that it would already be too late by then for her to do anything about it. That incident made me very wary in the future.

Di and I had meanwhile had our own quite dramatic small animal experience. The house where we had been living while I was a student had already been sold by the time I went to do my locum stint for John – Dad making a handsome profit of £13,500 on his original £6,500 investment! – so Di and I moved in temporarily with a friend, Alastair Mitchell, who lived on the other side of Cambridge. By this time we had acquired two cats, Face and Tommy. Face, the female, was very clingy whereas Tommy was quite the opposite, being rather shy and unsociable, and on the day we loaded our belongings into a hired van and moved across the city we couldn't find him anywhere. We searched and searched and I then went back several times to look for him again, but there was no sign of him and we had pretty much given up on him when, three weeks later, he suddenly turned up at Alastair's house. He'd never been there before, so how he managed to find us I'll never know. To get there he'd had to cover a distance of well over a mile, crossing at least one very busy main road along the way. It was a great moment when we suddenly spotted him in the garden, so totally unexpected that for a moment we couldn't really believe it was Tommy. But as soon as we opened the door and called him he came stalking in, none the worse for wear. From then on, we kept a close eye on him until the day came for all of us to make the move to Hook Norton, a new home and a new life.

5

Walker & Son

It was in the middle of August 1981 that we loaded all our possessions into a hired van and headed for Hook Norton. I drove the van while Di, heavily pregnant by this time with our second child, followed in our little Fiat 500, with twenty-month-old Lucy strapped firmly into a baby seat in the back.

For me, this was a time of mixed emotions. The excitement of at last joining my father in practice was matched by the anxiety that came with worrying about whether I would be up to the job, whether I could win over all those old clients of his who, I knew, would be queuing up to tell me: "You'll never be as good as your Dad". Added to that was the great responsibility I felt for my wife and growing family, all of whom would be relying on me to make a success of this challenging new venture that I was taking on. My mother, as ever, was the one who gave me confidence, quietly encouraging me with the words: "I know you can do it – now go out and show everyone else".

Burmington continued to be the main focus of the existing practice, the brand new Portakabin now properly equipped with our purchases from Seer Green. With help from Keith Haine, a local farmer friend with an interest in photography, an old outside lavatory was converted into a dark room where plates from the X-ray machine could be developed. At Hook Norton, meanwhile, the garage had been converted into a small waiting room, just about big enough for four chairs, and an even tinier consulting room. The doors to both had to open outwards to compensate for the lack of space inside.

At father's insistence, the little garden plot outside was put to good use as a place to grow some of the herbs and plants that he included in his traditional medicinal preparations. We transplanted some *Hellebore foetidus* (Stinking Hellebore), comfrey, rosemary and sage and I must have inherited my mother's green fingers because they all flourished. Father also wanted me to make sure I had access to plenty of dock leaves, gorse and mallow. "You'll find they all come in useful when those modern medicines fail," he promised.

I had meanwhile purchased a second-hand Fiat from our local dealer, Jack Wood, at The Firs Garage, stocking the boot with everything that I thought I would need for a day's calls – hoof testers, twitch, blindfold, assorted antibiotics in bottles and tubes, syringes, needles, stitching equipment, cleansing materials, waterproofs, wellies and a trusty brown smock, just like the ones my father and grandfather had always worn. With Di on standby to field telephone calls at Hook Norton and Mum doing the same at Burmington I was ready for action, a bundle of nervous and excitable energy as I prepared to set out on my first full round of calls.

As it happened, I had already had what had turned out to be a baptism of fire a few nights earlier when father unexpectedly asked me to answer a late night emergency call from a long-standing client named Mrs Tustian, a leading breeder of German Shepherd dogs. One of her pedigree bitches had gone into labour, but was having difficulty whelping. I raced over to Hookerswell, near Great Tew, arriving to find both the expectant mother and her anxious owner in a state of some distress. I was then up for most of the night, during which eleven puppies were eventually delivered, although, sadly, only four survived. Not the most positively encouraging start.

There were no mobile phones at the time and communication when I was first out on the road was still made by either Mum or Di telephoning to the client where I was scheduled to be – not that I was always necessarily there on time. I then invested in a bleeper which, when it sounded off, meant finding a phone box to ring into the Surgery, so I always kept a pile of change in an old tobacco tin in the car. However, technology was developing fast and we next invested in a radio transmitter, which we called 'Air Call'. This was a large piece of equipment that sat on the passenger seat. It worked quite well, although it could be temperamental – but at least you could speak to your Surgery base and receive messages much more efficiently. The first mobile phone I had was very unreliable. It had to be charged daily, the charge did not always last a full day and the cigarette lighter adaptor was, to say the least, not very effective. Apart from that, the area in which we operated was not well covered by the transmitters so you couldn't get a signal half the time. Now, of course, we all take mobiles for granted and we forget how difficult it was to keep in touch with people once you left your house or office.

My official first day with the practice – September 1st, 1981 – was a busy one, father having filled my appointment book with visits to regular horse-owning clients who had been waiting patiently for weeks for routine, non-urgent treatments for their animals, tasks that he had been physically unable to carry out himself due to his failing health and increasing immobility. Rather than opting to go off and find another vet, these loyal clients had agreed to hang on "until my boy Alan gets here to help me out".

Number one on the list of calls was Mrs Wood, wife of the Firs Garage owner from whom I'd bought my car, who kept miniature ponies that were stabled just down the road from the Hook Norton surgery at the bottom of Oatley Hill. Her four ponies and a donkey all needed to have their feet trimmed. Then it was on to a riding school run by Jill Harwood at Tudor Hall, just outside Banbury, where six horses were due to have their teeth rasped, another job that can be quite physically demanding. My time at Newmarket served me well in this respect as I had had plenty of experience of rasping teeth while helping out there.

The next call took me to Marston St Lawrence and Norman Mawle, one of father's oldest friends. Norman had a great old horse called Elm Boy whose feet required a trim. Then, in the afternoon, I drove all the way over to the other side of Stow-on-the-Wold to visit Judy Hanks, the doyenne of the Heythrop Pony Club. I arrived there to find no less than twelve ponies being lined up to have their teeth rasped. After that, it was back to Hook Norton for evening surgery, where my first patient was an off-colour rabbit belonging to the local Post Office owner, Laurie Heath. By the end of the day I was knackered.

My aim was to take at least £100-a-week at the Hook Norton surgery in order to cover the cost of the mortgage repayments. By the end of the first week I had taken £103 and felt very pleased with myself for having successfully followed Mr Micawber's recipe for happiness. But the next week I took only £94 and, by the same token, was instantly plunged into misery, convinced that we were going to go bust and that I wouldn't be able to support my family, which was due to be increased at any moment by the arrival of our second child. In fact, that second week was to be the only time that the takings ever dipped below £100.

Father had been busy holding impromptu gatherings and small parties for his friends and clients in order to spread the word that "our Alan" was back at last and would gradually be taking over more and more of the practice work from him. "I can't do so much now, so you will have to rely on him," he told them, adding: "I've tried to teach him all I know". I knew, however, that nobody would simply take his word for my abilities, that I would have to go out and prove myself before I could earn people's confidence and respect. It helped that, at thirty-five, I was a fair bit older than most young vets starting out on their careers, which meant that I didn't seem quite so obviously wet behind the ears. And having been born and bred locally, I not only knew the area like the back of my hand, meaning that I had no difficulty finding my way around even to the most remote outlying farms, but I had also been well acquainted for years with many of our clients and their families. I had been a member of the Young Farmers Club along with a lot of the local farmers' sons, many of whom were already in the process of taking over from their fathers and although I had been away for quite a long time, they remembered me.

On September 16th, 1981, just two weeks after my first day in the job, Di gave birth to our son, George. He came rushing into the world and was very different to his sister Lucy – extremely lively right from the word go. Di took his arrival very much in her stride and was soon able to resume working with me in the practice. In those early days we had no staff and Di doubled up as my receptionist and nurse, while my mother helped out at Burmington, fielding calls from clients and looking after Lucy and George when Di and I took animals over there for operations. That was something she really enjoyed and the kids loved it too, especially when they were a little bit older. The house was so big and there was so much more to do there than in our tiny little home. Mother would take them out to feed the pigs and the chickens, to collect the eggs and to pick the vegetables from the kitchen garden. Lucy particularly loved being allowed to pop the broad beans out of their furry pods.

We had a routine at Hook Norton whereby any cats that needed to be neutered or spayed would be dealt with first thing in the morning, before we had breakfast. In those early days Di would give George his 6.00am feed and then put him back to bed and we would then strap Lucy into her high chair and give her a slice of toast and something to drink while we operated on the cats. Still less than two years old, our little daughter used to find our antics hilarious and we would hear her chuckling away in the background as we grappled with often very reluctant moggies who, quite understandably, did not want to be held and injected with an anaesthetic.

After their operation, the cats would be left in their baskets to recover while we went off to have our breakfast. On one occasion, having operated successfully on two cats, we left them sleeping peacefully while we went and had our breakfast, only to find when we got back that one of them was missing. It is amazing what narrow spaces a determined cat can squeeze through. In this instance the basket hadn't been securely fastened. A few minutes of frantic searching ensued before we eventually discovered the escapee asleep in a cupboard.

Nearly all other routine operations apart from the spaying and neutering of cats were carried out at Burmington on Wednesday mornings. Again, Di would act as my nurse, holding the animals while I administered the anaesthetic, assisting me during the operation and helping to clean up afterwards. Because the surgery was so small, it was important to make sure that everything was kept neat and tidy and in its place, allowing us the space to move about as freely as possible while operating. The place was so cramped that not even father was allowed in while an operation was in progress!

As well as looking after the kids while we were out in the surgery, my mother would always prepare a proper two-course lunch for us all. While I then went out on my rounds, Di would stay until the animals we had operated on had fully recovered before taking the kids home, along with any of the animals that had come over with us from Hook Norton that morning. Their owners would then come and collect them later in the day. After finishing my afternoon calls I would go back to Burmington to discharge any animals that had been brought straight there, returning to Hook Norton in time for evening surgery from 5.00 – 6.30pm.

Even then, the working day was far from over. I would often have to go out again to make further calls immediately after evening surgery and then we would have to clean up the surgery itself, ready for the next morning. If it was a wet day the floors would be left very muddy, especially if we'd had farmers coming in and out in their wellies, on top of which there would be the usual mess associated with poorly and nervous animals.

We couldn't do the cleaning up until George had got to sleep because his bedroom was right above the surgery and in the days when he was having a 10.00pm feed this meant the job sometimes wouldn't get done until getting on for midnight. And somewhere in between all that I would have to find time to do all the paperwork.

Our new accountant, Bob Coombes, had given me a stern lecture about the vital necessity of making sure I always kept my paperwork up-to-date. "No matter how hard you work, the effort will all be wasted if you don't keep your books in order," he warned. He urged me to write up my bookings religiously every day, to send out invoices at the end of every month and to pay in any cheques every week. He said I should never tolerate debts and should pay my own bills on time. Sound advice, but not always easy to follow, especially at the end of another hard day when dealing with a load of tiresome paperwork was the last thing you wanted to do.

Despite doing my best to take care of the business side of things it was only a matter of months before I faced my first financial crisis. The biggest regular outgoings for any veterinary practice tend to be drug company bills. Reps from all the major companies are constantly knocking on your door, trying to sell you the latest wonder drug. I have dealt with many over the years and there were some real characters among them. Those I remember most vividly include Trevor Oliver, who worked for what was then Smith Kline & French and who did very well out of us with a horse wormer called Equitac and a cattle and sheep wormer called Valbazen; Brian Davis of ICI who eventually went off to live the good life in America, where he bought some log cabins overlooking a lake and ran them as Bed & Breakfast accommodation for fishermen; and Glaxo's Mike Rae.

Mike was the Noel Coward of reps. Well-spoken and very dapper, always elegantly dressed in a smart suit, he would puff on a cigarette and say: "Dear boy, this is what you need." He would then proceed to make up the order for me – and that was fine with me because, unlike some others, he never once tried to oversell to me. Hoescht's rep was a very dry old character called Tom Worsfold, who would never give you any kind of discount but had such good products that we were almost forced to deal with him. Others like Ted Armitage from Bayer, Dave Weaver from Intervet, Jane May from Mycofarm and Keith Porter from Upjohn all became great friends of the practice, helping to guide and educate me in the early years.

Where I nearly came unstuck was when, right at the very beginning, I was unable to resist the temptation of a generous introductory deal offered by the Veterinary Drug Company, who were prepared to let me have my first three months' supply of their products on interest-free credit, plus a decent discount, as long as it was then paid off in full at the end of the three month period. Payment fell due on December 21st, 1981 and when the bill arrived I found to my horror that I owed them just over £9,000 at a point when I had only £8,750 in the bank. I had gloomy visions of a rather unhappy Christmas until, by the greatest good fortune, a cheque for £300 from one of my clients came through in the post the very next day. The relief was palpable.

Within six months of setting up the new practice I found myself on my own, father having finally been forced to accept that he was no longer fit enough to carry on. He had continued to do the odd job here and there for the first few months until his hips became so painful that he had to go into hospital for a series of operations. Unfortunately, these were not a great success and he never worked again. However, he was still there to dispense advice, which was often invaluable, especially so given that I was still relatively inexperienced.

Meanwhile, the practice had been rapidly getting busier and busier as people I hadn't seen for years began beating a path to our door, both at Burmington and Hook Norton. In particular, the fact that more and more local farmers and horse owners were coming to me was very encouraging.

As had been the case ever since my student days helping out at the Crowhurst practice in Newmarket, my main ambition was to specialise in working with horses, and racehorses in particular. So it was a real red letter day when, towards the end of 1981, I got a call from trainer John Webber asking me if I could carry out routine blood tests on some of his horses. I had only met him for the first time a few months earlier at one of the small parties my father had organized with the aim of introducing me to a few people he thought I should know as I prepared to set up in practice. Father had been a friend of the Webbers for many years and was regularly called in to castrate their colts. Even so, I was amazed when John turned up at the little drinks party held at the Duke of Cumberland in Clifton, Oxfordshire, which was run at the time by keen racing fans Roger and Jenny Croft.

Here, after all, was a trainer then at the top of his trade, having won the Massey Ferguson Gold Cup at Cheltenham for local owners Mr and Mrs Richmond-Watson with their home-bred horse Snipe. Based at Cropredy Lawn, just outside Banbury, John and the entire Webber family were steeped in horse folklore as a result of their exploits in hunting, racing and showjumping. John's father, Captain Webber, was a former cavalry officer who went on to become a leading showjumper and who, as Secretary General of the British Showjumping Association, effectively ran the sport for thirty years. Described by the legendary Colonel Sir Harry Llewellyn as "one of the most popular men ever to grace our sport", he also had a livery stable near Amersham, where he mostly looked after hunters for the landed gentry, while also teaching their sons and daughters to ride. He retired to Cherington where, when I first started in practice, I would occasionally visit him to treat his little terrier dog. Father, who had enormous respect for him, made it clear that he should never be sent a bill.

John Webber had started out as a dairy farmer, with a large herd of Jersey cows grazing Cropredy Lawn's 400 acres, but horses were always his great passion. As an amateur jockey, he rode very successfully in point-to-points around the country for more than twenty years, with a total of seventy winners to his credit, before giving up farming to become a full-time trainer in 1970, selling the cows and turning the cowsheds into stables. His sons, Anthony and Paul, were both champion amateur jockeys, Paul going on to work as an assistant trainer to Jeremy Hindley and then as a director of the Curragh Bloodstock Agency before eventually taking over from his father at Cropredy Lawn, while Anthony became a successful equine chiropractor and also a steward. And elder daughter Teresa, who died tragically young from cancer, was a top class lady point-to-pointer for many years, with horses like Brockie Law and White Paper.

It boosted my confidence enormously to have someone as well-known and highly respected as John was throughout the equine and racing world going out of his way to be friendly and encouraging, wishing me all the best in my new veterinary enterprise and also giving me some sound bits of advice about dealing with horses. "Make sure you never get into a situation where they can hurt you and never fall out with anybody over them," were among the tips I remember him giving me during our chat that evening.

We got on very well, but I didn't really expect anything to come of it in the near future, so it came as quite a shock when just a few months later I received his phone call out of the blue. "John Webber here," he said, adding without further preamble: "Do you do blood tests?" I replied that, of course, I did – the prospect of being able to do a bit of work for such a highly-regarded trainer being far too tempting for me to admit that, actually, I had no proper laboratory and no means of carrying out the tests.

"Good," he said. "In that case, I would like you to come over to Cropredy Lawn tomorrow morning and take samples from three of my horses."

I put the phone down and, trying not to panic, rang Derek Knottenbelt, the Stratford vet with whom I had spent time 'Seeing Practice' and who, I knew, had the lab facilities needed to analyse the samples. Derek agreed to carry out the tests for me as long as he could have the samples by 10.00 am, in which case he would be able let me have the results the same evening.

Much relieved, I drove over to Cropredy early the next morning, took the samples and delivered them to Derek at Stratford. Then, armed with the results and displaying a certain amount of bravado, I went back later the same day to see John – 'the Guv'nor' as he was known around the yard – and to inform him that while one of the three horses was in tip-top condition the other two had mild infections for which they would need to be treated. The one I had passed fit duly won next time out and the test results for the other two merely confirmed what the Guv'nor had already suspected, so I was seen to have done a good job and earned an all-important seal of approval. From then on I was regularly called in to carry out blood testing, continuing to take them to Stratford for analysis until the time, some years later, when I installed my own set-up. I am not certain if the Guv'nor ever knew exactly where the samples were being tested, but suspect that he probably did. He was so shrewd that nothing really escaped him. Anyhow, it was the start of an enduring and hugely rewarding professional and personal relationship with the Webbers that helped to establish my credentials in the racing world and that has lasted to this day.

By the early summer of 1982 the business and the pressure of work had expanded to the point where I felt I needed some part-time help in the practice and employed Jessica Moseley, another fellow student from the Cambridge days who lived in Cirencester, to take one evening surgery a week. This was mainly so that I could spend just a little bit more time with the children. Looking back, one of my regrets is that I missed being involved with George during the first few months of his life in the same way that I had been with Lucy, when I was still a student. With Jessica there to hold the fort, there was at least one weekday evening when I could be involved in bath time and bedtime story reading. Later on, I did make every effort to go to school events, such as sports days, plays, carol services and the like, but even so there were occasions when I had to let the kids down. Seeing the hurt in their little faces when we met up later always made me feel terribly guilty. But my father had brought me up to accept that work must always come before everything else – when it came to supporting your family, that had to be your only priority. And, of course, he was right. That was how everybody of his generation thought. Today, attitudes generally have softened.

Jessica was only available to work for me over a three-month period before taking up a full-time job elsewhere, but having her around for that short time made me realise that I could actually do with some permanent help. This became more of a necessity when the small animal branch surgery run by Banbury-based vet Joy Spiers from her home in the nearby village of Sibford Ferris closed down after Joy decided to retire following the death of her husband, Austin. A great character and a very popular vet, much in demand locally, Joy passed many of her clients on to us at Hook Norton.

At around the same time, and again with a lot of very generous help from Derek Knottenbelt in Stratford, I had succeeded in qualifying as a registered Local Veterinary Investigator (LVI), enabling me to carry out valuable inspection and testing work for what was then still the Ministry of Agriculture and Fisheries, now the Department of Environment, Food and Rural Affairs.

It was at this juncture that I was very conveniently introduced to Kiwi Sue Blaikie. A relative of Nicky Lay, wife of one of father's longtime clients, Sue had qualified as a vet back in New Zealand and, having recently moved to the UK, was looking for work as a locum. I took to her from the moment we first met and immediately offered her a job. She proved to be a fantastic help and we worked well together – Sue mostly looking after the rapidly growing small animal side of things, thereby freeing me up to concentrate on the horses and other large animals.

With Di increasingly having her hands full looking after the children, I decided at the same time to employ someone else to answer the phone and to look after the booking of jobs, the banking of cheques and other day-to-day office administration. Valerie Smith worked for me in this capacity for two years. Not exactly in the first flush of youth when she joined us, she was admirably neat and tidy in her work, very calm and well-organised and extremely adept at dealing with any awkward or difficult clients. When she sadly succumbed to the ravages of breast cancer she left a big gap that was not easily filled.

Towards the end of 1982, just over a year after setting up in practice, things were going much better than I had ever dared to hope. The practice turnover in the twelve months since I had taken over amounted to £44,000, compared with £15,000 for the previous year, father's last on his own. But then, just when I was beginning to think that it was all now going to be plain sailing, I found myself facing a major financial crisis that threatened to ruin everything.

6

An Inspector Calls

Most people would probably find it hard to imagine what might be worse – answering a knock on your front door to be confronted by two stony-faced police officers demanding entrance before then accusing you of a crime you have not committed; or the arrival on your doorstep of an equally unsmiling inspector and two assistants from the Inland Revenue wanting to grill you about the not-so-small fortune they claim you owe in unpaid tax. Di and I between us having once had the misfortune to suffer both these ordeals in the space of just a few months, I can say with some authority that there's not much to choose between the two.

My father had just gone into hospital for the second of his hip operations in September 1981 when, out of the blue, one of those dreaded buff envelopes marked HM Revenue and Customs dropped through the practice letterbox, addressed to him. Opening it in his absence and anticipating nothing much worse than a routine reminder that our annual tax return was due, I was horrified to read that the business was under investigation for what appeared to be a considerable sum of unpaid tax and that we would be visited shortly by an inspector.

An appointment was made and a Mr Armstrong duly arrived with his team and revealed the stunning news that the sum involved, which related to a period going back over several years, was estimated at a mind-boggling £70,000! Much else of what he had to say at that initial meeting flew over my head because I was, understandably, in a state of shock. I explained that I had only been with the practice for a few months, that I had no idea how such arrears could have arisen and that having to come up with that sort of money would bankrupt the business. Making it clear that I was willing to co-operate, I requested a further meeting in the presence of our accountant, Bob Coombes.

Bob, who clearly relished the opportunity to pit his considerable wits against those of the Revenue, was in his element, but as he and the inspection team went through the books together and analysed the figures it became clear that there had indeed been an underpayment. This was due to the failings of Bob's predecessor – the accountant in whom I had never really had much confidence and who I had insisted should be sacked before I would agree to join the practice. However, I could quite honestly say that neither father nor I had ever knowingly signed off false accounts. At one point, when the same question was put to me over and over again, I asked Mr Armstrong, point blank, if he thought I was telling lies. He replied menacingly: "If I thought you were lying, Mr Walker, there would be a couple of extra noughts on the bill."

In fact, he was very fair and understanding. Although the settlement eventually negotiated by Bob was for less than the original £70,000 it was a still an eye-watering sum, money that we clearly didn't have and couldn't possibly raise overnight, so I was given the option of paying it off in instalments spread over a period of four years. Even so, it was a shattering blow that, for a while, put the practice under severe financial pressure.

We were still reeling from this devastating setback when we were suddenly hit by a second extremely distressing and totally unexpected run-in with the authorities. This time it was the police who came calling, with Di becoming an unlikely and totally innocent suspect in a bizarre crime investigation.

It began late one afternoon while I was out answering an emergency call from trainer Walter Charles at Guys Cliffe Stables in Warwick. One of his horses had gone down with colic so I was detained there longer than anticipated and when I eventually returned home in the early evening I walked through the door to find Di distraught and in tears. For an awful moment all sorts of terrible thoughts flashed through my mind and I then listened in stunned disbelief as she told me that she had answered a knock on the front door an hour or two earlier to be confronted by our local police constable and a Sergeant from Banbury wanting to question her about a hoax call that had been made to Marks & Spencer in Banbury warning that a bomb had been planted in the store. The call had been traced to our number and although the switchboard operator who had taken it had described the caller as sounding like a young male, Di was told that her voice could easily have been mistaken over the phone for that of a young man.

Asked where she had been at 1.00pm, she said that she had been feeding the children their lunch. But because there were no witnesses, apart from the children themselves, this didn't count as an alibi. By now, she was in a state of shock. Of course, she hadn't made the call, she told the officers, protesting her total innocence. What possible motive could she have had for doing something like that? It was ridiculous. They must have somehow got the wrong number. But they were adamant that our number was the one from which the call had been made. The two officers eventually left, threatening to return with further evidence that would enable them to charge her.

Not surprisingly, Di had a sleepless night, but by the next morning she was absolutely determined that if she was charged, she would fight it all the way. Sir Geoffrey Howe, then Chancellor of the Exchequer and the father-in-law of Steve Glanvill, one of my fellow students at Cambridge who had become a close friend and was godfather to our son George, even wrote a character reference on her behalf. Meanwhile, there was no further word from the police and no follow-up visit. Days and then weeks went by and we heard absolutely nothing more and yet the worry hung over us like a cloud. I eventually took the initiative and got in touch with the police to be told that the case had been dropped because it seemed there was a possibility that the call could have come from the numbers on either side of ours. Fortunately, the case was never made public so Di's good name was in no way tarnished. However, we were very angry that nobody had bothered to contact us to let us know what was happening. It could have saved us a month of unnecessary anxiety.

While all this was going on we also found ourselves having to deal with the worrying fact that my mother's health had started to deteriorate rapidly. She had been suffering terribly with arthritis for some time and at first this masked the fact that she had developed a much more serious underlying problem. By the time breast cancer was diagnosed it was too advanced for anything to be done about it and she died a few months later in the summer of 1983, shortly after being admitted to the Ellen Badger Hospital in Shipston-on-Stour. She was sixty-nine.

Mother had always been a very strong lady, the driving force behind the whole family. My father, it has to be said, liked a drink and we all know what drinkers can be like – some days they're good, some days they're not. Mother was the consistent thread that held the family together. She it was who pushed father to make the move to Burmington and who then almost single-handedly supervised the transformation of the crumbling manor house into a solid family home and the land that went with it into a valuable source of extra income; she it was who got the money together to pay for private education at good schools for me and my two sisters through her various little cottage industry enterprises – her poultry, her pigs, the produce from her kitchen garden and the things she cooked for sale in the local market stalls; and she it was who insisted that we must all have a week's sea air once a year, organizing holidays in Bournemouth, Clacton and Pwellhi.

Mum was always working, always grafting. And she had a wonderfully positive attitude, which, especially as far as I was concerned, manifested itself in the way she provided constant encouragement throughout those long years when I was struggling to gain the qualifications that would enable me to realise my ambition of becoming a vet, urging me to believe in myself whenever I experienced moments of self-doubt. In that and many other respects I owed her an enormous debt of gratitude and it was a great comfort to me to know that she lived long enough to see me beginning to justify the confidence she had always shown in me by successfully taking over and re-establishing the family business. At the same time, I knew that she had taken a special delight in being able to see her grandchildren, Lucy and George, starting to grow up. So, one way and another, I like to think that she will have died a very proud woman.

Left on his own, father decided that he wanted to move from Burmington. The house was too big for him to rattle around in by himself and, no longer being in the best state of repair it needed a lot of work doing on it. Apart from that, the place suddenly seemed to hold too many painful memories for him. I understood how he felt and while he started looking around for a more manageable property I set about making arrangements to relocate the Portakabin, parking it temporarily at my friend Tom Heritage's farm at Oxhill.

Father eventually found a bungalow in the nearby village of Stourton where he was to spend the last six years of his life with his companion and carer, Annie Baker, an old family friend who had been godmother to my deceased sister Margaret. She and father were very happy together. Given his state of health, the old man needed somebody to look after him, so Annie did us all a favour. She also loved being able to get involved with our children, Lucy and George, and they, in turn, were equally fond of her, adopting her as a surrogate grandmother.

At around the same time that father moved out of Burmington, I suddenly got the chance to expand both our home and the small animal surgery facilities in Hook Norton when the other half of our semi-detached house came up for sale. The price asked for 'Calafel' next door had now risen to twice what we had paid for 'Dunromin' just two years earlier and whilst I couldn't really afford it, I equally couldn't afford *not* to take advantage of such an opportunity. Not only would we, as a family, have more space to ourselves, but it would also enable me to develop the surgery and provide accommodation for any future employees.

In the latter respect, the investment paid off within a couple of years when Steve Glanvill came to join the practice and moved into the house with his wife Amanda. Steve had been a fellow student in the same year as me at Cambridge and right from the start we had got on well together. He was a farmer's son from Woodbury, near Exeter, and I had always rather assumed that he would eventually return home to Devon to work down there. However, as we parted company after graduating and went our separate ways – Steve to start a job in Horsham – I made him promise to keep in touch. I explained that I was going home to take over my father's one-man practice and suggested that if I could make a real go of it then maybe there might be an opportunity for him one day to come and work with me.

We again discussed this possibility a couple of years later at George's christening in 1983, when Steve became a godparent, along with Rob Pilsworth and Jan Guilbride, another good friend from Cambridge days. At that point I was able to report that things were going well, that the practice was building nicely and that I had already taken on a locum. Steve, for his part, made it clear that he would be interested in joining me and we agreed once more to keep in touch. By 1985, with the business expanding and Sue Blaikie having moved on, I decided that the time had definitely come to bring in a second full-time vet and when I duly contacted Steve he was more than happy to accept my offer of a job.

Steve and I worked very well together. He looked after the farm animal side while I concentrated on the horses and we shared the small animal duties between us. With the business rapidly expanding, we soon decided that we needed to employ a full-time veterinary nurse. Although not formally qualified, Bloxham farmer's daughter Sue Hemmings was blessed with great common sense and also had a wonderful way with both animals and their owners, who all liked and respected her.

At the same time, we also found it necessary to upgrade our office set up. Margaret Stratford had been doing the book keeping and invoicing for some time, but as the volume of business continued to increase she was finding it difficult to cope manually with all the paperwork involved and suggested that we should invest in a computer. Unlike Steve and myself, Margaret was computer literate and after a few teething problems the new system was soon up-and-running and proved a great success.

With everything going so well and our confidence growing, Steve then felt that we should expand the small animal side of the business, and after looking around we opened a new surgery in the Spendlove Centre at Charlbury, which had been the old school and was just twelve miles from Hook Norton. We initially leased a unit on the first floor of this local community business centre, but that turned out to be less than ideal since we often had to carry animals upstairs for clients who were unable to do so themselves for whatever reason. Fortunately, a unit soon became available on the ground floor and we were able to move in there instead. Meanwhile, I had found a site in the Station Yard at Shipston-on-Stour at which to relocate the Portakabin. So – two vets, a nurse and a secretary, along with Di as a general helper and holiday relief, and two branch surgeries in addition to the main one in Hook Norton. With more than enough work coming in to keep us all busy, life was indeed sweet!

Within a year it had become clear that the surgery at Hook Norton was getting far too busy for Di and I and the children to continue living 'above the shop' at Dunromin. We were finding that we had no real privacy there any more. The final straw came one Sunday evening when I was playing with Lucy in the back garden and a client suddenly marched through the gate demanding to be seen right away. In 1986 we moved round the corner to a brand new house at Bell Hill, built by local builder Ray Manning, whose yard was located immediately behind the surgery.

As soon as we moved out of Dunromin, work started on converting the downstairs part of the house into consulting rooms, an operating theatre and a drug store and the upstairs into a laboratory, plus a small self-contained flat in which, if necessary, a nurse could live. When the alterations were complete, we decided to hold an Open Day at which we could show clients around the new facilities while at the same time also generating some useful publicity.

The official opening ceremony was conducted by Ray Gasson, a local dairy farmer, District Councillor and Land Manager who had also become a good friend despite – or maybe because of – an awkward incident that could well have got our relationship off on the wrong foot. I had only just started in practice when he called me out to look at one of his cows that appeared out of sorts. In all good faith, I treated the animal with drugs that later prevented it being slaughtered for human consumption, thereby reducing its value. Ray came knocking on the back door at Dunromin on a Sunday morning with his jaw set at an angle that suggested he was not a happy man.

"What are you going to do about it?" he demanded, claiming that I had been responsible for costing him money. I hadn't actually done anything wrong, but rather than argue the toss I simply asked him how much he was out of pocket and, without further ado, wrote out a cheque for the suggested amount. He was shocked into silence and departed in a much better frame of mind. He says now that, of course, I have recouped my outlay that day many times over as a result of continuing to look after all his animals. Well, it's true that I would have been very stupid to give away money when I didn't really have to if I hadn't thought that my generous gesture would pay off in the long run!

As the practice continued to grow and with horses now taking up more and more of my time, I very soon found myself contemplating the need to expand both our facilities and our staff even further. Since moving away from Burmington we had nowhere to stable horses and any operations had to be carried out in the field. By 1988 it was clear the time had come to rectify this situation. The perfect opportunity then quite naturally arose when I was called out early one morning to treat a case of colic at a livery yard run by Tessa Emblem and her partner Lionel Hayward in the middle of Hook Norton, where they had eight stables in the yard behind their house, Peverel. The entire property had been on the market for some time but I hadn't really considered it until I got chatting to Lionel that morning after treating the horse and, in the course of conversation, asked casually if he'd had any offers for the place. "We've had a few people showing interest, but nothing concrete so far," he shrugged, adding in his characteristically dry manner: "I reckon you ought to buy it!"

I thought hard about it all day, went back that same evening to have another look around and then straightaway made what seemed to me like a sensible offer. It was less than the asking price, but Lionel accepted it on the spot – on condition that I paid Tessa an extra £1,000 for the carpets. It's always a bit worrying when somebody appears to bite your hand off in that way because you start to wonder if you've paid over the odds. However, I was happy with the deal, which was done on a handshake and went through smoothly and quickly. Shortly afterwards, a third vet, Robin Kernohan, joined the practice and moved into the house with his wife, Ruth, who helped out with the horses, a steady stream of whom soon started arriving at Peverel for treatment.

Operations were carried out in a special area enclosed by large bales of straw. My first case involved a Hobday operation – a procedure aimed at improving a horse's breathing – which I carried out on a good old hunter chaser called Rugy, owned by George and Rob Weaving, old friends of father's who had used him to look after their racehorses. They were originally from Sherborne in Warwickshire but had moved to a farm near Newport Pagnell, some sixty miles from Hook Norton. They dropped the horse off on their way to Heythrop for the annual point-to-point that always used to be held there on the first Tuesday of April and then picked him up again on the way back. The operation was a success and Rugy went on to win several more races over the next few years.

Despite the fact that the practice now boasted three full-time vets it hadn't got to the point where I was able to devote myself exclusively to working with horses. I was still taking my turn to be on-call in the evenings and at weekends and was also doing my share of the small animal surgeries and farm work. All this was never a problem for me, the level of job satisfaction I got from successfully doing exactly what I had always wanted to do more than making up for the long hours and hard work. I've always been able to get on well with people and there were plenty of wonderfully colourful, interesting and often very entertaining characters to be found not only among our clients but often among their animals as well. And the joy and relief that people often experienced when I was able to treat a beloved pet successfully was tremendously rewarding.

In this respect, I have a particularly vivid memory of an elderly couple, Will Shirley and his wife, coming in one evening with their dog, Beau, who had collapsed suddenly. I knew the Shirleys well. They lived in Wigginton, where Will had worked for many years for local farmer Tom Lovell, one of father's oldest clients. In fact, as father would often proudly recall, five generations of Walkers had served as vets to five generations of Lovells. Like Jack Sprat, Will Shirley was a small, slightly built man, while his wife was a huge lady, and they were both in tears when they arrived at the surgery with Beau. The dog was actually an ugly, snappy little thing and my main concern while examining him was to avoid getting bitten, but they clearly adored him. Unable to find anything obviously wrong, I suggested that they leave him with me overnight. I set up a drip and gave him some fluids and when I checked at 11.00pm I found, somewhat to my surprise, that he was still alive and his colour had improved. We continued to check him through the night and at one point found him sitting up, looking much better. By the next morning he had recovered completely and I concluded that he must simply have been dehydrated for some reason. The Shirleys were completely overcome when they returned later that day expecting the worst only to find Beau sitting up bright and cheerful. Tears again streamed down their faces, only this time they were tears of happiness rather than despair. Will insisted that it was a complete miracle and the couple's joy was so palpable as to be infectious, everybody in the surgery sharing their delight.

Mrs Shirley cradled Beau in her arms and I watched them walk to their car, a light blue Reliant Robin three-wheeler. Will ushered his wife into the passenger seat at which point the car tilted considerably to that side. When Will got in on the driver's side, it seemed to make no difference at all to the angle of the car and as they set off for home, both of them so happy, I wondered what would happen if they cornered to the left a little too quickly!

Another case firmly rooted in my memory concerned a lady named Cathy Beaumont from Whichford and her collie, Cindy, who was brought to the surgery in a very bad way, having been hit by a car and left with a shattered hind leg. Cindy had been a present to Cathy from her husband, who had then died tragically not long afterwards, so there was a very special sentimental attachment and Cathy naturally wanted everything possible done in an effort to save her dog. The leg was so badly damaged that it was immediately obvious to me upon examination that there was no way of repairing it. The only option would be amputation – and I had to admit to Cathy that this was a procedure I had never carried out before. Completely undaunted by this, she told me to go ahead, so, with instruments in hand and Di reading out instructions from my textbook on surgery, the leg was removed. Happily, Cindy proved to be a model patient and not only recovered quickly but soon mastered the art of walking and then sprinting on three legs.

I later found myself having to carry out the same operation

on a sheep. Derek Strong, a farmer from Chadlington, had imported some very expensive, pink-faced Rouge de l'Ouest ewes from France, intending to breed from them. One of these ewes, Peggy, then damaged a hind leg so badly that it could not be repaired and amputation was the only option, given that she was far too valuable to be put down. Part of the lower leg was removed at the surgery and Peggy then went home to recuperate in her pen in the shadow of the church at Chadlington. Like Cindy, she was a brilliant patient, but although she could get around quite happily on three legs we doubted that she would be able to stand up to the rigours of breeding in that condition, so we got Tracy Hapgood, a local saddler, to make an artificial limb. Tracy crafted a prosthetic that featured a wooden leg with a soft, leather-lined attachment that fitted over the stump. This was so successful that Peggy produced twin lambs for the next four years and reared them all without any problem.

There were always clients who wanted to see father rather than me, never missing an opportunity to remind me of how good he was. This was especially true of the Romany gypsies who would regularly pass through the area in their traditional, brightly decorated caravans drawn by lovely horses that were always well cared for. One of them called in at the surgery one day, asking for father, and was clearly disappointed to be told that he wasn't around and that he would have to make do with me instead. Having rather grudgingly accepted this, he explained that one of his horses, a gelding, was having a problem urinating. "You'll have to come and have a look at him," he said.

After surgery had finished, I drove over to the encampment just outside Milcombe, where four or five horses were tethered nearby, grazing happily. I was taken to the one with the problem and having asked the Romany to hold the animal steady whilst I had a look I managed surreptitiously to inject a relaxant into a vein without him being able to see exactly what I was doing. I then told him to stand back and he watched with an increasingly puzzled frown on his face as I started repeatedly stroking the horse's flank with a circular motion. "What the hell are you doing now?" he inquired.

"Surely you know father's old trick of getting a horse to relax and let its manhood out?" I replied. "With your hand, you stroke ten circles clockwise, ten circles anti-clockwise and then wait for a few minutes. It never fails." His response was unprintable, with the suggestion that I must be trying to take the p*** out of him rather than his horse. But sure enough, the patient was soon fully relaxed, enabling me to set to and clean his sheath, removing a large deposit of solid material from his urethral fossa.

"That should sort him out," I said, stepping back. "But you will need to repeat the treatment daily for a while. So, remember – ten times one way and then ten times the other."

A week later the gypsy burst into the surgery, demanding to see me. "How many times did you say I had to do it? I've spent hours trying to get him to relax and I'm buggered if I can!"

With a self-satisfied smile I replied smugly: "Well, perhaps I'm a bit better than you thought, after all."

7

Horse Whisperer

My father's health had been steadily declining throughout the 1980s and in November 1988 he was finally admitted to the Ellen Badger hospital in Shipston-on-Stour, where he died peacefully on December 23rd. It was only during the days that followed, leading up to his funeral in Long Compton, that I came fully to appreciate just how widely-known, well-liked and highly-respected he had been, not only within the farming, horse-owning and racing fraternity but generally, throughout the whole area and beyond. The church at Long Compton was packed to overflowing with people from all walks of life who had come from miles around to see him off. And the letters of condolence, sympathy and goodwill that poured in served to remind me of many great anecdotes, mostly concerning friends, acquaintances and countrymen involved in racing and point-to-pointing, people who, over the years, had regularly either dropped in on him at Burmington or had invited him into their own farmhouse kitchens after a professional visit to gossip and reminisce, usually over a drink or two.

The names that spring to mind include trainer Earl Jones and his wife Bridie from Roel Gate near Guiting Power. Every summer they would go down to Torquay for a busman's summer holiday, taking a few horses with them and racing them at Newton Abbot and what was then known as Devon & Exeter, located up on top of Haldon Hill just outside Exeter. On one occasion, when I was a young boy, they took me along too, to help look after the horses. It was a great adventure. I slept in the horsebox and on the days when they weren't racing we would all go to the beach for an hour or two before Earl went in search of a suitable watering hole. Bridie was a larger-than-life character. Very Irish, she had a broad accent and spoke so fast that it was sometimes difficult to understand her. The two of them were both great fun and very entertaining.

They had some good horses, including a mare named Good Gracious, who, as a youngster, had once beaten Arkle. And Forty Secrets, a stayer who won a New Year's Day chase at Cheltenham. Earl also trained Honey End, who, having then been moved to Ryan Price's yard at Findon, much to Earl's chagrin, went on to finish as runner-up to Foinavon in the famously dramatic Grand National of 1967. Honey End, the 15/2 favourite, was going well while Foinavon, a 100-1 outsider, was lagging far behind when a mass pile up at the 23rd fence, caused by a loose horse careering into the field, effectively brought the race to a temporary standstill. However, Foinavon was so far behind that jockey John Buckingham had time to steer him wide of the melee and through a small gap to jump the fence cleanly on the outside. Honey End's jockey, Josh Gifford, was one of seventeen riders who remounted and gave chase but by then Foinavon was almost out of sight and went on to win by fifteen lengths. Some years later the 23rd was officially named the Foinavon Fence.

Edward Courage, a member of the Courage brewing family and a director of the company, was also a successful breeder and trainer who produced some wonderful horses at Edgecote, his estate on the Northamptonshire/Oxfordshire border north of Banbury, where he had a superb grass gallop in the days before all-weather gallops came in and where his tally of winners included Tibretta, Tiberina, Spanish Steps and Royal Relief. He employed two Welsh brothers in the stables, Jack and Tom Morgan, whom I got to know well through visiting the yard with my father. When I first qualified in 1981, they presented me with a beautiful set of wolf tooth extractors, still very much treasured to this day.

Mr Courage himself was confined to a wheelchair and father had to go and report to him after his visits. On one occasion he was called in to geld an unruly colt named Quintus, who by all accounts was extremely difficult. In those days no adequate sedatives were available, so a twitch and blindfold was used, with the horse's tail held over the stable door by two strong men so as to raise the hind legs off the ground, making it impossible for the animal to kick. Despite the best efforts of the Morgan brothers, Quintus did manage to lash out as he was being manoeuvred into position, smashing Jack's pocket watch in the process. Father mentioned this when he went to make his report to Mr Courage as usual and the next day, when he went back to check on the horse and remove the pegs, Jack proudly showed him the brand new watch that the guv'nor had gone out and bought for him as a replacement.

Father got on really well with Mr Courage and liked to tell the story of a visit the two of them had made to Aintree in the days when it was still owned by the legendary Mrs Mirabel Topham, a former Gaiety Girl who ran the course in truly dictatorial fashion in the years before the family sold it to a developer in 1973. Mrs Topham lived in a house near the present parade and on this particular occasion she asked the two of them to join her there for drinks after the racing had finished to celebrate a Courage winner. Father obviously celebrated in style because as they were leaving he made a complete horlicks of steering the wheelchair, with the result that both he and Mr Courage ended up on the floor, much to the amusement of Mrs Topham and her other guests.

Fred Hillman was a cousin of my mother and, along with his brothers, ran a stud at Stockwood near Redditch, where they owned a particularly good premium stallion named Vimadee. In order to get a premium qualification a horse had to be shown at the Stallion Show in Peterborough and be passed fit by a panel of judges. It was usual in those days for each county to have one premium stallion that would be used to cover a selection of mares, travelling the county with an itinerary published in advance. Fred had a stutter and would address people as "me old pal, me old beauty", just like Walter Gabriel, the much-loved village ancient who featured in the *The Archers* for many years. Speaking with a broad rural accent, Fred loved to give the impression that he was a bit of a simpleton, whereas he was actually as sharp as a needle.

He had a colt foal by Vimadee, out of one of his best mares, but it had contracted a bacterial infection known as 'joint evil'. In the days before antibiotics were available this was very difficult to treat and often ended in a disastrous outcome, the joint becoming increasingly ravaged by the infection and rendering the horse unfit as an athlete. Father, who'd had some success in treating the condition with Hellebore Foetidus (stinking hellebore), was duly summoned to Stockwood. There, he proceeded with the treatment that involved taking the stem of the plant, the circumference of which would be similar to that of a pencil, trimming it to about three inches in length and then inserting it into a small incision made in the horse's chest. After about five days it was reported that the foal seemed to be much less troubled by the joint problem, but had developed a nasty looking swelling on his chest. Father greeted this news with great delight, announcing that it showed the treatment was working. He went back to Stockwood to lance the swelling and before very long the patient made a complete recovery, the chest wound healing uneventfully and the joint giving no further trouble – another triumph for father's natural, traditional remedies that further enhanced his reputation when word got around.

Jack Bletsoe, from Deddington, was an outstanding horseman. Although primarily a dealer and breeder he was also a renowned riding instructor, heavily involved in hunting and in showing, taking horses into livery to educate and prepare both them and their owners for the show ring. Father used to say that he was the best judge of a horse he had ever known, with a wonderful eye for conformation. The two of them developed a great mutual respect after father sorted out one of Mr Bletsoe's horses that had been suffering from persistent lameness. Father thought that the problem stemmed from the shoulder and recommended swimming exercises for the horse. This was back in the 1950s when swimming a horse was virtually unheard of and was certainly not something for which there were any readily available formal facilities; it was a matter of finding a suitable river, pond or lake. In this instance, father decided that Somerton Deep Lock, on the Oxford Canal between Somerton and Aynho, would be ideal.

The horse would be coaxed into the canal at a convenient point where the bank was not too steep and with a sturdy head collar and a rope on each side, father on one rope and a groom on the other, would be guided into the lock. The gate would then be closed behind it and the gate at the other end opened and as soon as the level of the water rose, the horse would start to swim. When it got to the other end of the lock the handlers crossed over, turning it around and swimming it back, repeating the manoeuvre several times. After three such sessions, which took place early on consecutive Sunday mornings, when there was little or no traffic on the canal, the horse was seen to have improved significantly and was soon declared fully sound. Mr Bletsoe was highly vocal in his appreciation and the Sunday morning sessions at Somerton soon became a regular feature, with up to six horses being exercised there. Of course, it was very thirsty work for the handlers, who refreshed themselves liberally once the treatment was complete.

Jack Bletsoe was succeeded at Park Farm, Deddington by Peggy Pacey, a highly accomplished horsewoman who had already won international honours as a rider and polo player long before going to work alongside Jack. Like him, she then went on to become a highly respected judge and breeder. My father and I both worked for her over a period of many years – she always claimed that I was still in short trousers when she first met me at Park Farm! She herself was almost always dressed in a beret and a smock.

She was a truly remarkable woman. A lifelong equestrian, she won her first 'double bridle' showing events at the age of four and represented England at ten. With ponies such as Puck, Rhew, Lapiz Lazuli and Snap Dragon (bought in Banbury market for £18), she went on to win riding, show jumping and showing classes at all the major shows, including the Royal Windsor, Royal Highland, Bath & West, Olympia, Richmond, the Three Counties and the Horse of the Year Show. She also represented her country at polo.

During the war, she swapped horses for motorbikes, becoming an RAF despatch rider attached to 3 Group Bomber Command in East Anglia. On one famous occasion she was sent to London in the middle of winter to collect some urgently needed spare parts for a Flying Fortress and had to ride back to the base with them through bad weather on a freezing February evening. When she got there she was called in to meet Churchill, who was visiting the base and who made a point of thanking her personally for her effort. Sadly, she was bedridden with severe arthritis during her final years, dying in 2013, at the age of ninety-five.

John Bosley over at Haddon Farm, Bampton was a very old family friend. Leading amateur jockey after the war, he was a true Corinthian who loved horses, lived life to the full and was extremely good company, all of which helps to explain why he and father got on so well. He combined riding and farming for many years, often managing to do more of the former until he had a very bad fall and fractured his skull, which effectively ended his competitive racing career. When he eventually recovered he decided to start training point-to-pointers and bought a very good mare called Eyecatcher from Peter Wilsden, a fellow farmer and horse breeder from Abingdon. At the same time, he started looking around for a good, steady horse – something a little less lively than Eyecatcher – on which to get back into riding himself.

Popping in to see father at Burmington one day to pick up a morning suit that he had arranged to borrow for some formal occasion he was due to attend, he inquired as he was leaving: "Who owns that black horse you've got out there in the paddock, Jack?" Father explained that it was named Rustic Work and had been bred by Mrs Budgett at Kirtlington. It had been sent to him after sustaining a serious leg injury and as it seemed unlikely that it would ever be fit enough to race again, Mrs Budgett had kindly suggested that he might like to keep it in lieu of payment for any treatment he had already provided, an arrangement that suited him fine. In fact, the horse had gone on to make a full recovery. When John then revealed his interest he was invited to take it on permanent loan.

Rustic Work proved an able runner and actually won the Members' Chase at Lockinge, ridden by John Bosley's son, John Peter. From the celebrations that followed you might have thought that the Grand National and the Gold Cup had been won on the same day! As the party around the winner's enclosure got louder and louder it became rather obvious that Rustic Work was still technically owned by father, which was a bit of a problem because the National Hunt rules in those days stipulated that as a trainer only members of your own family could have point-to-pointers and hunter chasers with you if you were training with a permit rather than a full licence, although that has since been changed. An official who happened to be standing nearby twigged and threatened to ruin the day by reporting the Bosleys to the stewards for breaking the rules. Happily, after much discussion, good sense and humour prevailed and it all blew over.

Eyecatcher, meanwhile, proved to be a very good horse indeed, finishing 3rd in two consecutive Grand Nationals, despite having an irregular heartbeat which John treated with Vitamin E and Selenium. In 1976, when she came in as a 28-1 outsider behind the winner Rag Trade and Red Rum, she was ridden by Brian Fletcher, who had been replaced as Red Rum's jockey at the last moment by Tommy Stack, after falling out with trainer Ginger McCain. The following year, when Red Rum scored his record-breaking third National victory, Eyecatcher started at 10-1 and was again third past the post, this time behind Churchtown Boy in 2nd place.

When Eyecatcher retired, she went to stud, but never produced anything with the same ability that she herself possessed. However, events leading up to the birth of her first foal were unforgettable. Haddon Farm was right next door to Brize Norton airfield, with the perimeter fence running right behind the stables and banks of security lights on poles at regular intervals. These powerful floodlights were not routinely switched on every night, but on this occasion there was some sort of late night exercise going on and they were blazing away. One set was immediately behind Eyecatcher's stable and they were shining in and upsetting the heavily pregnant mare. Returning home from a night out to be confronted by this situation, John was furious. He jumped out of the car, ran over to the perimeter fence and, finding a security patrol parked nearby, shouted at them to turn the lights off. They duly obliged and John went to bed. However, an hour or so later he awoke to see that the lights were back on, whereupon he jumped angrily out of bed, announcing to his wife Sylvia that he was going to ensure that the 'effing' lights remained off for the rest of the night. Pausing only to pull on his wellies and throw a coat over his pyjamas, he loaded his shotgun, stormed outside and blasted away with both barrels until darkness was restored. Well pleased with his efforts, he again retired to bed only to be disturbed minutes later by the arrival on his doorstep of the local Bobby. "Been shooting a few rabbits have we, John?" the officer politely inquired.

"That's right," replied John, deadpan. "We're overrun with them at the moment."

"Oh well, that's OK then," said the Bobby. "I'll leave you in peace. Just be careful where you point the gun in future, won't you?"

Although a severe reprimand was later delivered by the Commanding Officer at Brize Norton, no further action was taken. Eyecatcher, meanwhile, produced a healthy foal without any more dramas.

John went on to train a lot of good horses – Corn Street, Pusey Street, Bridge Street Lady, Point Made, Fada the Knife, Numismatist and Goldyke, to name but a few. A lot of young jockeys also gained experience at Bampton, including Richard Dunwoody, Michael Caulfield and Richard Phillips, who later recalled that some of his happiest days were spent there.

Annual Open Days at racing stables are always very popular with owners and guests and those held at Haddon Farm by John and Sylvia, were always especially well attended. The horses would be paraded, food and drink would be liberally dispensed and there would be plenty of good-hearted banter. One year, however, John felt that the proceedings had fallen a bit flat and needed livening up. So, when nobody was watching, he sneaked off into the adjacent paddock where he put a head collar on his grey hunter, Mossman, leapt on bareback and then galloped across the field and jumped straight over the hedge and into the middle of the lawn where his guests were gathered, scattering them in all directions. This certainly had the desired effect of livening things up but Mrs Bosley wasn't too pleased.

Sylvia is a lovely, warm-hearted lady, but she is not one to be trifled with. Father would often call in to see John for a chat and a drink and would tease her, saying: "My word, but you're a fine-looking woman, Sylvia – give me a kiss and a whisky!" She would have none of it and would tell him either to behave himself or go home.

John used to rear turkeys at Christmas and the part of that job that he most enjoyed was delivering them. It would, of course, have been rude of him to turn down any hospitality that happened to be offered by his customers, so his delivery rounds became extended affairs as he stopped off here and there for a chinwag and a noggin or two, often ending up well and truly oiled by the end of the day. On one occasion he forgot where he had parked his car and had to call for one of his sons to come and pick him up. They eventually found the car the next morning.

There was never a dull moment when John was around. An all-round country sport enthusiast, owner of the largest collection of Snaffles paintings in private hands, he was full of fun and always ready for a few rounds of his beloved spoof. I still miss him enormously. One of my last memories of him was when I visited him at the hospice in Oxford. He was fairly heavily sedated and comfortable, but not really able to hold a conversation by that stage. Nicolette, his daughter, was also there at his bedside and I was telling her a story about one of his old owners and remarked casually: "I don't suppose John would remember them." Quick as a flash and clear as crystal, he exclaimed: "Oh yes, I bloody well do!"

Rest in peace, John. You were a great mate both to father and to me and I was so proud to be asked to deliver the eulogy at your funeral. What wonderful memories were shared by all of us who were present on that very sad occasion!

Tom Venn was a self-made millionaire businessman who started out as a bus driver before the war, then got hold of an old charabanc with solid wheels in which he ran trips to the seaside and eventually went on after the war to build up a major transport business, specialising in coach holidays in the UK and across Europe. He developed a passion for racing and kept a string of horses at the stables he had set up at his farmhouse home at Brooksby in Leicestershire. Larger than life, opinionated and quite difficult at times, he and my father were like two peas in a pod in many ways and loved each other's company. Father made regular visits to Brooksby to look the horses over and, along with John Craven, Tom's regular vet, would discuss any problems, swap ideas and make tactical decisions about when and where to race.

It was during one of these visits that father was first introduced to a young teenage stable girl who stood out as being way above average – keen, willing to learn and with a great understanding of the horses she was helping to look after. Father told Tom: "Her horses are cleaner and tidier than the others and her boxes are spotless – she will go far." That girl was Jenny Harvey, who later became Jenny Pitman, the most successful woman trainer in British racing history.

At the start of her training career, she often took on horses that were convalescing or had some problem or other. Newly married to jockey Richard Pitman and based at Hinton Parva, near Swindon, she soon established herself in point-to-point racing before graduating into full-time professional training following her divorce from Richard. It was in those early days that she called father in to treat one of her horses, Road Racer, who had a wart in his ear. Well aware of the court case in which father had been sued successfully by an owner who claimed that his horse's looks had been disfigured by father's treatment of an identical problem, Jenny asked only that enough of Road Racer's ear should be left intact for him to be able to wear blinkers. The treatment worked and Road Racer went on to race very successfully.

Among the other trainers with whom father worked over the years were Ben Lay, Walter Charles, George Smith and Mrs Pam Taylor. Ben Lay lived and trained at Broughton near Banbury and had many good horses, mostly ridden by his son Victor, the two best known of them being Torrabus and Headlight.

Walter Charles trained at Guys Cliffe in Warwick, where he also stabled horses for Irish trainer Arthur Thomas, who would bring a few horses over to race during the summer. Walter once told father: "Arthur says your opinion is worth its weight in gold."

George Smith was a builder from Warwick who trained a few horses for fun. Father used to say that George, who had an outstanding horse named Chiel, could train as well as anyone. Visits to Warwick usually ended with the customary good luck drink and on those occasions when the whisky bottle was emptied father would lay it on its side, proudly pronouncing: "A dead man tells no lies".

Mrs Taylor lived just down the road at Salterswell Farm in Little Compton and had horses in training with John Webber at

Cropredy Lawn. She was a charming and delightful lady who used to hunt side-saddle, an impressive sight famously captured by the celebrated equine artist Snaffles. Father would tease her, saying that she spoilt her horses, killing them with kindness by overfeeding them. She would tell him: "Jack, you are a devil – but a good devil!"

I suppose that pretty much sums up how I, too, came to think of my father. I didn't find him easy to get on with during my younger days and we were often at loggerheads. In particular, he thought I was a bit wild and that I spent too much time playing sport and generally enjoying myself and it is undeniably true that I didn't apply myself to my studies quite as much as I should have done and ended up rather a late starter as a result. He was a true countryman and a strong believer in manners, but he was moody. When in company he was the life and soul of the party and yet back at home, in the post euphoric phase, he was a completely different character. But whatever disagreements and angry confrontations we may have endured during what was often a tempestuous father/son relationship were happily resolved during his final years. And he left me with a valuable set of basic personal and professional principles: to work hard, play hard and always tell the truth; never to run away from a problem, but towards it; and never to be afraid of admitting to a client that you didn't know the answer to a particular problem or hesitate in turning to someone who did know.

Father was a very popular and highly-respected country character, a man with old-fashioned principles who was also steeped in the tried and tested traditions of animal husbandry and veterinary care handed down over the centuries through generations of Walkers. In particular, he had a tremendous knowledge of horses and experience of treating them, making him the closest thing you could ever get to a genuine 'horse whisperer'. For all these reasons he succeeded in building up a wonderful, loyal following in the local farming and equine community. The challenge for me was always to live up to the Walker name.

8

'The Guv'nor'

Racing stable yards are where, professionally, I have always felt most at home. I love the atmosphere of the yards, the humour, the banter and the many different and often very colourful characters that you find yourself working with – and I'm not just talking here about the trainers, stable lads, jockeys and owners, but also the horses themselves, all with their own distinctive personalities.

Being out on the gallops at daybreak on a beautiful crisp, clear morning to assess the general health of the horses as they are put through their paces; coming in afterwards to enjoy a hearty 'full English' breakfast with the rest of the stable staff, often served up in the 'Guv'nor's' own farmhouse kitchen; joining in the boozy Sunday lunchtime celebrations back at the yard after a big race win during the week; I have fond memories of many such occasions over the years when I worked regularly at both Cropredy Lawn and Weathercock House, the yards run by, respectively, the Webbers – first John and then, following his death, his son Paul – and Jenny Pitman.

I have already referred to John Webber and the vital part he played in helping to get my career as a racehorse vet up and running by calling me in to carry out routine blood tests on three of his horses not long after I had first set up in practice. Always respectfully referred to around the stable yard as 'the Guv'nor' or simply 'Guv', John was a true gentleman, a great character who personified the image of the traditional English country sportsman. A keen point-to-point rider from an early age, he had first started training his own horses under permit in 1957. He was still farming at the time – "I am a farmer first and racing is my hobby," he used to say. It was only when he retired from riding competitively in 1970, at the age of forty-five, that he decided to take out a public licence and go into training full time. His decision to give up riding had come immediately after a race at Bicester in which he finished down the field, well behind his younger son, Anthony. Dismounting in the unsaddling enclosure he said with a sadly resigned shake of the head: "That's it – time to call it a day. I'm too old, too fat and too frightened."

He was already fairly well established as a trainer by then, having produced most of the many horses that he himself had ridden to victory over the previous thirteen years. And he soon enhanced his reputation, enjoying a lot of early success with Ballyrichard Again and victories at Stratford, Uttoxeter, Warwick, Leicester and Newbury. His big breakthrough then came in 1978 with The Snipe's triumph in the Massey-Ferguson Gold Cup at Cheltenham. It was just three years after that famous victory, much celebrated locally, that I first started working with him.

At that time his regular vet was the highly respected Peter Scott Dunn, who looked after the Queen's horses and who also acted as veterinary surgeon to the British Olympic Equestrian team over a period of thirty-one years. John also regularly turned to Les Harris from Upton-on-Severn, renowned for his expertise in treating leg problems, mostly with acid firing. Senior men in the profession, both Peter and Les were extremely kind, understanding and generous with the help and encouragement they gave me in my early days in practice.

Having carried out those initial blood tests to the Guv'nor's satisfaction, I was asked back to do the same job for him on a regular basis. And once I'd got to know everybody at Cropredy Lawn a bit better I was also invited to provide emergency cover at night and at weekends. Peter Scott Dunn remained very much in charge, visiting at least once a week to check the horses over, but he lived more than an hour's drive away at Straight Mile Farm near Wokingham, where his Scott Dunn Equine Clinic has been based since the early 1970s, so it made sense to have standby cover provided by someone who was a bit closer to Cropredy. From then on, I was gradually handed responsibility for more and more of the routine work, always with Peter's full blessing.

After about a year I got a call one day asking me if I could go over to castrate a colt owned by Anthony Webber. I was told that it was always getting into trouble and that it was also something of a weakling. Unfortunately, about two months after the delicate operation the gelding died and I was duly summoned to Cropredy and told to bring my emasculators with me. I was terrified, certain that at the very least I was going to be sacked and possibly sued as well, assuming that the reason I had been told to bring my instruments with me was that they were going to be confiscated and sent away for analysis. However, my fears could not have been more misplaced. When I got there, the Guv'nor's first words were: "I hope you've remembered to bring your emasculators because I've got two more colts that need gelding right now."

Sensing my relief, he added: "It wasn't your fault that Anthony's colt died. Right from the start it was under-sized and backward. I always thought there was something wrong with it and a post mortem showed that it suffered from an underlying kidney problem." After that, I gelded colts for John every year. He had a taste for sweetbreads and enjoyed feasting on the fruits of my operations, so much so that I used to take him extra supplies from elsewhere during the season.

I always got on extremely well with John, just as my father had done before me. Forever puffing away on his pipe, he was a friendly, good-natured individual with an earthy sense of humour, a man who lived life to the full, liked a drink and never needed much of an excuse to throw a party. At the same time, he could be tough when he needed to be and was a stickler for detail, good manners and etiquette, insisting that everything had to be done in the right and proper way. He wouldn't stand for any nonsense and if you upset him you would certainly know all about it.

The strength of his personality was reflected in the way in which he dealt with the potentially ruinous setback that had led him to impose a strict rule whereby no one owner was ever allowed to have more than four horses in training at Cropredy at the same time. This had not originally been the case and there was a time when a particular owner had had no less than twelve horses at the yard. All went well until this owner suddenly got it into his head that not all the horses were performing quite as well as he thought they should be and announced that he was going to send three of them to rival trainer Fred Rimell at Kinnersley.

"If you send three you can send the whole bloody lot!" retorted John, understandably upset by what he regarded as unacceptable disloyalty and a completely unjustified sleight. And that was that. All twelve horses were duly taken away, leaving a large number of empty boxes and a serious cash flow crisis. In most yards that would have led to stable staff being laid off, but not at Cropredy, where John refused to allow loyal staff members' livelihoods to be threatened on the whim of a wealthy owner. Not one lad was made redundant. And having weathered the storm, the Guv'nor then introduced the rule limiting the number of horses that he would accept from any one owner, partly so that he could never again be left in the lurch in the same way by a sudden mass exodus and partly, as he explained, to avoid a situation where an owner with a lot of horses in training started to think he owned the trainer as well.

John had various funny little sayings that he would come out with from time to time. For instance, if he didn't like somebody, or didn't rate an individual for some reason, he would say: "I wouldn't want him in my cave!" This came from his habit of assessing someone's character on the basis of whether or not he or she was the sort of person you would want to have by your side if you found yourself trapped in an imaginary cave with a hungry tiger blocking the entrance and needed to fight your way out. He had made up his mind that he would rather be on his own in the cave than with that particular owner.

He could be very outspoken, although usually with an edge of humour, and had strong views on many things, such as where and when it was best to go racing. He had his favourite courses, especially Towcester, Worcester and Warwick, and some that he wasn't so keen on. He always said that those who raced at South-well were "either needy or greedy" and he never liked running horses at the four Fs – Folkestone, Fontwell, Fakenham and "eff-ing Plumpton"! He also hated Sunday racing, not because of any religious convictions, but because he felt that his staff and horses all needed a day off. Besides, if there had been winners in the previous week he liked to invite the owners to Sunday lunchtime celebrations that were always great fun and tended to go on a bit, with the booze flowing freely. If I ever got an emergency call-out on a Sunday I had to make sure I was in and out as quickly as possible because if I stayed for a drink afterwards it wouldn't be just one drink, regardless of whether or not there was a celebration party in full swing, and I knew I'd never get home sober!

John always enjoyed the fun side of racing, the 'craic', as his Irish friends would call it. His great friend and fellow trainer, the late Captain Tim Forster, who ended up with three Grand National winners to his credit, said of him: "John loved hunting and point-to-pointing. He had no time for those who took racing too seriously. If you beat him, he was always the first to come over and congratulate you – and he meant it. He could also see the ridiculous side of racing. I will always remember that marvellous chuckle, hearing him say: "It's only a horse race. There'll be a dozen more tomorrow and another twenty-four on Saturday."

Although undoubtedly gracious in defeat, John was also highly competitive and hated being beaten. He was always looking for new ideas to improve his training methods and the care of his horses. For instance, he was one of the first trainers to have an all-weather surface on which to train – a wood chip gallop with a round canter and a curved seven-furlong stretch. He would drive out and park his car up on a special mound from where he could observe the horses being put through their paces, using a stopwatch to time them over various distances and keeping precise records of their performances. Following his death, the stable staff and his friends got together to have a stone memorial laid at that regular vantage point where he had been such a familiar presence over the years.

John was also one of the first to recognize the value of scanning horses' legs, having seen during a trip to America how this could help to anticipate potential problems before they started to show, allowing trainers to take preventative measures by resting the horse before any real damage was done. Racehorse vets spend ninety per cent of their time looking either at lungs (scoping) or legs (scanning), because if a horse isn't running well and isn't suffering from an obvious injury then it will almost certainly be down to something either in the respiratory system or the legs. Most often it is the legs. If you watch closely as a horse is galloping you will notice that with every stride the fetlock almost touches the ground, so the tendons have to be extremely flexible, continually stretching and slackening like a piece of elastic. The fibres in the soft tissues have to run in a straight line. If they get over-extended, tendonitis develops and these fibres start to break when put under stress. An experienced vet can feel by touch when things are not quite right, but regular scans enable you routinely to assess the condition of the legs, pinpointing impending trouble spots that much earlier and with greater accuracy, removing any element of guesswork. At John's insistence I purchased a scanner and although it was pretty basic compared with the latest versions, which provide superb pictures and diagnosis, I soon became an enthusiastic convert.

Something else that the Guv'nor was very keen on was cold laser therapy, a non-invasive process that accelerates the healing process and is most useful in the treatment of sore shins, splints, tendon injuries and some muscle problems. Again, I was encouraged to invest in a laser, which, at the time, came in the shape of a hefty piece of equipment like a space gun, whereas the state-of-the-art versions you get today are not much bigger than a ballpoint pen and much more advanced. That first one I had was such a new and delicate piece of technology that I was reluctant to let anyone else use it. John would come into the stable to watch me operating it, sitting on an upturned milk crate and chatting away as I worked. I valued those moments, welcoming the opportunity to listen and learn from his vast experience and knowledge of horses.

John had a wonderful eye for a horse and those he had at Cropredy Lawn were always of the correct conformation, beautifully turned out and well schooled. Of the better known and more successful ones, those that stood out for me and that I remember most fondly were Auntie Dot, Elfast, Townley Stone, Knock Hill, Land Afar and Flying Instructor.

Auntie Dot, home-bred at Cropredy Lawn, was one of the yard's most successful horses. Named after one of John's aunties, she was a tough, talented little mare, but was not easy to handle. She had problems with her hormones and whenever she was coming into season she would become very difficult and would not perform, leading the Guv'nor to comment drily that most of the problems at Cropredy Lawn seemed to be caused by sex! In order to get the best out of her it was necessary to keep a close check on her cycle so that it could be carefully monitored and the timing of ovulation controlled to help with race planning. The trouble was that Dot was neither regular nor consistent. You could tell by her mood roughly where she was, but to assess the exact stage of her cycle I would have to carry out a rectal examination to feel for follicles in her ovaries. Once they reached a certain size I could then inject her with a release hormone that would facilitate ovulation and sort out her PMT. After many examinations, Dot and I came to an understanding of mutual respect and she would allow me to handle her without restraint, giving the equine equivalent of a shrug of the shoulders and accepting the inevitable. This treatment became so routine that the Guv'nor would often introduce me as Dot's gynaecologist.

Despite ending up with a total of eighteen wins to her credit, Dot is perhaps best remembered for her 3rd place finish in the 1991 Grand National. The event coincided with a potentially critical period in her cycle and in the two weeks leading up to it she needed four examinations on consecutive days before the follicles were large enough for the treatment to go ahead. As it happened, that particular Grand National also provided me with one of the proudest moments of my own career, with horses that I looked after filling three of the first four places – Jenny Pitman's Garrison Savannah being just beaten into 2nd place behind the winner, Seagram, while Over The Road, trained by another of my clients, John Upson, and, like Dot, a 50-1 outsider, came in 4th.

Elfast looked anything but a future winner when he first arrived at Cropredy Lawn as a foal, so weak that he hardly had the strength to get up into the horsebox that brought him home from the breeder. He had a decent pedigree and, despite initial appearances to the contrary, the Guv'nor reckoned he had potential, so he bought him for his wife, Diana. It proved to be a shrewd purchase, Elfast going on to record eleven victories, including two at Cheltenham. I'll never forget the rousing reception he got from the crowd as Diana and John together led him back into the winner's enclosure after his second win there, a special moment for everybody concerned. After his retirement, he developed Lyme's disease, an infectious condition carried by blood-sucking ticks that can be difficult to deal with. Initially, it affected his balance but after prolonged treatment he made a full recovery and lived on to a ripe old age.

Knock Hill was owned by an American named Peter Thompson and was known affectionately in the yard as 'Knockers'. He was a good, steady, long-distance chaser and won many times, but he was also very temperamental and fussy – a bit of a wuss, you might say. He didn't like being away from home overnight and flatly refused to drink any water other than that served at Cropredy, which meant that when it came to the more distant meetings, special arrangements had to be made involving very early starts on the day of the race, along with a plentiful supply of local Cropredy water in churns.

His most unlikely and amusing claim to fame is that he is the only horse ever to have become a Page Three pin-up in the Sun newspaper. This came about when he was briefly the pre-race favourite for the Grand National and the Sun, for obvious reasons, seized on the fact that his nickname was 'Knockers' as an excuse to feature him in their Page 3 slot – with a busty model posing astride him! The picture was shot at Cropredy, where the model's arrival was eagerly anticipated not just by the stable lads, but also by the Guv'nor himself. John insisted on personally supervising the shoot, an onerous task that naturally included hands-on involvement in helping the young lady safely into the saddle! Needless to say, he loved every moment of it. Sadly, 'Knockers' remained less impressed and was a faller early on in the race.

John reckoned that the best horse he ever trained was Townley Stone, who was bred at Cropredy Lawn and then sold to local businessman Mike Townley. Mr Townley was a demanding owner and he and the Guv'nor didn't always see eye-to-eye about when and where to race the horse, who, although very successful, was also quite fragile and needed very careful handling. Two weeks before he was due to run in a valuable Novice Handicap at Ascot he went lame in one of his hind legs. This was potentially disastrous. Mr Townley had such great expectations of his horse in this important race that he had gone to the lengths of taking a box at Ascot and inviting all his friends and business colleagues along so that they could witness what he hoped would be a glorious triumph. As a result, John was under great pressure to make sure that Townley Stone not only ran, but ran well. A non-runner would be an absolute catastrophe, possibly leading to the horse being moved to another trainer.

We could find nothing obviously wrong with the leg, so John decided that he would simply rest him in his box for a few days and then re-introduce some very gentle exercise. The horse soon regained full soundness, but rather than putting him back on full training, thereby risking the possibility that the problem might return, John decided to stick with nothing more testing than walking, trotting and slow cantering, with no fast work at all. "Walker, my boy," he told me, "that's all I'm going to do with him between now and the race. If I have to tell Townley his horse is not really ready to run he will go ballistic, so we'll say nothing, make sure he is fit enough to start the race and then just see what happens."

As they lined up at the start, with the owner and his friends looking on excitedly from the box, we waited with bated breath, only to watch in amazement as Townley Stone then hammered a high-class field. The further they went, the further he forged ahead, eventually winning by a country mile and showing absolutely no adverse effects afterwards. The Guv'nor turned to me and, with that trademark chuckle of his, said: "It just goes to show – the more you think you know about horses, the less you actually do. They are all individuals and need understanding."

Land Afar was a tough little pony with a heart of gold, who could always be relied upon to give it his all out on the racetrack. He never knew when he was beaten and won some decent hurdle races before eventually developing leg problems. The routine way of treating his particular condition would have been tendon splitting, but the Guv'nor was very keen to try a different technique that he referred to as micro splitting and that involved using a needle. I wasn't looking forward to this too much, because, game little horse that he was, Land Afar also had a tendency to buck violently, so I knew I would have to be on my guard.

There are few things more painful than being kicked by a horse. For a vet, it is obviously an occupational hazard. I've been kicked plenty of times, as the many indents on my legs bear witness, but I've been lucky insofar as I've never been really badly hurt. The way to avoid getting into trouble with almost any animal, but especially horses, is to approach them with confidence. Even so, they can sometimes catch you by surprise.

My most painful experience actually came not from being kicked but from being butted. The culprit was a horse named Numismatist. Owned by Andreas Sofroniou and trained by John Bosley at Bampton, he ran successfully in the Ayr Gold Cup several times without ever quite managing to win. I had just finished blistering his front legs and was helping John put a cradle around his neck to stop him bending his neck down to rub at his legs when he took great exception to this and head butted me under the ribs with such force that I was lifted clear off the ground – and I'm a pretty hefty six-foot-four! I saw stars – and colours I never knew existed! I didn't suffer any broken ribs but it hurt like hell for days afterwards. To add insult to injury, John Bosley, who was a great friend, could only see the funny side of it and greeted me with mock sympathy and stifled guffaws as I crawled out of the stable. His reaction was rather like that of cricketers when an unfortunate batsman takes a low blow from a fast bowler!

My most frightening moment came very early on in my career, shortly after I had set up in practice with my father. His health was already failing by then and he was no longer able to carry out castrations, so I was sent along to cut a colt for one of his regular clients, John Robbins. I was still relatively inexperienced at the time and the colt must have sensed it. He had been sedated in preparation for the procedure and was held on a twitch in a corner of the stall, but as I approached him, he reared up and knocked me down and as I lay there, with the knife in my hand, all I could see was this young horse collapsing down on top of me. For a split second I thought: "That's it!" I simply shut my eyes and waited for the inevitable impact. But it never happened. The half-doped colt fell just to one side of me – a very lucky escape.

Back to Land Afar. Despite my slight apprehension he behaved very well while I administered the needle, the treatment proved successful and he went on to win again before eventually being retired to the Racing School at Cropredy Lawn, where he was used to teach young jockeys, regularly testing their mettle with his bucking bronco tendency.

Flying Instructor was one of those horses who will live in my memory forever – a true professional, a terrific competitor and a wonderful character who, like Land Afar, would always give his very best. I had vetted his dam, Flying Mistress, who was known as 'Twiggy' and was owned by Lady Lyell, a lifelong friend of the Webber family. There was great excitement when Twiggy's son arrived at the yard to be trained. He came with the nick-name 'Bugsy', because he had been a complete bugger to break in – not a bad sign as it is often said that a wild colt makes a good horse. When Lady Lyell died she left Bugsy to Diana Webber in her will and all his great success came under Diana's owner-ship. Although John was responsible for his early education, it then fell to Paul Webber to develop the grey gelding's full poten-tial after he took over the reins at Cropredy Lawn following his father's death in 1995. A truly top class horse, Flying Instructor went on to become the most consistently successful horse in the yard's history, with thirteen wins, plus five runner-up spots and eleven 3rd place finishes from a total of sixty-three starts during his long ten-year racing career. He was a great favourite in the yard and even after his retirement at the age of thirteen he could often be seen being ridden up the gallops by Paul, still trying his heart out, as usual.

It had been terrible to watch John's health deteriorating. He had been diagnosed with bladder cancer and towards the end he went downhill rapidly. He bore it bravely, carrying on as long as he could. I was about to leave at the end of a routine visit to the yard one morning when he called me into the kitchen, admitted for the first time that he really was not feeling too good at all and went on to explain that Paul would be returning to Cropredy to help with the training. There was a pause and then he said: "Walker, I want you to speak at my funeral." I was completely overcome. With tears in my eyes, I told him that it would be a great honour to be able to pay tribute to someone who had been such an inspiration, not just to me but to so many others in the equine world.

Apart from anything else, I found it deeply moving to have been accorded what seemed to me the ultimate mark of true friendship and to have been entrusted by John, himself, with such a personal responsibility, especially given the many much more eminent and better-qualified people that he knew so well.

At his crowded funeral in the Catholic church in Banbury I was shaking like a leaf as I stood up in the pulpit and prepared to deliver my eulogy. I was proudly wearing one of John's monogrammed white shirts with his initials J.H.W – John Huyshe Webber – on the pocket. We were both roughly the same size and he had given me the shirt as a personal memento, along with his British Field Sports tie, which I also wore on the day. In addition, I was sporting a pair of his great friend Peter Scott Dunn's trademark flamboyant floral braces that Peter had given me for the occasion.

I had worked hard on my eulogy, knowing that the only way I could do myself and John justice would be to write it all down in my own hand and then pretty much learn it off by heart. But then, on the day that I had set aside to work on it, I got an emergency call from John Richardson down at Andoversford – a colt had been castrated and complications had set in. Dealing with that took up most of the day and, as a result, I was up half the night trying to find the right words to say and then rehearsing them over and over again. Fortunately, when it came to the moment of truth I managed to overcome my nerves and said everything I wanted to say without losing my way, drying up or letting emotion get the better of me.

Having had to accept long before the end finally came that John's illness was terminal, the family had already started making plans for the future of the yard, Paul eventually making the difficult decision to give up what was a very good job at The Curragh Bloodstock Agency, gradually reducing his involvement there and returning home to begin the process of taking over at Cropredy Lawn.

Shortly after John's funeral I rang Paul and asked to see him. We walked around the yard, checking the horses, and I told him: "Just because I worked for your father doesn't mean you have to stick with me. You are young and you will very likely have different ideas about how things should be done and will want your own team around you. I quite understand that. However, I do have one favour to ask of you. Over the years I have become very fond of your mother and I would always like to feel free to come over and visit her from time to time for a chat."

Paul replied that, of course, I was welcome to visit at any time. "As for us continuing to work together, let's give it six months to see how we get on and then we'll just take it from there."

I was delighted by his response. And right from the start we got on really well, so that it soon became apparent that my relationship with Cropredy Lawn would be carrying on much as before. I had the advantage that Paul and I had already got to know one another quite well both personally and professionally before he took over, not just through having met on his regular visits home to Cropredy but also as a result of being called in to vet horses on his behalf while he was working as a bloodstock agent. That is by no means an easy job. To ensure that the right horses end up with the right owners and trainers can be taxing and involves not only a thorough knowledge and understanding of breeding, the performance of a horse's antecedents, its conformation and action, but also an understanding of human nature as well. As I have seen all too often, clients can very soon become disgruntled if their investments do not bear fruit.

Paul realised that he had a hard act to follow at Cropredy Lawn, but it wasn't long before he started putting his own stamp on the place as he set about gradually updating and improving the facilities there. He built a swimming pool, replaced the old all-weather gallop with a new one featuring a state-of-the-art surface, introduced a water splash that enabled the horses to walk through natural stream water after exercise and built new stables.

More importantly, Paul was very much in tune with the changing fashions in the breeding and training of National Hunt horses. For years, the tradition in this country, particularly, had been for big, strong, late-maturing horses, correctly made, with a good jumping shoulder, strong hindquarters and an honest head. This was what people looked for in the days when courses tended to be less well drained and were therefore softer, deeper and heavier, meaning that horses had to be the sort of stayers that could gallop all day long as well as being good, safe jumpers. But as tracks started to become better drained and maintained and the ground got firmer, the requirement was for horses that were lighter and faster.

The changing nature of the courses was just one of several factors involved in the overall transformation of the National Hunt racing scene that has taken place over the last twenty years or so. Most significantly, perhaps, a new type of owner has emerged during that time, with many of the country landowners and farmers who once dominated the sport having gone out of it to be replaced increasingly by syndicates and wealthy individuals who naturally tend to have a more businesslike approach and want a quick return on their investment. And whereas those old traditional owners mostly wanted to breed their own winners at home and were happy to wait five or six years from the time a mare was covered to the time that her offspring was mature enough to make its first appearance in a race, today's owners don't expect to have to wait more than three or four years. This, along with the trend towards lighter, faster National Hunt horses has led to moves away from the traditional breeding principles and training methods.

Instead of being bred in the shires, horses are now bought in from all over the world. Martin Pipe was one of those who led the revolution in training, bringing in smaller horses from abroad, mostly from France, and then training them up to be super fit. Others soon followed suit. At one time I found myself going to France to vet horses as often as I went over to Ireland – Nantes, Chantilly, Pau, Maison Lafitte, all over the place. Today, horses are coming from even further afield – everywhere from Argentina to Eastern Europe. And Paul, with his eye for a horse and the expertise he gained through working as a top bloodstock agent, has led the way in this field. He has contacts worldwide and will happily travel thousands of miles if he thinks there is a really good horse on offer.

As far as we vets are concerned, all these developments have not altered the basic way we work – all that's changed is that we now have a lot more highly advanced diagnostic equipment at our disposal. We don't treat very much differently from the way we did thirty years ago, but we do know more about exactly what, where and when to treat. That's where sophisticated state-of-the-art scanners, in particular, are such a boon. They can warn us about leg problems long before they become obvious and then, when they are healing, enable us to avoid running horses before they're ready to go. However, we still can't heal injuries any quicker. There is always pressure from owners and trainers to get their horses ready much sooner. You tell them that it'll take three months and yet they always want you to give the go-ahead after a month or six weeks.

One of the great plus factors associated with today's smaller, lighter National Hunt horses is the versatility that enables them to race on the flat as well as over jumps. Back in the old days, jumping used to finish in early June and didn't start again until mid-August, which meant that the horses would have two months off during which they would most often go home to their owners. At the peak of the summer holiday season Cropredy Lawn would be virtually empty. It would be a time for the staff to clear out the stables and go on holiday. But that gave trainers a cash flow problem. So-called 'dual horses', capable of winning on the flat as well as over jumps, helped to solve that problem – and Paul had several good ones.

Both Full House and Ulundi won at Royal Ascot as well as over hurdles and fences, Ulundi chalking up a notable victory in the Scottish Champion Hurdle. He was a top class horse despite suffering from breathing problems that required him to be treated with an inhaler. Initially, he resented this and I had to tread carefully, but he gradually got used to it and it proved very effective. He ran an absolute blinder in the prestigious Arlington Million in Chicago, the first race to offer a purse of $1 million, only just beaten into fourth place by a distance of six inches. Oh, for just another few strides! He was then invited to run in the Dubai Horse Festival, only to catch an infection that meant he then had to be quarantined there until it had completely cleared up. That took about ten weeks and, sadly, he was never the same again afterwards and was retired.

Carlito Brigante was another who won well on the flat before going on to record a major victory over the sticks by winning the Imperial Cup at Sandown Park. Australia Day, known as 'Skippy' in the yard, has proved to be even more versatile, having won on the flat, over hurdles and over fences, and is still going strong.

Since retiring from the partnership to work part-time, I still go over to Cropredy Lawn regularly to look at the horses and to have a chat with Diana Webber over a cup of coffee, bringing her up to date with all the gossip. They say that behind every successful man is a strong, wise and hardworking woman and that was certainly true of John and Diana. Petite and birdlike in stature, Diana could nevertheless be formidable when she needed to be and was very much the matriarch of the family, hence her nickname 'Moccy'. The original Moccy was an old friend of the family, Monica Dickinson, another strong personality who wouldn't stand for any nonsense. Whenever Diana put her foot down over something her children would complain: "You're being just like Moccy!" And, of course, it stuck.

She showed tremendous fortitude in facing up not only to John's death, but also that of her daughter, Teresa, who succumbed to the ravages of liver cancer at the early age of fifty-nine. What a terribly cruel blow that was. Teresa's memorial service at Cropredy village church was deeply moving and served as a great tribute to a wonderful, kind, talented person of the sort who was always ready to go out of her way to help others and was the jolliest company. The church was packed – standing room only – with her devastated husband, Robert, and the rest of the Webber family displaying an outer courage and dignity that must have belied their true inner feelings. We all miss her.

Despite such sad and, especially in Teresa's case, premature losses, Diana remains full of boundless enthusiasm and energy and it is always a pleasure to spend time in her company, hearing all about her latest travels and sharing her delight in the progress and achievements of her four grandchildren – Sophie, Hugo, Harriet and Joanna and her great-grandson, Max. It is a great tribute to the family as a whole that loyal staff like Jerry and Pauline Walsh, Trevor and Suzanne Heath, Maureen Foster, the farrier Richard Morgan, Martin Archer, John Buckingham and John Gregory have all been at Cropredy Lawn for so long, working first for John and then for Paul. It is a privilege for me to be able to include myself among them.

9

'The Missus'

I have vivid memories of my first meeting with Jenny Pitman. It took place at Nottingham racecourse one bitterly cold winter afternoon in 1984. Nottingham was still a jumping track in those days and I had gone along with my father, who had a horse running there. The weather was absolutely freezing and it was touch and go whether there would actually be any racing at all. As it turned out, the programme for the day had to be abandoned immediately after the race in which our horse came in 3rd.

At the age of seventy-two, dad was already struggling with his arthritic hips and had to use two sticks to get about, so as we got ready to leave I sat him down and told him to stay exactly where he was while I went to collect the car, which was a ten-minute walk away. Despite strict instructions not to move away on any account, he was nowhere to be seen when I got back with the car. I was not best pleased about this because, apart from anything else, I was anxious to get back home. I asked a gate steward if he had happened to notice a gentleman wearing a flat cap and walking with two sticks and he replied that indeed he had and that the gentleman had been heading in the direction of the bar. Typical, I thought, and strode off in pursuit.

The scene that greeted me when I entered the bar momentarily stopped me dead in my tracks. The atmosphere inside the place was fantastic, with a real buzz among the lively crowd who had sought refuge from the cold and were busy drowning their sorrows and disappointment at having had their racing cut short. Right in the middle of them all, at the very centre of everyone's attention, was my father. And perched on his knee was Jenny Pitman.

Dad was beaming from ear to ear as he introduced us, saying: "Jenny – this is my boy, Alan."

He had known her since she was a teenage stable girl, working for owner Tom Venn and the young Jenny Harvey, as she then was, had made an instant impression on him as being quite out of the ordinary – keen, willing to listen and to learn and with an obvious natural affinity with the animals that she was working with. Apart from that, I think he had anyway developed a bit of a soft spot for her. Later, after she had married Richard Pitman and had set up in business on her own with a small stable at Hinton Parva, specialising in the rehabilitation of horses that were recovering from treatment, she had occasionally called dad in, mostly to treat wart cases, although Hinton Parva was too far from Burmington for her ever to be a regular client. When her career as a trainer then really started to take off they had kept in touch, but hadn't actually seen each other for a few years until their reunion that afternoon at Nottingham.

It emerged that he had forever been going on to her about "my boy" and telling her: "One of these days when he qualifies and follows in my footsteps he will come and do some work for you". As a result, I think that in her mind's eye she probably had a mental image of me as a little lad in short trousers with knobbly knees, so it must have come as a surprise when she eventually met me face-to-face only to discover that I was actually six-foot-four and eighteen stone!

By then Jenny was already well established at Weathercock House, the former pub on the outskirts of Upper Lambourn that she had bought as a derelict property following her divorce from Richard Pitman and had then painstakingly transformed into a lovely timber-framed home with a purpose-built stable complex in the grounds. And she had just made racing history the previous year when, with Corbiere's victory at Aintree, she became the first woman ever to train a Grand National winner.

As we were saying goodbye that day at Nottingham her part-ing words to me were: "I've got some really lovely horses – you must bring your father along to have a look at them."

By the time dad and I got round to taking her up on this invi-tation a few months later in the summer of 1985, one of those horses, Burrough Hill Lad, had added the Cheltenham Gold Cup, the King George VI Chase and the Hennessy Gold Cup to her growing list of major trophy wins, which also included earlier back-to-back Welsh Grand Nationals with Corbiere in 1982 and Burrough Hill Lad in 1983.

Jenny's father, George Harvey, was at Weathercock House when we visited and he and my father instantly took to one another. They were like two peas out of the same pod – both true countrymen who were imbued with the same values and who knew their horses inside out. In particular, George's powers of observation when it came to judging horseflesh were phe-nomenal. He didn't care how well bred or how expensive an animal was, it just had to be made as near perfect as possible. He would stress this to his daughter time and time again and it was through him that she developed such a good eye for a horse.

While the two old-timers were busy chatting away, Jenny took me aside and explained that she had had a difference of opin-ion with her regular vet and would like to give me the oppor-tunity to cover some of the routine work during the summer, which would include getting all the flu vaccinations updated. I couldn't believe it. I straightaway wanted to shout yes, yes, yes! But, keeping a cool head, I pointed out that there was a practi-cal difficulty in that I lived more than forty miles away, which meant that every visit would involve a round trip of well over two hours. And as we were a small team of only three vets at the time I wasn't sure that my practice colleagues would appreciate me taking the time to venture so far afield. But in characteristi-cally forthright fashion Jenny brushed this aside as a rather fee-ble excuse. "Let's give it a try and see how we get on," she said.

As things turned out, we got on very well indeed right from the start, soon establishing a good professional relationship that was to develop over the years into a firm personal friendship that has lasted to this day. I have often been asked: "What's Jenny Pitman really like?" The answer is that as a boss, 'The Missus' – as she was always respectfully referred to around the yard – was a truly formidable character, an unashamedly down-to-earth woman who was more than capable of holding her own in what was predominantly a man's world. Running her business very much hands-on, with military precision and strict discipline, she liked everything to be right, hated sloppy work and wouldn't stand any nonsense from anyone. It was never wise to try and pull the wool over her eyes – it would drive her mad. And if you made a mistake you could expect the most monumental bollocking from someone who, in her less ladylike moments, has never been afraid to call a spade not so much a spade as an 'effing' spade!

As far as any working relationship was concerned Jenny was a classic example of somebody who was hard but fair. She had very strong opinions about how things should be done and would let you know in no uncertain terms if she thought you'd got it wrong. "What are you doing about my effing horse then, veterinary?" she would demand if an animal did not respond to treatment quite as quickly as she had hoped. She could be like a Rottweiler if you took her on and there were several occasions when she slammed the phone down on me after a disagreement over a treatment I was proposing, leaving me convinced that our business relationship was about to be terminated. However, once she'd calmed down she would always ring back and you would realise that she had listened to everything you'd said and had taken it all in. Even so, you had to accept that she would always have to have the last word!

We quickly developed a routine whereby I would visit Weathercock House every Thursday, which tended to be the least busy day of the week at the stables, setting off from home at the crack of dawn in order to arrive there by 7.00am, just before the first horses went out onto the gallops.

Like most yards, Weathercock House adhered to a strict daily timetable, starting at 5.30am when the head lad or his assistant would give the horses an early morning feed, each horse having their own individual ration according to the work they would be doing. The previous night the boards would have been prepared, with the horses divided into two or three groups or 'lots'. Next to the name of each horse would be that of the rider, who would have been selected according to what work was being done – cantering, fast work or schooling. Those already identified as having a problem of some sort were listed under the heading 'See Breakfast', which meant they would be seen at the equivalent of a surgery that would be held immediately before or after the hearty breakfast that would be served up to the senior stable staff when they came back from the gallops.

Blood tests would be taken before the horses were tacked so as not to excite them, and woe betide if you delayed the process. All the stable lads and lasses work extremely hard and care deeply for their allotted horses, making sure they are turned out in tip top condition with all the tack fitting correctly. And they themselves would have to be careful that they passed muster too. Jeans, for instance, were strictly forbidden. "This is not your first day at Pony Club – go and get yourself some decent kit!" Jenny would bark at anyone she considered to be too casually dressed.

The horses would next be walked in hand to the tack room where Jenny, Dave or one of the assistants would check each of them over before giving the rider a leg up. They would then be walked around the house, the string gaining numbers as more arrived from the stables. When the first lot were all present and correct, the riders would be given final instructions as to what they were to be doing that session and would then be led out by a senior member of the staff. They would often be joined by visiting jockeys who had come to sit on or school a horse that they were going to be riding at a later date.

Once the first lot had gone out there would normally be a lull in the proceedings during which I would go to the office to go through various administrative duties such as checking all the horses' passports to make sure that their vaccinations were up-to-date. After that I would usually pop up to the gallops to see how things were going and to listen to any horses that had wind problems. My time on the gallops was well spent because it enabled me to assess the health and wellbeing of the horses for myself, instead of simply relying on what I was told by Jenny and the stable staff.

After completing their various pieces of work and exercise, the horses would be ridden back quietly to Weathercock where they would be taken to the paddock, dismounted and allowed to have a pick of grass for about as long as it took to smoke a cigarette. Any horses that needed scoping would be dealt with at that point because, unlike blood testing, scoping is a waste of time unless it is done immediately after exercise.

The horses on the 'See Breakfast' list would mostly be suffering from lameness of some kind, while others might just be generally out of sorts for some reason. A few might be undergoing long-term treatment and one or two might have been racing the previous day and would just need to be checked over. One by one, they would be trotted up in front of the wooden stables under the watchful eye of Jenny and her team. Jenny being a stickler for regular, accurate records, detailed notes would be made on each 'patient'. Notes from the previous week would be consulted and decisions made about further treatment. Depending on how many horses there were on the list – it could be anything from two or three to twenty – this would be done either before of after breakfast.

Breakfast was a grand affair. Usually the 'Full English', it would be eaten in a dining room adorned with a whole range of glittering trophies and paintings of famous horses. Here, the senior stable staff would often be joined by visiting owners, jockeys and racing journalists for what was often a lively and entertaining combination of work and pleasure, enjoyed by all.

After breakfast the second 'lot' of horses would be prepared and assembled before being dispatched for their allocated exercise for the day. This might sometimes include a full work-out, especially if an owner had come to see how his horse was getting on, but would normally be reserved for those which were doing less strenuous exercise. During the racing season, the day's runners would meanwhile be undergoing final preparations before being collected for their trip to the races.

Once the second lot had been sent out more routine work would be carried out. This might include treatments such as firing or blistering, the removal of stitches following previous procedures, vaccinations, teeth rasping, sedation for clipping, cleaning of ears for head shakers and the scanning of legs. X-rays were normally carried out in the Surgery, the resulting pictures being of much better quality. When your list had been completed it was time to write it up and also to prepare reports for owners, or meet owners to explain procedures, or insurance. Also I was often asked to read reports and sometimes interpret the terminology. Each horse had its own separate file containing all relevant details pertaining to that animal.

I would normally have completed my workload by late morning before heading back to the practice, armed with my blood samples. I liked to get back by 1pm to enable our laboratory nurses to get on with the analysis of the samples as soon as possible because come 6.00pm the phone would be active with a polite but urgent enquiry from Jenny about the results.

It was shortly after I had started doing work for her that Jenny notched up her next big winner with Stearsby, jockey Graham Bradley riding the seven-year-old to victory in the 1986 Welsh Grand National at odds of 10-1. Owned by Terry Ramsden, Stearsby was a big strong horse of the sort that Jenny always favoured. Then there was Gainsay, owned by Errol Brown of Hot Chocolate fame. Gainsay had big flat feet that were causing him problems. Jenny always paid particular attention to the condition of her horses' feet. One of her favourite sayings was "No foot, no 'oss", simply meaning that if the feet weren't right for any reason then there was nothing you could really do with a horse. In Gainsay's case she eventually had special glued-on shoes made and fitted rather than conventional nailed-on shoes and this seemed to put him right. Following a number of big handicap successes, a delighted Errol Brown presented Jenny with a gold necklace bearing the legend 'No Foot, No 'Oss'.

In retrospect, 1986 can be seen to have been a key date in Jenny's career success story, thanks to some very astute buying in that year's summer sales. Before summer racing was introduced in the mid-eighties it used to be the tradition for National Hunt jump racing to end on the first weekend in June with the Horse & Hound Cup at Stratford and an evening meeting at Market Rasen. There would then be a break until early August when jumping started again at Newton Abbott and Devon & Exeter. In between, trainers were mostly kept busy visiting the big sales at Doncaster and Ascot and also in France and Ireland with the aim of replenishing their yards and also buying on behalf of owners. Some owners would pick a horse out of the catalogue, while others would ask their trainers or agents to look out for something with potential. Trainers would also buy horses on spec and sell them on when they got home. "The bank owns that one", Jenny used to say.

Jenny would go to the sales accompanied by David Stait – her training assistant at Weathercock House and long-time partner who eventually became her second husband after they had been together twenty years – along with her father, George, and her son Mark. Although a good judge herself, she relied heavily on her father's eye to pick horses out and David would then do the bidding for her. Altogether that summer they brought back nine horses of which no less than four went on to win major races, helping to establish Jenny beyond dispute as by far the UK's most successful woman trainer ever.

As is routinely the case, all the newly purchased horses came from the sales unnamed and identified only by the lot numbers stuck on their rumps. Jenny always made a point of personally welcoming each newcomer into the yard, ensuring that these youngsters, some of whom might not have travelled well, were tucked up comfortably for the first night in their new home, having first had their lot numbers gently washed off. "They don't feel at home until that's been done," she used to say. It would be up to their eventual owners to choose names for them – often but not always linked to their pedigree in some way – and until then they would be referred to around the yard as 'the chestnut by Alflora' or 'the grey by Presenting' or 'the big stroppy bugger by Roselier'.

The four stars to emerge from that 1986 intake were Garrison Savannah, who won the Sun Alliance Chase in 1990 and the Cheltenham Gold Cup in 1991 before going on to finish as runner-up in the Grand National later that same year; Royal Athlete, who won the Grand National in 1995; Willsford, whose total of seven wins included the County Hurdle at Cheltenham in 1989, the Midlands Grand National at Uttoxeter in 1990 and the Eider Chase and Scottish Grand National, both in 1995; and Esha Ness, winner of the highly controversial 'Grand National that never was' in 1993, the race being declared void after a bungled start.

Garrison Savannah, named after the Caribbean racetrack venue in Bridgetown, Barbados but known around the yard as 'Gary', was a very special horse and Jenny absolutely adored him. However, he didn't like vets and it was always a battle to treat him. I normally always wore a brown smock for work, but Gary hated it and wouldn't allow me into his box until I had taken it off. I used to say to Jenny: "I know why you like him so much. You two are kindred spirits – awkward and difficult to deal with, but sweet as a nut once you're up and running!"

In the months leading up to the Gold Cup in 1991 Gary was suffering from stubborn lameness after jumping awkwardly during a race at Haydock the previous autumn. He hadn't actually fallen, but had taken a false step and had pulled a muscle in his shoulder. We weren't too bothered at first, thinking he would quickly recover, but the injury proved stubborn. Anti-inflamma-tory drugs, faradic treatment and physiotherapy all proved inef-fective. Eventually, with Cheltenham looming, Jenny rang me with the characteristically blunt observation: "Hey, veterinary, you ain't put my effing horse right yet and we're running out of time! You got any more bright ideas?"

Somewhat in desperation, I suggested nervously: "Well, I have heard there is a vet operating just down the road from you in Stanford-in-the-Vale who specialises in acupuncture. Maybe we should give that a try." There was the briefest moment of silence at the other end of the line before she erupted: "Acupuncture? Have you taken leave of your effing senses!" And with that the phone was slammed down. I turned to my wife, Di, and said: "That's blown it. I've really upset her this time." The next day she rang again and I braced myself for another, possibly ter-minal, bollocking. Instead of which she simply said casually: "Hello, Alan. What was the name of that acupuncturist you were telling me about?"

A homeopathic vet, Chris Day didn't deal with horses on a regular basis and I wasn't quite sure what I was letting us all in for. Given Gary's dislike of any kind of veterinary treatment, I couldn't see him taking kindly to being used as a pin cushion by a complete stranger. That, along with Chris's relative lack of experience with horses, didn't augur well. I was also con-cerned that Chris's penchant for open-toed sandals and large round spectacles would only serve to increase the scepticism with which Dave Stait, especially, viewed the sort of alternative treatments he specialised in.

However, to everyone's amazement Gary actually tolerated Chris and allowed him to insert the acupuncture needles at all the key points without any hint of the violent reaction we had rather expected. And after a few treatments, even Dave Stait, who had been convinced that the whole exercise would prove to be a complete waste of time and money, had to admit that there were definite signs of improvement. After two or three more sessions Gary was trotted up in the middle yard for inspection and it was clear that he really was on the mend. Jenny made him trot up again and again and we all thought: "Amazing! He's nearly there!" Not long after that he was sound enough to start full training and there can be no doubt that a lot of the credit for that must go to Chris Day.

A few weeks later I stood next to Jenny in the Owners and Trainers enclosure at Cheltenham to watch as her son, Mark Pitman, rode Gary to victory in what turned out to be one of the most thrilling Gold Cup races of modern times, beating the great French horse The Fellow by the shortest of short heads with the legendary Desert Orchid in 3rd place. In what was probably the best ride of his career, Mark got Gary in front, but The Fellow kept coming at him and at the end was gaining on him with every stride. The photo finish was so close that everybody was on tenterhooks as they waited for the result to be announced. People were excitedly clapping Jenny on the back, telling her she'd won it, but she wasn't so sure and TV race commentator Peter O'Sullevan was telling viewers that he reckoned The Fellow had probably just edged it. One more stride and that would undoubtedly have been the case, but the photo showed that Gary had just managed to hold him off. It was a glorious, wonderfully dramatic moment, marking another landmark in Jenny's career – a second Gold Cup to add to that won by Burrough Hill six years earlier. And it caused an upsurge of interest in equine acupuncture when the story of Gary's treatment was revealed.

Sadly, Jenny's celebrations were cut short when, later that same afternoon, Mark went out on Gary's stable mate, Run To Form, and suffered a crashing fall that resulted in a fractured pelvis when the horse landed on him. So, instead of being able to paint the town red at the end of the day, an anxious Jenny spent the evening in Cheltenham hospital with her injured son. Fortunately for Mark, although it was very painful he was young and fit and healed quickly. After just two weeks he was back riding, albeit rather gingerly at first, determined, like his mother, that he was not going to miss Aintree

Gary, meanwhile, had come through his race really well and was sound and bouncing and generally unscathed apart from an overreach – a slight laceration resulting from the hind hoof clipping the heel of the front hoof at full gallop – and a few other small cuts. Overreaches can sometimes turn septic and with Gary due to go for the Gold Cup/Grand National double at Aintree just three weeks later we decided to give him a course of antibiotics as a precaution. This involved a series of injections – one-a-day for four days. I gave him the first jab in his backside during my regular Thursday visit to Weathercock House and Jenny herself then administered the second one in his neck the following day. As she was away racing over the weekend it fell to her assistant Ian Williams to complete the course of treatment.

Gary was being particularly difficult by this time so Ian decided to inject into the chest muscles, which is easier to do but carries the risk of swelling. Saturday's jab went OK but the Sunday one caused a real reaction with enormous swelling. Ian rang me in a panic and asked me what he should do. I told him to put a cold compress on it four times a day, exercise him as usual and hope for the best. Well, the best didn't happen.

Evening stables is always an important element of every yard's training routine and Weathercock House was no exception. Each horse would have its rug taken off before being stood up for visual inspection, as a result of which notes would be recorded along with a treatment action plan if necessary. Accompanying Jenny on that Sunday evening round, Ian and head lad Adam Kyte were both extremely apprehensive, having not dared to tell her in advance about the state of Gary's chest. The box next to the one Gary was in was occupied by Villa Recos and as a result of his inspection it was decided that he needed worming. Ian seized on this as an excuse to go and get the wormer straightaway, in the hope that he would be able to escape the wrath that was about to ensue.

No chance! As he tried to hurry away Jenny turned her attention to Gary and was onto the situation in a flash. "Who did this?" she exploded. "What's been going on? Get that bloody vet here NOW! There must be something wrong with his effing drugs."

I was duly summoned and arrived to find Jenny still steaming. "He's got a bigger chest on him than Samantha Fox!" she told me. The swelling was indeed very big, but it was also soft and I was pretty sure we would be able to move it. Calm was eventually restored and Gary was soon back in shape, but not before he'd missed a couple of days' training on the gallops.

Come the National and Gary, ridden once again by Mark, who had made a near miraculous recovery from the injury sustained at Cheltenham just three weeks earlier, gave it his all. Going over the last fence he was four lengths clear of Seagram and seemed set to make history by becoming the first horse since Golden Miller in 1934 to do the double in the same season. But in the long run-up to the finish his stride shortened and Seagram caught up and went past him as if he was standing still, going on to win by five lengths. Jenny always claimed that it was those missed training gallops that robbed Gary of victory. Was that really the case? We'll never know for sure. But at least Jenny managed to retain a sense of humour about it. A few months afterwards she announced that she'd got something for me and presented me with a framed print entitled Ailments of The Horse. It was an illustration of a broken down horse exhibiting every known equine fault – except one. Jenny herself had added an enlarged chest with an arrow pointing to it and the caption "Big Tits". It was signed "Love, JP". It hangs on my wall to this day.

The horse that was to become Jenny's second National winner was Royal Athlete, affectionately known around Weathercock House as 'Alfie'. Alfie was very talented but also somewhat fragile, requiring frequent veterinary attention, mostly to do with his legs. Pure white, they gave him a distinctive appearance but were constantly causing him problems. For reasons to do with pigmentation, horses with white legs, or 'socks', are especially prone to the skin infection known as 'mud fever' that commonly affects horses and ponies in the winter and early spring when they are standing around in wet, muddy fields. Continual dampness of the skin causes a breakdown of the protective barrier of the epidermis, allowing bacteria and fungal organisms to get in and cause infection, usually around the pasterns and heels. This can be both irritating and painful for the animal and can result in lameness if not treated promptly and properly. Alfie suffered one particularly severe attack that took weeks to resolve, as did any cuts to his beautiful but rather delicate pins.

On another occasion he sustained what was a potentially life-threatening cut around his pastern while racing at Newbury. Charlie Schreiber, who by then had become Jenny's other regular vet, was on duty at the course that day and he did a magnificent job of repairing the wound on the spot. And with regular applications of the Missus's patent sugar paste – sugar and honey are natural healers and work very well on keeping wounds dry and clean – Alfie made a full recovery.

Charlie Schreiber and I were from very different practices – Charlie was with Mike O'Gorman at Newbury – but our approach was similar. We were always very open with each other and discussed any problems that arose at length. We saw some things from different perspectives and there were obviously times when we didn't totally agree, but we had great mutual respect and were ultimately only interested in coming up with the right answers. We were also never afraid to admit it if we didn't know the answer to a particular problem, in which case we would refer the horse to a specialist. But not before we had been made to consult what Jenny and many others regarded as the bible – Captain Horace Hayes' Veterinary Notes For Horse Owners, a comprehensive manual of horse ailments, medicine and surgery dating back to 1877.

When Alfie developed yet another leg problem, this time as

a result of strained tendons, it was agreed that I should line fire him, a procedure that I knew would be a challenge, given those snow white legs of his. Having managed to get the job done, we gave him plenty of time to recover and the leg eventually settled, only to start niggling him again as soon as he resumed full training. Jenny once more had to stop working him to let it settle and in characteristically blunt fashion told me to "have the balls to do it properly next time".

"Bloody cheek," I thought. But I bit my tongue and did it again, pin firing as well as line firing him the second time around. Known clinically as thermocautery, pin and line firing are controversial procedures aimed at stimulating tendon repair by setting up a counter irritation that effectively increases the blood supply to the affected area. This involves first clipping the leg and then, having applied a local anaesthetic, using a red hot firing iron to burn lines around the back of the leg and then touching the tendon sheath with a hot pin.

There is no denying that firing is a highly controversial procedure that was actually banned in the UK for a brief period in the 1990s, and veterinary opinion remains strongly divided. Many younger vets today tend not to use it, but if you talk to racehorse vets up and down the country you will find that they all use it because it works. I have certainly used it very successfully over the years.

Alternative options include blistering, carbon fibre and stem cell treatment, tendon splitting, injection with various substances and simply resting. But none of these are totally successful, while firing has stood the test of time. The main objection is that it is painful for the horses and therefore cruel, but the anaesthetics and painkillers that are available today mean that any discomfort can be reduced to a minimum. The main disadvantage is that horses that have been fired then have to be rested for a year afterwards before they can get back to full training.

With Alfie, it was just one thing after another. He was also prone to the painful and often totally debilitating muscle cramps known variously as 'tying up', 'setfast', 'azoturia' and 'Monday morning disease' – the latter because the condition is usually brought on by the resumption of training on the gallops following a day of rest on Sunday. It affects the hind quarters and back and can sometimes be so severe that a horse will be reduced to a complete standstill, unable even to walk, in which case it has to be transported from the gallops back to the stables. In Alfie's case, it wasn't until Jenny resorted to "my dad's juice", one of her father's old traditional recipes, that the problem was finally resolved.

As late as the February before his 1995 National win Alfie was still not absolutely right. This time it was his knees that were troubling him. I gave him some injections that seemed to transform him, but although he was soon back to his best, every day was a challenge. Whenever his owners, Libby and Gary Johnson, rang to check on him Jenny's reply would be: "Don't ask! I haven't dared look today."

In fact, Jenny, who ended up with a record total of six runners in that year's National, hadn't initially wanted to include Alfie, urging his owners to enter him instead in the Scottish Grand National, but the Johnson's understandably wanted their day at Aintree and overruled her. In a post-race television interview with Des Lynam Jenny admitted in typically blunt style: "I told them they were mad bringing him here because he could win the Scottish National doing triple toe-loops!"

Partly because of his history of chronic leg problems and also because of his age – he was twelve years old by then – Alfie lined up at Aintree as a 40-1 outsider. In the saddle was a young Irish jockey, Jason Titley, who had not at that stage had many rides for Jenny. She told him that Alfie was the least fancied of her six runners that day, but that he had started coming into form. "He's a good jumper provided you don't interfere with his light mouth, so just sit still and let him get on with it," she instructed.

He did just that and after staying back in the early stages started moving up the field until, by the halfway stage, he was jumping neck-and-neck with 5-1 favourite Master Oats, who, like Garrison Savannah four years previously, was bidding to repeat Golden Miller's 1934 double. By the time they reached Valentine's the two of them were four lengths clear and with Master Oats tiring Alfie fairly cruised the last five fences to win by seven lengths. His homecoming and the celebration party at Weathercock that followed were memorable.

Alfie never won another race after that – despite Jenny's confident predictions, he couldn't match his Aintree heroics at the Scottish Grand National that followed, a race that was actually won by his stable mate Willsford. I had a soft spot for Alfie, a tough, game little horse who, despite all his problems, was always easy to deal with. Following his retirement he was given to John Chugg, a former trainer and highly respected judge at horse shows and championships, whose daughter rode him in show jumping and dressage events. An old friend of Jenny's, John later broke his back when he was twice thrown from an excitable young horse he was judging at the Dublin Horse Show in 2004. He was in a cast for ages, forced to lie on his back for much of the time in a room that overlooked the paddock where Alfie, by then nearly twenty-one years old, used to graze, coming up to the gate right outside John's window every late afternoon for his evening feed. That little ritual was one of the highlights of the day for John, helping to relieve the boredom during his long convalescence. One evening Alfie didn't arrive and when John's wife Jenny went out to look for him she found him lying peacefully in a corner of the paddock. He had passed away, quietly and on his own, a contented and much loved horse.

Willsford, winner of the 1995 Scottish National for which Jenny had originally earmarked Alfie, was the smallest but in many ways the most endearing of that 1986 sales quartet – a bright, sparky, cheeky character who was always ready for some good craic. And what a trier! Named after the apartment block in Willsford Green, Edgbaston where two of his three joint owners lived, 'Little Willy', as he was more familiarly known around the yard, always gave everything he'd got and actually chalked up more wins than the other three put together.

It was on a very wet day at Cheltenham in 1989 that he secured his first victory, winning the County Hurdle in style. The wetter it was, the better he liked it, so we were all very hopeful in advance and Willy didn't disappoint, coming in at 11-1. He had it won a mile from home. He took up the running at the top of the hill and from then on there was no stopping him. He went on to achieve great things in the long distance chasing world. There was a point early on when he seemed to lose his sparkle and sense of fun, but he then gained a new lease of life when assigned to a girl groom. It was almost as if he was saying: "Hey, look at me, I've pulled this bird – now aren't I just the bee's knees!"

That 1995 Scottish Grand National victory at Ayr turned out to be the last and most significant of his career. By that time he was twelve years of age, making him the oldest ever winner of the race. Ridden by Rodney Farrant, he hit the front a couple of fences from home and although the others came at him there was no way in the world that Little Willy, with his will to win and his great staying ability, was ever going to let anyone get past him. Part owner Arnold Kaplan later recalled that the celebration party went on for three days afterwards!

In complete contrast to his stable mate Alfie, Willy did not fade away quietly in a retirement paddock. In the November of the year after his triumph at Ayr he was taking part in a race at Cheltenham when he suddenly collapsed and died of a heart attack as he approached the second last fence. It was a terribly sad day for all concerned, but a glorious way for such a grand little horse to go down, with all guns blazing.

It is hard for owners, trainers and all those connected with a horse to bear such a tragic loss. At least in Willy's case death was instantaneous. It is so much worse when a limb is fractured beyond repair or when, for some reason, pain is unremitting and incurable and the dreadful decision has to be taken to put the horse out of its misery. At all of the yards I have dealt with, the loss of a horse for whatever reason – whether at home in the stable after colic surgery, out on the gallops or at the races – has always left a huge dark cloud hanging over all concerned. Personally, I will never get used to putting an animal of any kind to sleep. I hate it. But under those circumstances where it is necessary I will do it without hesitation, as quickly and efficiently as possible, either by lethal injection or with a humane pistol.

Esha Ness, an Irish horse named after a lighthouse in the Shetland Islands, was the last and, in terms of recorded results, the least successful of Jenny's four star 1986 buys. And yet his one claim to fame is likely to remain unique for all time in the annals of racing history, although not in the official record books.

The 1993 Grand National was unforgettable, but for all the wrong reasons. As always, I was present at Aintree as part of the Weathercock House team so as to be on hand if there were problems with any of our horses. Esha Ness was a 50-1 outsider as he lined up with thirty-eight other runners, including stable mates Garrison Savannah and Royal Athlete, for a start that proceeded to go catastrophically wrong. A spectacularly chaotic situation that was afterwards likened to 'Fred Karno's circus' began with a false start, when several riders became entangled with the starting tape and the rest of the field had to be recalled.

At the second attempt the tape again became entangled, this time around the neck of jockey Richard Dunwoody, and starter Keith Brown, officiating for the last time before his retirement, went to call yet another false start. But on this occasion his red recall flag failed to unfurl and thirty of the thirty-nine runners set off determinedly, oblivious to the farcical drama that was unfolding behind them. Despite the frantic efforts of officials, trainers and spectators to alert them and have the race stopped they carried on. The jockeys later explained that they thought all the feverishly gesticulating figures were animal rights protestors, a group of whom had invaded the course earlier in the afternoon.

It was not until the water jump at the end of the first circuit that many of the riders realised what was happening and pulled up, leaving just fourteen horses to carry on racing. Falls and refusals had further reduced the field to seven as they came round the elbow and summoned the last shreds of their energy for the final quarter mile run-in to the line. And it was Esha Ness, ridden by John White, who was first across.

By then, Peter O'Sullevan and the BBC commentary team had already been telling viewers for some time that the race would have to be declared void. O'Sullevan described the fiasco as "the greatest disaster in the history of the Grand National". There was vague talk of a re-run, but this was ruled out by the Jockey Club and bookmakers had to refund £75 million worth of bets. So, Esha Ness's and John White's gallant efforts were all in vain and they will never go down as National winners, although, ironically, they actually recorded the second fastest time in the history of the race.

For everybody concerned it was a crushing disappointment. Jenny was in tears and, in the immediate aftermath, did seriously consider giving up training altogether. What very nearly finished her off was seeing Esha Ness's owner, Patrick Bancroft, who had dreamed for years of having a runner in the National, enter the weighing room ashen-faced, in a state of inconsolable despair. She wrote in her autobiography: "It was like looking at a dead man, as if there was no-one inside his body".

With Royal Athlete having fallen at Valentine's and Garrison Savannah being one of those pulled up at the Water Jump, we were all in a sombre mood as we loaded up and headed home down the M6 that day.

Over the twelve years that I worked with Jenny I met all manner of interesting and colourful personalities from the world of racing – owners, jockeys, stable staff, press and sundry hangers on. And yet it is the great characters among the horses that I remember most vividly.

In addition to those leading lights from the Class of '86, there were many other star equine personalities who made a lasting impression for various reasons. One of my favourites was Mudahim, whose victory in the 1997 Irish Grand National at Fairyhouse completed Jenny's grand slam set of Grand, Scottish, Welsh and Irish Nationals. Owned by civil engineering magnate Salvo Giannini, Mudahim came to Weathercock House quite late in his career, having already won three races under trainer Chris Broad, but having then unaccountably lost his way. We had him thoroughly examined, with blood samples taken, to see if there was any physical reason for his problems, but none was apparent.

"He was as weak as a kitten and hadn't got the strength of a junior dispirin," as Jenny later recalled in her usual forthright style. "He needed lots of TLC and nursing." This was duly administered and he started to pick up, his confidence gradually returning, showing first in his outlook and then in his work. Starting with the smaller fences – and with an excellent lead horse in Gary Savannah – his jumping also improved. In February 1997 he followed a 2nd place finish at Uttoxeter with a good win in the Racing Post Chase at Kempton. He had already been entered in both the Grand National and the Irish National, but Jenny then decided that the Grand National might be too quick for him, preferring to wait for the Irish. With his owner wanting Aintree and the Missus wanting Fairyhouse, arguments inevitably followed. Eventually the debate was settled when Jenny insisted: "Look, Salvo – why don't you stick to digging foundations and I'll stick to training! I'm telling you, he will go close in Ireland."

The rest is history – victory by a short head after a great fight back in the run-in to the line, trainer justified, owner delighted. And I was chuffed to have played a part in helping to make it happen.

Toby Tobias was a very talented horse and a perfect gentleman, but he was a little bit on the soft side, a bit precious and a bit of a prima donna – in human terms, you might even call him effeminate. He had all the ability in the world, but lacked the mental toughness of a Garrison Savannah or a Willsford. You only had to startle him and he'd sulk in his box for hours; any change in his routine or a bit too much work and he would develop a tummy ache, nothing serious but enough to take the edge off him. Whether you were training him or treating him, you found yourself having to walk on eggshells, but he was well worth the effort. Although narrowly beaten by Norton's Coin in the 1990 Gold Cup he still came in ahead of Desert Orchid and in the same year he was 2nd in the King George VI ahead of The Fellow before going on to win the Betfred Bowl at Aintree.

One of my most vivid memories of him relates to an occasion when I was asked to scope about fifteen horses at Weathercock House after some of them had developed a persistent cough. Coughs and sneezes are a common problem in any yard, especially when young horses are newly arrived. It's just like kids going to school for the first time and inevitably picking up coughs and colds.

Endoscoping is the most effective way of checking out the respiratory system, but feeding the scope through a horse's nostril can obviously be a tricky procedure, especially if the patient is at all highly-strung or jumpy, and Jenny was never a great fan of it. She was always concerned about the risk that the scope itself might pass on an infection if it was not cleaned thoroughly enough after each treatment and she also worried about the fact that the pharynx would almost inevitably become slightly bruised during the procedure, which could lead to a weakening of the body's natural defences, setting the animal up for infection. On top of all that, horses could find it uncomfortable and upsetting. Because Toby was such a wuss, Jenny, who was especially protective of him, told Dave Stait: "Don't let that vet scope Toby until I am there." It was therefore agreed that I would leave him until last.

All was going well as I moved from box to box, scopes being successfully carried out and notes made. Then, as I was working on the horse before Toby, the light bulb in my scope blew. Of all the times for your kit to let you down! And to make matters worse, I hadn't brought a spare with me. In a dilemma, I decided on the spur of the moment to carry on and scope Toby as if nothing had happened and then pretend that the bulb had blown as I was proceeding. As expected, he was a little bit fussy and delicate and as I was inserting the scope, with Jenny standing by and offering plenty of advice, a tiny trickle of blood appeared in his right nostril. Jenny immediately exploded. "Look what you've done now!" she cried. "You've damaged my effing horse. You were too rough with him. Get that thing out of his nose and leave him alone." I tried, in vain, to explain that this often happens when a horse tenses up, the turbinate's in the nostril being rich with blood vessels. But Jenny was convinced it was my fault and was no way going to allow a second attempt – which was a result insofar as it meant my oversight in failing to bring a spare bulb went undetected amid all the fuss.

The only horse of Jenny's that I was never able to scope successfully was Superior Finish. A talented, multiple winner but very highly-strung, he was always quite difficult to deal with and when it came to the scope he made it plain that he was having none of it. We tried everything to try and coax him into it, all to no avail. Feet, legs, teeth – all defences went into overdrive. Head lad Adam Kyte, who was holding him, was big, strong and fearless and when he was tossed into the water trough, clean as a whistle, we decided it was time to give up, at which point some bright spark suggested that we could perhaps sedate him. The Missus did not find that at all amusing. "How can I run him at the weekend full of dope?" she snapped and then added thoughtfully: "As it happens, he's been a bit dull lately and at least you've livened him up, so let's just leave it at that." He duly went out and won the following Saturday.

Toby Tobias was one of several horses trained by Jenny for Robert Hitchins, a self-made multi-millionaire who once famously stunned the chief executive of the Injured Jockeys

Fund by unexpectedly presenting him with a cheque for £1m. Among the others were Princeful and Golden Freeze.

Princeful was well named, insofar as he was strikingly handsome in appearance, but he did have a few problems with his back when he first arrived at Weathercock House. His muscles were constantly monitored and worked on, but in the end it was Horace Hayes' old traditional 'cider vinegar' treatment that eventually settled him down and enabled him to start fulfilling his promise. He won the Stayers Hurdle at the Cheltenham Festival ridden by 'the little pigeon' Rodney Farrant. The Missus knew he was spot-on that day. And I was glad to be there to witness a sight that will always be with me – that of a beaming owner, by then in the autumn of his life, leading his own horse into the winner's enclosure at his home track. Mr Hitchins then spotted me watching from the rails and made his way over to shake my hand and say: "Thank you, Alan." I felt truly humble.

Golden Freeze was actually owned by Asil Nadir of Polly Peck fame when he first came to Weathercock House. He was another good horse, but he had his own ideas about his personal space and was quite selective about those who would be allowed to invade it. Having run a close 2nd behind Joint Sovereignty in the 1989 Mackeson Gold Cup, he returned from Cheltenham with tell tale signs of some heat in his left fore. It was treated but didn't settle and needed to be scanned to assess the full extent of the problem, about the existence of which everybody was sworn to secrecy.

At the time, he was stabled just next door to Weathercock House in Les Hamilton's yard. We all assembled there, armed with the scanner, but as soon as I started clipping his leg in preparation it was clear that Golden Freeze was not amused. He would not stand still for the scan and it took several attempts before an area of tendon damage was eventually located – nothing serious, but enough to put his racing career on hold.

Jenny wanted to re-bandage the leg and sent one of the lads off to get some bandages and Gamgee surgical dressing. We waited and waited until an increasingly impatient Jenny barked: "Where's that bloody lad with my bandages? If he doesn't hurry up and get here soon we shall have to use my effing knickers!" Whereupon one of the Irish lads piped up: "I didn't think he was quite ready yet for blistering, Missus!" At that point we all burst out laughing, including Jenny herself. Our patient was the only one present who didn't seem to see the funny side.

However, it was no laughing matter for anybody when, having been sold to Robert Hitchins following the collapse of Polly Peck in 1990 and Nadir's subsequent flight to exile in Cyprus, Golden Freeze was at the centre of the infamous 'stalking horse' controversy that surrounded the 1992 Gold Cup and led eventually to a Jockey Club inquiry.

Jenny was accused of using outsider Golden Freeze as a spoiler to unsettle and knock the stuffing out of rival trainer Martin Pipe's red hot favourite Carvill's Hill, with the aim of paving the way for Toby Tobias to come through and win. Ridden by Jenny's brother-in-law Michael Bowlby, Golden Freeze certainly set a cracking pace early on, jumping shoulder-to-shoulder with Carvill's Hill, the two of them well ahead of the rest of the field throughout the first circuit. Both then faded in the later stages and Golden Freeze dropped out, with Cool Ground going on to win from The Fellow with Toby Tobias coming in 4th, while Carvill's Hill, completely spent, was walked over the line by jockey Peter Scudamore.

It was Jenny herself who, in the face of continued allegation from various quarters that her race tactics on the day had amounted to unsporting behaviour, eventually insisted that the Jockey Club should hold the official inquiry that went on to clear her of any malpractice. It was, as she had claimed all along, a simple case of sour grapes, fermented by bitterly disappointed supporters of Carvill's Hill, whose performance had itself initially been the cause for a steward's inquiry in the immediate aftermath of the race. As far as she was concerned, Golden Freeze had every right to go head-to-head with Carvill's Hill, whom she had good reason to think might not last the distance, something that was borne out in the inquiry.

In her autobiography Jenny talked about the Press pouring petrol onto the flickering flames of a false controversy and there is no doubt there were those in the media who perhaps saw her as a legitimate target, partly because of her naturally abrasive and unashamedly forthright manner. I remember her calling me one day to ask the meaning of the word 'virago', which a reporter had used to describe her in one of that morning's papers. I was mischievous enough to reply: "How about 'cantankerous old cow'?" There was a pause and then she replied with a chuckle: "I see. Well, he might be right then."

There is no denying that Jenny has always been a tough cookie – she had to be in order to succeed in what is a very tough business. But having worked closely with her for many years and having been a friend for even longer, I can vouch for the fact that underneath the sometimes fearsomely hard exterior she is good-hearted, generous and fiercely loyal to those she knows and trusts. And while she can certainly dish it out, she can also take it, too. She has a great, often very earthy sense of expletive-undeleted humour and can laugh at herself.

The rather oddly named horse Bizage Motors was responsible for an incident that resulted in everybody else enjoying a chuckle at Jenny's expense. He developed a problem that made it necessary to take a urine sample from him. You might think that would be pretty straightforward, but some boys get shy with an audience and we ended up having to catheterise his bladder. After suitable sedation a catheter the size of a garden hose was gently inserted into his urethra.

Jenny wanted to keep an eye on the proceedings but had to go off to the races immediately afterwards, so during the pre-liminaries she went off to change and then waltzed back in looking very smart and wondering why it was taking so long to get the sample. I tried to explain that it was not easy and that things needed to be done slowly for obvious reasons, but she pooh-poohed this, insisting that I needed to be more positive. By way of demonstration, she then leaned forward and gave the tube a push, whereupon a flood of urine gushed out of the catheter and all over her fancy shoes. Amid a torrent of unprintable abuse she stormed out of the box, accusing me of setting her up on purpose and threatening to have my guts for garters. I was used to that sort of outburst by then and knew it would all be forgotten by the next day, so it was like water off a duck's back, to coin a rather apt phrase! The main thing was, I'd got my sample and, following analysis, was able to provide the effective treatment.

Saleel, owned by Lucy Wadham's Waterhall Racing syndicate, was not a famous horse but I remember him well, mostly because he had one bad habit that we all hate – he was a biter. When a horse's jaws snap shut they do so with some power. The tables of their front incisors are flat so that they don't pierce, but when clamped together they do cause an extremely painful pinch. He nipped me on a couple of occasions and although I didn't suffer any serious damage it certainly helped to blow away the morning cobwebs! He was looked after by a mercurial French lad named Freddie, the only person in the yard for whom he seemed to have any respect. The two of them understood each other perfectly. Freddie knew how to handle him and was always able to control him, although he had to put a muzzle on him to stop him getting at the other horses in the string.

Saleel reminded me of my father and his rather unusual but very effective way of dealing with biters. Father always wore a flat cap wherever he went, to the point where people used to joke that he must have been born with one already on his head. He had just purchased a new one, of which he was very proud, when, walking through the stables at Dunthrop owned by Heythrop hunt stalwart Miss Nancibel 'Nan' Gregory, one of her hunters leaned out of his stall and sunk his teeth into the precious titfer. Father was furious.

"Nancibel, I will cure that blighter of his biting habit once and for all," he promised and Nan replied that she would be delighted if he would. So he had a leg of mutton boiled up and when it was cooked he cut off a sizeable chunk, speared it with a short fork and then walked past the offending horse with the steaming mutton prominent. The horse duly sank its teeth into the very hot meat and then quickly retreated to the rear of its stall with a burnt tongue. It never bit anyone again. There were one or two occasions when I was sorely tempted to suggest that we should give Saleel some of the same treatment, but I don't think it would have gone down too well with the Missus. I suspect I would be the one who would end up getting a verbal roasting!

One day in the early summer of 1997 I got a phone call from Jenny who said excitedly: "Bet you don't know what's happening on July 18th!"

I replied that as a matter of fact I did – because it was my birthday.

"Well, in that case there's a double reason for celebration," she chuckled. "Because Dave and I are getting married. And we want you and Di to come to the wedding."

We were thrilled to be included among a small group of only around twenty guests who attended the register office ceremony in Southampton that was followed by a reception aboard the P&O cruise liner Orianna, on which the happy couple were to sail off on their honeymoon. It was one hell of a party that developed as the champagne flowed under the watchful gaze of an ice carving of a horse's head. It was still in full swing when, rather unfortunately, it was cut short by the announcement that the ship was about to set sail and we needed to leave. By then, the girls among the guests had already made sure that the bridal cabin and the bed were strewn with confetti.

Later that year, during one of my routine visits to Weathercock House, I happened to notice that Jenny seemed rather under the weather. When I mentioned that she didn't seem her usual self she admitted that she was worried about a tiny lump the size of a pea that she had found in her throat and asked me if I would take a look. I didn't like what I saw and told her: "If you were a horse we'd be looking for specialist treatment. I suggest you go and get it checked straightaway." Charlie Schreiber had apparently given her exactly the same advice.

What at first appeared to be no more than a benign cyst was eventually diagnosed as thyroid cancer. After two operations and several months of treatment, during which Jenny kept the true nature of her illness a secret from all but her immediate family and closest friends, she was thankfully given the all clear shortly before the publication of her autobiography in October 1998. But the illness had taken its toll on her energy levels and the following year, at the age of 52, she decided the time had come to retire from training, handing the business on to her son, Mark. She herself then went on to forge a successful new career for herself as a novelist, writing books set in the racing world, rather as former jockey Dick Francis had done. At the same time, her contribution to racing was acknowledged with the award of an OBE. She also became the inaugural recipient of the BBC TV Sports Personality of the Year Helen Rollason Award for 'outstanding achievement in the face of adversity'.

She and I have remained good friends, still speak regularly on the phone and see each other from time to time. I have nothing but admiration for someone I regard as a wonderfully entertaining, larger than life character with a great heart. A true professional, her sheer force of personality and her forthright, no-nonsense manner made it inevitable that she would rub some people up the wrong way as she pursued a high profile career in the tough and fiercely competitive world of horseracing. And let's face it – she could certainly be an awkward customer if you upset her. But even when she was dishing out another bollocking she tended to do it with style.

And when the chips were down, she would always be there for you – literally so in my case. When my disciplinary hearing came up before the RCVS and I needed someone to attend in order give me a character reference, she didn't hesitate. "Anytime, anywhere, I'll be there to support you," she said. And when it came to it, she postponed a long-awaited knee operation at the last minute just so that she would be free to come up to London for the hearing.

There have been many other little kindnesses over the years that pointed to the other, softer side of her otherwise formidable character. When my daughter, Lucy, was trying to get her badges as a Girl Guide, one of the tasks she was given was to interview someone famous and she wondered whether Jenny might agree to be her subject. I had a word with Jenny, who said that, of course, she would. I then told Lucy that although it might possibly be on, she herself would have to contact Jenny to arrange it. Lucy was only about fourteen at the time and understandably quite nervous about the whole thing, but got on the phone and spoke to Jenny who suggested that it could be done the following Thursday, immediately after my regular visit to Weathercock. As it turned out, that particular day was not the best – things had not gone well, bad news had been dispensed and Jenny was not pleased with any of us. I was feeling for my daughter, worried that this was not going to be the right moment for her interview as a very cross Jenny dismissed us with the angry comment that she had better things to do with her time than waste it talking to us lot, adding: "I've got to go now anyway as I have a very important prior engagement." And turning to Lucy she said quietly: "Come on, Luce, we'll go upstairs where we won't be disturbed." She then proceeded to give a generous amount of her time to a young girl who still treasures the tape of that interview to this day.

10

Extra Training

Following closely in the professional footsteps of a successful parent can be a hard thing to do, as I myself had discovered in the early days of my veterinary career when I often struggled to live up to the expectations of clients who had held my father in such high regard. I therefore had a lot of sympathy for Mark Pitman when he took over from Jenny at Weathercock House.

Having first ridden for trainers David Nicholson and Martin Pipe, Mark then became No 1 jockey at Weathercock House, he and his mother together enjoying several major race victories as jockey and trainer that included the 1991 Cheltenham Gold Cup. Top jockey at the Aintree festival of 1990, Mark rode a total of nearly three hundred winners before retiring at the age of twenty-six to become Jenny's assistant trainer at Weathercock House. Quite naturally, he had his own ideas about training methods, leading to occasional differences of opinion between mother and son, and after three years it became apparent that he wanted to go it alone.

Having taken out his own licence, Mark's solo training career then got off to a flying start when his very first runner, Sailin Minstrel, came in a winner. Sailin Minstrel was one of the two horses with which he got started, the other one being Marble City. Both were purchased in Ireland and Mark initially stabled them at his father's property in Denchworth before renting the yard at Saxon House. Marble City was a rather bad-tempered individual, putting down a marker early on by delivering a double-barrelled kick to Mark's thigh when he went into his stall at night to straighten his rugs. He was the first horse bought by wealthy entrepreneur Malcolm Denmark, with whom Mark was destined to have a long and successful relationship.

At Saxon House, Mark and his wife, Natasha, set about building the business, soon acquiring about twenty horses, but after the initial success of Sailin Minstrel things didn't go so smoothly. Coughing, dirty noses, poor appetites or simply feeling off-colour for no apparent reason – it was one thing after another, with horses constantly having to be declared unfit for training. Then, within a couple of years, Jenny retired and Malcolm Denmark purchased Weathercock House. Mark moved in as trainer and a new era dawned.

It was pleasing to see that all the old values – discipline, cleanliness and attention to detail – were strictly adhered to. Mark had an experienced assistant in Paul Price, who had worked for Jenny and knew the racing game inside out; and also a head lad, Murty McGrath, who was a very knowledgeable young man. It wasn't long before the new team started to turn out the winners.

Monsignor was bought from renowned Irish dealer Tom Costello. A big chestnut gelding, he was a lovely horse, a gentle giant with a wonderfully kind temperament; and what an engine! He won eight of his ten career starts, with two victories at the Cheltenham Festival, including the 1999 Champion Bumper, the most prestigious flat race in the National Hunt calendar, followed in 2000 by the Sun Alliance Novice Hurdle, which he won in record time. His racing career ended prematurely because of a persistent leg injury, but in his retirement he went on to become a hugely popular equine ambassador for the charity Homing Ex-Racehorses Organisation Scheme (HEROS), to whom he was gifted by Malcolm Denmark in 2006, going out to racecourses for 'Meet the Racehorse' sessions and parading at Lambourn and Epsom open days. And in 2012, he was asked to carry the Olympic Torch and Frankie Dettori around the parade ring at Ascot. Sadly, he had to be put down the following year, at the age of nineteen, having suffered a serious foreleg injury in his field at the North Farm Stud, near Wantage in Oxfordshire, where he was stabled.

Ever Blessed was another lovely horse. He had many problems – none major and yet all cumulative – but was a very willing patient and always tried to please. However, getting him fit, ready and at his peak for a big race on time required considerable teamwork. As Mark once remarked: "Keeping him right is like holding together a fragile piece of china." Paul Price and Murty took him swimming, massaged his muscles and gave him extra, controlled exercise, never galloping him with another horse in case he got too competitive and risked damaging himself, while Charlie and I weighed in with our veterinary contributions. But it was Mark who always conducted the orchestra. Between us, we managed to get him absolutely spot on for the 1999 Hennessy Gold Cup at Newbury and when he strutted into the paddock he was full of himself, confident and blooming. And he did not disappoint. Jockey Timmy Murphy held him back during the first lap before moving him through the field to win by three-and-a-half lengths after fighting off a determined challenge from Splendid over the final four fences. Mark thus became the third Pitman to win the Hennessy, Jenny having trained 1984 winner Borough Hill Lad while his father, Richard, had ridden Charlie Poteen to victory in 1972. The celebrations were memorable.

Tracy Brown had some good horses with Mark. Ashley Park was a bonny little stallion, with a heart as big as his body. Talented but fragile, he was the nearest I got to being associated with a winner of the Champion Hurdle when, in 2000, he crossed the line a fast-finishing 4th, very close behind three-time Champion Hurdle winner Istabraaq, one of the great all-time hurdlers. Tracy also owned Smarty, who came 2nd in the 2001 Grand National behind Red Marauder. It was very wet that year and only four horses lasted the distance, although the ground was so soft and the pace so slow that, despite the many fallers, there were no serious injuries to either horses or riders.

Red Marauder took many liberties with the fences and although no-one who loves horses wants them to fall, there were a few of Smarty's supporters who were hopeful that day!

Malcolm Denmark loved to be involved with his horses. His team would meet for dinner at one of the local hostelries before the start of each season to discuss the previous season's problem horses, how he wanted them dealt with and his hopes and plans for the coming season. He bought a lot of his horses from Tom Costello. Based at Newmarket-on-Fergus in County Clare, Tom was a very shrewd man. He had a wonderful eye for a horse and bought most of his as weaned foals or yearlings. Malcolm and Mark would fly over to Ireland to see what was on offer before bidding for the ones they liked the look of. I would then get a call to go over and vet the ones they had managed to buy. Tom always treated me courteously even when a horse failed, provided he could see the reason why. And on those few occasions when they didn't work out, he would have them back and exchange them. When you were walking around anywhere with Tom he had this rather disconcerting habit of sticking very close beside you – if there had been a Steward's Inquiry he would have been done for taking your ground! He also had a favourite saying: "You would wear a set of tyres out before you could find another horse of such quality". On one visit, Mark cheekily asked as he was inspecting a particular horse: "How many sets of tyres would we wear out before we found another as good as this one, then?" Quick as a flash the answer came back: "Two sets of tyres and an effing engine!"

There was another occasion when Malcolm was looking to buy a three-year-old with a view to winning the Triumph Hurdle the following year and it was reported that there was a suitable candidate at Coolmore. Malcolm, Mark and I flew over to Cork and from there up to Tipperary where we were regally entertained and shown round the impressive Coolmore complex before being taken to Ballydoyle to look at the horse. Unfortunately, it wasn't nearly as good as it had been cracked up to be and we left fairly quickly. Malcolm was rather annoyed that it had turned out to be a wasted trip, but all that changed on the way back to Cork. We passed a shop selling old-fashioned fireplace surrounds and Malcolm asked Mark to stop the car while he went in and had a look around. After what seemed an age he came out beaming, having found just what he wanted for one of his development projects.

Mark eventually found that juggling the demands of family life with those of a trainer was very hard and, despite having been involved in the racing world all his life and having enjoyed considerable success as both a jockey and a trainer, he became somewhat disillusioned and decided on a complete change of lifestyle. He wanted to spend more time with his wife Natasha and two young daughters, Darcy and Talia, and so, in 2006, he moved the family to Spain.

Mark's place at Weathercock House was taken by assistant trainer and stable jockey Carl Llewellyn, who almost immediately had his first big winner when, just a couple of weeks later, he rode Run For Paddy to victory in the Scottish Grand National, getting up in the last stride to win. It was one of Carl's mates who remarked that he would have worked out his percentage winnings as both rider and trainer before he got back to the winners enclosure! Three years later he had another prestigious win with Hennessy in the Betfred Gold Cup at Sandown, before returning, to Naunton to rejoin Nigel Twiston-Davies.

Martin Bosley, youngest son of my father's great friend John Bosley, is someone else who found that following in a well-known parent's professional footsteps can be hard going. Having retired as a jockey, Martin took over the training licence from his father when they moved from Haddon Farm to Kingston Lisle. His wife Sarah, who was still a leading lady rider at the time, worked with him.

The life of a trainer can often be very tough. It involves getting up at dawn every morning to check on the horses, supervising their feeding, sorting out any problems and generally making sure that everything in the yard is OK; then working with the horses on the gallops before going into the office to do the paperwork, making declarations for runners, planning and preparing race entries and talking to owners; after that, maybe going racing, then hurrying back for evening stables and sometimes having to give gloomy or disappointing news to owners; and, in between all that, compulsory socialising and looking for both new horses and new owners. It really is a labour of love and can be soul-destroying, especially if you are working most of the time with horses of only limited ability. Martin and Sarah, who are now based in a lovely yard at Chalfont St Giles, fall into this bracket, doing their best but having to work all hours for scant reward. Their owners are wonderfully supportive, but don't have unlimited funds with which to buy horses so they are constantly on the lookout for a bargain – the one magic horse that will light the touch paper and put them on the map.

Makarim was a good buy and we thought he might be the one to ignite Martin's career. He did indeed go on to win several races in a row, but had to have things all his own way and, in the end, never really fulfilled his promise. And then there was Rhubahunish. He was owned by a syndicate of London taxi drivers, to whom Martin was introduced by jockey Luke Harvey, who was still riding at the time before going on to become a BBC radio and Sky Sports television racing reporter. The horse had ability and was the subject of a huge bet by his owners in a good race at Sandown, but could only manage to finish 3rd. However, he did then win two or three races for Martin and finished 2nd to Swinton at Haydock before getting 'a leg' and having to be rested. Once he had settled down, I fired him to help repair his legs. He recovered and Martin and Luke were looking forward to getting him back on track, but the owners had other ideas and sent him instead to Nigel Twiston-Davies. A brilliant trainer and a really good man, Nigel trained him to win at Ascot, Punchestown and Cheltenham.

Although I was pleased for Nigel, I would have preferred the wins to be Martin's. I was at Cheltenham on the day of the horse's victory there and a bunch of us went on afterwards to The Hollow Bottom, that well-known watering hole in Guiting Power. Nigel had a marquee set up in the garden there in which to entertain his guests, among whom were Rhubahunish's owners. Flushed with a few drinks and full of confidence, they were none too impressed by my lecture on the subject of loyalty!

As previously mentioned, respiratory problems can be a major concern with racehorses, because at the speeds they travel they need an uninterrupted flow of oxygen to enable them to perform to their maximum ability. There are several different types of problem that arise. Surgery on the larynx or palate has become very sophisticated over the last fifteen years or so and in some treatment centres laser surgery is used, but prior to all these very modern developments a horse with a breathing problem would be tubed, a procedure whereby a metal tube consisting of three interlocking sections would be inserted into the windpipe to provide an air inlet. In truth, it was not a very satisfactory means of treatment; it was messy, the tube needed to be taken out twice a day to be cleaned, and if you left it out for any length of time the tracheotomy hole soon healed over. On top of all that, the horse had to learn to adapt to a slightly different way of breathing. However, there were some horses for whom it worked very effectively, Party Politics famously winning the 1992 Grand National with a specially-adapted tube.

The Bosleys had a horse called Pusey Street Boy who suffered breathing problems until a tube was put in, whereupon he was transformed and became a multiple winner – but not before we had made a further modification. Pusey Street Boy was at his best on an all-weather surface, but in the early days of all-weather tracks there was a problem with what was known as 'kick-back', sand kicked up by the horse in front being inhaled by those following. When all-weather racing first started we couldn't initially understand why, on scoping a horse after a race, we would find all these small bruises in the upper airway and it was a while before we realised that this was caused by the sand particles they were breathing in. It doesn't happen any more because the modern surfaces are superb. Anyway, at the time when this was still a problem it was Sarah Bosley's idea to take Pusey Street Boy's tube apart and put a piece of material cut from an old pair of nylon tights across the aperture, enabling the air to pass through while filtering out any sand particles. It worked brilliantly.

Because my working relationship with the families spanned two generations I felt a particular affinity with the Webbers, the Pitmans and the Bosleys. Working first for the parents and then the sons, having already been through the father-to-son transition myself, I had a deeper understanding of the problems involved in the handover and a special interest in watching the younger generation get established and doing what I could to help. From being taught, I found myself becoming the teacher.

The horseracing fraternity is full of colourful and often very strong personalities and I am fortunate to have worked with some of the best of them over the years, including owners, jockeys and stable staff, but mostly trainers.

John Upson had a lot of good horses at his Highfields Stables in Adstone, many of them again purchased from Tom Costello. When I first went to the yard the late Terry Casey was training for John, who, although very much involved with his horses and racing, was also a very busy and successful businessman and did not have the time to do everything himself. It is fair to say that Terry was not the most organised person in the world; just when you thought you had finished your work for the day and were getting ready to leave he would announce casually: "Oh, by the way, there are ten horses that could do with a saline wash – you might as well do that while you're here." He was a great fan of this old-fashioned treatment, which is not much used today but which he always maintained would help to freshen up a horse. It involved mixing up about two gallons of saline solution with various additives and then passing a tube up the horse's nostril, carefully locating the oesophagus and feeding the tube from there into the stomach. You needed to be certain you were in the right place and not in the windpipe, which led to the lungs. When satisfied that everything was in place you then attached a stirrup pump to the free end of the tube before gently pumping the solution into the stomach. Not all horses will stand still and tolerate this invasion and even with the most docile ones the procedure would take at least fifteen minutes, so it wasn't really a job to be done at the last moment.

Terry was also the only trainer who has ever kissed me full on the lips. John's horse Over The Road had picked up a few problems in the lead-up to the Cheltenham Festival one year, but we managed to overcome them and he was showing signs of a return to top form. Terry was bullish about his chances, especially after being 'freshened up'. Sure enough, he won his race at Cheltenham and Terry was so pleased as he crossed the line that in his excitement he jumped up and planted a smacker on me before I could move out of range.

Soon after that Terry moved to Derek Ancil's yard at Thorpe Mandeville. Derek, who died in 2010, was a kind, modest and greatly respected man who became a real legend during a successful career as both jockey and trainer, achieving the rare feat of training and riding Knucklecracker to victory in the Hennessy Gold Cup in 1960 and then coming 2nd in the Grand National on Merryman the following year. Terry was with him for two years before moving to Beare Green, Dorking to train for Andrew Wates, enjoying his greatest success there when Rough Quest won the 1996 Grand National.

I visited him several times at Beare Green to treat horses for sarcoids. He later developed throat cancer and although he did gain some remission following surgery and chemotherapy it took a heavy toll. The last time I saw him was at Stratford Races in 2001, by which time he was very poorly and had to keep taking sips of water to moisten his dry mouth. We had a chat and he was the same old, ever-optimistic Terry, a good horseman and trainer with an eye for the ladies. I was saddened to hear of his passing shortly afterwards at the age of just fifty-six.

Going back, Terry's place as trainer at John Upson's yard had been taken by Tom Costello's oldest son, John, and his wife, Gronya. I got to know them both well, little knowing that I would later find myself regularly visiting Tom's yard in Ireland on buying expeditions with Mark Pitman. John was anxious to make a success of his time training in England and he certainly did that. He was very willing to learn and you would often see the two Johns together, deep in earnest conversation, the boss with his ever-present Havana cigar. He stayed a couple of seasons before returning to Ireland to become more involved with the family business there.

John Upson was still heavily involved in his business interests and so, while he held the training licence, he promoted a young red-haired Irish lad, Brian Rothwell, to manage the day-to-day running of the yard. Brian was helped greatly by John's secretary, Angie Smith, the daughter of local neighbours Syd and Jane Smith – farmers, stud owners and the most charming, genuine people. Angie worked for John for many years, remaining a steady and continual thread throughout the yard's most successful years.

Perhaps the best horse they had was Nick the Brief. The most handsome of horses – big, black and with a superb temperament – he came very close to being top class, winning many races in England and Ireland. Others that remain firmly in the memory were Thar an Barr, who, like Party Politics, overcame breathing problems by having a metal tube inserted into his windpipe, and Zeta's Lad, another multiple winner and one of the favourites in the void 1993 Grand National.

During Brian's time there a new owner, Andrew Cohen, came to the yard, initially with three horses and then, as time went on, lots more. One summer, a fresh batch of young horses arrived. They were turned out into the paddocks and as I was checking them over and giving them their annual vaccinations, one big, cheeky grey horse stood out. I fell in love with Suny Bay who went on to become a great favourite with racing fans, recording eight wins from eleven starts, including the 1997 Hennessy Gold Cup. He was also runner-up in the Grand National in both 1997 and 1998. Unfortunately for John, all his success came after he had been moved to Charlie Brooks' Uplands yard.

Peter Hiatt trains at Six Ash Farm, near Hook Norton, and has been a friend for many years. I first met him on the cricket field, where he proved far too canny a bowler for a batsman of my limited ability. A farmer and livestock dealer, Peter had always had a keen interest in racehorses, first point-to-pointers and then under rules, but he was already getting on for sixty when he took out a full trainer's licence in 1997, since when he has consistently enjoyed terrific success, with a total of well over 260 winners. He tends to buy less expensive horses, gets them fit using his rotavated earth gallop up on Oatley Hill and then places them very shrewdly, only entering them in races he thinks he can win.

An early example was Royal Circus, a little horse for which he paid just six hundred guineas, but which went on to win fifteen times, both on the flat and over hurdles. Other great successes included Lost Spirit, who was pretty wild when he first arrived at Six Ash Farm, but was eventually calmed down and, having won first time out at 33/1, went on to record multiple victories. Also, the mare Tight Squeeze, who was also blessed with a fierce temperament and was highly competitive, with many wins to her credit. I admire Pete tremendously and it certainly pays to follow his horses. I remember reading an article in the local Banbury Guardian newspaper in which it was calculated that if you had put £10 on every runner the stable sent out that year you would have made a profit of £200!

The late Chris Treitline, who trained near Stratford-upon-Avon, was a real character. As wide as he was tall, he was not known as Porky for nothing! He had some good horses – Judge's Fancy, Aldington Belle, Kilbannon and Gembridge Jupiter.

When he first rang asking if I would be interested in doing his horse work I replied that I would indeed, but that I was particularly busy at that very moment and wouldn't be able to come and see him straightaway. Two days later he rang again and asked where I had got to.

"I did warn you that I was busy," I reminded him, promising to come the next day. When I arrived he again asked what had taken me so long. "Well, I had to do my homework on you, just as I'm sure you had done on me," I told him.

"Oh! And what have you found out?" he inquired.

"Two things," I said. "One, that you have got a very short fuse and a vile temper and, two, that you are a bad payer."

"Who told you that?" he barked.

What a great start to our relationship!

He liked me to make my visits in the afternoon. Each time a checklist would be provided and his head girl, Jane, would show me the horses. When I had finished it would be back to the office to report. At first, he did pay his bills and we got on well – he was having a few winners at the time and all was rosy. But as time went by the bills weren't settled quite so promptly and when I pressed him he came up with the usual excuses.

I knew from his constant breathlessness that he had a heart problem and I noticed as he sat smoking yet another cigarette that if he got agitated he would reach into the left-hand draw of his desk to get his tablets. On one particular occasion he was so far behind with his payments that when he came out with the usual excuses I lost patience – I felt he was taking the mickey and I was not at all happy. Neither was he. His blood pressure clearly rising, he reached into his desk drawer for his tablets and as he did so I quickly leaned over and pulled the drawer sharply closed, trapping his hand. He turned blue and started gasping. I told him: "You're right-handed so you can still sign the bloody cheque and then I'll let you go!" He duly signed and quickly recovered. There's no doubt that he could be very difficult but, even so, I liked him.

If George Baker had listened to me and had taken my advice he would never have become the highly successful trainer he is today! I first met George when he was working as an assistant to Paul Webber, and Candida, his lovely wife, used to come and ride out at Cropredy Lawn. He helped Paul with the placing of horses and the general running of the yard but, although keen, he was not a natural horseman, as was demonstrated one day when one of Paul's fillies, who had been on box rest, needed to be re-assessed for lameness. As she was fresh, I advised him to put a chifney bit on her to discourage her from rearing. He ignored me and with just a leading rope, no helmet and the fateful comment "no woman ever gets the better of me", led her out of her box. Well, talk about famous last words! As soon as this filly saw the light of day she became playful, reared up and came down on the hapless George's head. He went down in a heap and was very fortunate to get away without serious damage to anything other than his pride.

George, who liked a punt and spent most of his afternoons investing, left Cropredy Lawn to become a racing correspondent for The Sportsman, a publication that was short-lived. I next bumped into him at Wincanton, he in his role as a reporter and me on a tour of all the country's racecourses in my capacity as Chairman of the Association of Racecourse Veterinary Surgeons. It was then that he expressed his burning desire to become a trainer. I told him he was mad to even think about it, that it was the last thing I would do if I were him. Once again, he ignored my advice and the next I heard he had bought land and stables near Warwick and was going ahead. Where he had been very shrewd, however, was in going into partnership with Pat Murphy, a brilliant rider who had been Paul Webber's work jockey.

Pat was smart. He knew the best horses and their abilities and when he was at Cropredy Lawn and he fancied a punt on one in an up-coming race he would always appear out of the blue to find out if it had been scoped clean – a useful tip in itself. George could not have made a better choice – Pat rode and trained the horses with terrific support from his wife Val while George made the contacts and got the horses. They made an excellent start and the yard was soon buzzing and brimming with confidence, so much so that George decided they needed better facilities to enable them to compete at the highest level and moved the operation to a new state-of-the-art training centre at Whitsbury Manor Racing Stables in Hampshire. The winners kept coming and in 2012 he moved again, this time to the Barton Yard on the Sangster estate at Manton, near Marlborough, where he operates alongside fellow trainer Brian Meehan. At the last count he had a career total of nearly two hundred winners to his credit. So, as he always takes great delight in reminding me, it's just as well he didn't listen to my well-intentioned advice to forget the whole idea!

George's success was in complete contrast to the disappointment of Mark Wilkinson's ill-fated training career. Mark started training at Trafford Bridge on the Courage estate – his wife, Sandy, being related to the Courage family. He made a superb start, with Smart Tar winning at Cheltenham in 1989 and for a while he was seen as an up-and-coming star, even the Queen Mother visiting his yard. But in the end it never quite happened for him. Smart Tar sustained a fatal injury not long after his Cheltenham victory, as did another good horse, Andrew's First, just when carrying all before him. Mark had better luck with Mister Drum, a lovely honest chaser who won many races. However, being in the public eye and under pressure to produce results puts a great strain on family life. Some owners seem to think that their trainers should live, eat and breathe their horses and not have any time for themselves. Mark's marriage cracked under the strain and he and Sandy split up. I liked them both very much and would not take sides. Meanwhile, Mark's career was effectively over and he handed in his licence, going to work instead for the family estate agency business. I last saw him at the wedding of Culworth trainer and mutual friend Paul Cowley in 2008. Finding ourselves sitting at the same table we reminisced and I could see how much he missed all the hurly-burly of training and how he still entertained hopes of starting again one day.

Dave Lewis trained at Upton on Severn and I first got to know him when he purchased a horse from Jenny Pitman. Celtic Laird was a bright chestnut with some ability. He was a kind, calm horse until you went anywhere near his ears and so it was always tricky putting a bridle on him; it had to be taken apart and then carefully slid over the top of his head before being put back together again and then he was fine, but the whole operation was time-consuming. The reason for his sensitivity in this area was that he suffered from a chronic build-up of calcium deposits and fungus in his ears. Two or three times a year he would have to be sedated and the build-up of plaque removed, but even under sedation it was not easy. It was through repeatedly carrying out this procedure that I got to know Dave well. He was a building contractor who loved his horses and enjoyed quite a bit of success as a trainer. I remember going on one of my regular visits to his yard and finding him in a particularly good mood and when I asked why he was in such good spirits he explained that one of his lifelong ambitions was about to come true. He told me how a local businessman had wronged him in a deal many years previously and that he had born a grudge ever since. So why was he now so pleased about it?

"Well, " he said. "I had always promised to put him in the ground and now I can. He died recently and I run a grave-digging business used by the church where he is being buried. I'm actually aiming to do the job myself!"

I first met Ian Williams when he joined Jenny Pitman as her assistant at Weathercock House. He was a fresh-faced, clean cut, polite young man whose father, Billy Williams, was a trainer down in the West Country. He was somewhat vague about his true age when he first arrived at the yard; in fact, he was a lot younger than I thought he was – just eighteen – but mature beyond his years. He and Jenny got on well together. As well as being a quick learner and a hard worker, always very clean and tidy, he had the priceless quality of knowing when and when not to speak.

One funny story that he will not thank me for recalling concerns a visit we made one day to Ashdown, where some of the resting horses were cared for by Jenny's sister and brother-in-law, Mandy and Michael Bowlby. Among the horses they were looking after at the time was Do Behave. Never the easiest of animals to handle, he had leg problems that were due to be treated. After managing to sedate him, not without some difficulty, I started to prepare his legs by first clipping and cleaning them before injecting local anaesthetic. Then, all of a sudden, just as I started the firing procedure, I heard a crash and looked round to see that Ian was no longer standing there holding the horse but was in a heap on the floor, having passed out. Fortunately, the horse was well doped and blissfully unaware that his handler was no longer in a position to be able to restrain him, so I simply carried on and by the time the treatment was finished Ian was beginning to stir. Thankful that I had not had to give him the kiss of life, I administered some basic first aid and he was fine.

Before Ian eventually launched out on his own as a trainer in 1997 he went on to gain further invaluable experience by also working for a time as assistant to both Martin Pipe at Pond House and then to Francois Doumen at Chantilly in France. He is now a hugely successful trainer based at Hob Hill Farm, just off Junction 3 of the M42 at Alvechurch, where he and Patrick Kelly, a businessman with a passion for horse racing, created the Dominion Racing Stables, a state-of-the-art training facility. At the last count Ian had more than seventy-five horses in training, with a total of more than five hundred wins to his name.

Ian is still as youthful-looking and as charming as ever and remains a very good personal friend, very kindly helping my daughter Lucy to prepare for her GCSE French oral exam in 1996, the subject being 'The Differences Between French and English Horseracing'. It is a real pleasure to see him doing so well.

11

A Grand Tour

The practice continued to grow and develop throughout the 1990s, especially the equine side of the business. Simon Richards joined us in 1991 and it was clear from the start that he was going to be a great asset. I had been told by one of his previous bosses, Ken Ferguson from Sherbourne, to make sure I didn't let him slip through my fingers. "He is far too good to lose," said Ken. How right he was. Simon was not only an excellent stud vet, something that I certainly could not claim to; he was also an extremely hard worker and a most likeable individual who soon became highly popular with the clients.

Simon and I worked well together. With our very different personalities – he is quiet, I am noisy! – we complemented each other rather well and as our equine workload started to increase he rapidly established himself as a valuable and indispensable member of the team. I clearly remember the moment when, as Steve Glanvill and I were sitting in the office one morning, there was a knock on the door and Simon came in asking if he could have a word. "What are my chances of being made a partner?" he wanted to know. Steve and I exchanged glances and replied in unison: "Very, very good!" And that was that. Now we were three.

I have been fortunate in my life to have such wonderful partners both at home, where Di has been a loving and wonderfully supportive wife, and at work. Steve, Simon and I haven't always agreed, but we have never disagreed in public. On those few occasions when we were at odds for any reason we made sure we got it sorted out between us without the staff ever suspecting that there was a problem. And we very happily shared the administrative duties. Steve dealt with the buying in of drugs, a time-consuming job that involves seeing reps, attending meetings and keeping up-to-date with all the latest developments and offers; Simon was responsible for the various insurance policies and the purchase of new equipment; and I took responsibility for keeping an eye on the practice finances generally and also looked after the personnel side of things.

It all worked well and, as the business expanded even further over the next few years, it became fairly apparent that we were once again running out of space. We were starting to feel cramped. It was also difficult at times to get the increasing number of lorries and transporters in and out of the yard, a situation that was made worse by the fact that a school had been built opposite us in Sibford Road, the start and finish of the school day coinciding with our busiest time when clients would be bringing their animals in and collecting them. With children milling about on the road outside, extra care was called for. Happily, there were no accidents, but we were aware of the potential danger and it was a worry.

It was clearly time for a change, so we started to look around for an alternative site to develop, although, in truth, we were already so busy and overworked that our efforts were initially rather half-hearted. Simon eventually suggested that we should employ a local agent to find suitable premises. Ian Sloane from Bankier Sloane was duly engaged and it wasn't too long before he came up with several possibilities. We did try to buy some land between the new school and the Redlands Farm dairy unit, but that didn't work out for various reasons.

The Christmas party season was in full swing in Hook Norton when I happened to find myself at a drinks party chatting to Ray Gasson, the local District Councillor, Land Manager and good friend who had officiated at the opening of our original surgery in the Sibford Road. My tongue loosened by a few drinks, I told

Like father, like son: dressed for work in exactly the same sort of brown smock that father always wore, along with his flat cap (below). The twitch that he has in his hand had been passed down to him by his father – and I still have it.

(Top) With Steve Glanvill (left) and John Webber at the opening of the extended surgery in Sibford Road, Hook Norton. (Below) Treating an equine patient in the stable yard there and (right) lasering a horse at Cropredy Lawn with John Webber looking on.

The current surgery at Whitehills includes (below) a fully-equipped operating theatre. It's all a far cry from my father's surgery in the white shed at Burmington (left). The girl on the bicycle is my sister Margaret, whose tragically early death from cancer devastated the family.

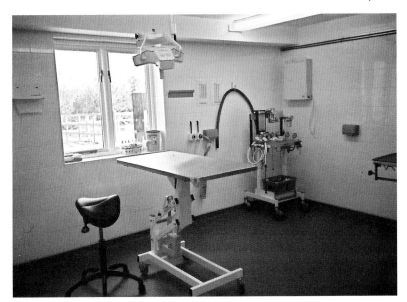

Three of Cropredy Lawn's best: (left) Elfast with Diana and John Webber and jockey Michael Jenkins, (below) Auntie Dot and (bottom) Flying Instructor in full flight at Wetherby.

Jenny Pitman welcomes Royal Athlete home
after his 1995 Grand National triumph.
(Right) Me offering congratulations and
(below left) Mark Pitman on Cheltenham
Gold Cup winner Garrison Savannah.

Star of the show: Royal Athlete makes a guest appearance
at our charity fund-raising Donkey Derby while (below)
daughter Lucy shows her delight as she pips my practice
partner Steve Glanvill in the main event.

Lucy with Scampi, my constant walking companion, and Folie, who belongs to our good friends Jim and Andrea Kiernan and sometimes stays with us when they are away.

Son George (on the right) has inherited a liking for the horses.

Enjoying retirement:
with Di on holiday
in Cuba and (right)
proud grandfather with
Lucy's son Jack Lindsay.
Maybe he will one day
re-establish the family
tradition by becoming
a vet.

him what we were looking for and added half-jokingly: "Can't *you* find us a site, Ray?" When he replied that he didn't really have anything suitable I cheekily suggested: "Well, what about that property at Whitehills?" Located about a mile north of the village, this consisted of buildings and land that he owned. It wasn't on the market and I didn't seriously think he would let us have it, but to my surprise he said he would have a think about it. A site meeting was duly arranged shortly afterwards and although he made it clear that he would not sell the property he told us that he would be prepared to lease it.

The negotiations that followed were frank and open, both sides making compromises as we hammered out a fair and long lasting agreement with which we were all happy. Our existing premises were then put on the market and were soon bought up by a property developer. Meanwhile, we started work on converting the buildings at Whitehills in November 2000. We had to insist that the work there must be finished before the end of July 2002 because the sale of our existing property was due to be completed on July 31st. Our building contractor was well aware of this, but in March he informed us that he was eight weeks behind schedule. You can imagine our reaction; no way was this acceptable. Heavy pressure was exerted and, happily, most of the project was ready on time and although not all of the work was fully completed, it was far enough advanced for us to be able to move in. Four days later, on August 3rd, a demolition company arrived back at Sibford Road and completely flattened our old premises. So, the whole operation – which had been master-minded with great efficiency by Simon and Practice Manager Lucy Warner – was almost seamless!

The new premises were officially opened three months later, in November 2002, with Paul Webber kindly agreeing to do the honours. It was a memorable occasion, with more than two thousand people attending the ribbon-cutting ceremony or dropping in at various times during what was an extended open day to look the place over and wish us well. My two partners and

I were extremely moved by all the support we had received, not only from our much-valued clients, but also from our suppliers, both veterinary and non-veterinary, who provided sponsorship.

Horse racing has always figured prominently in my life, my interest in and love of the sport extending far beyond mere professional commitment. And with Simon taking a bigger role in the practice I was able to become more involved with racing activities outside the practice. When Brian Needham retired as the senior on-course veterinary surgeon at Stratford-upon-Avon racecourse after forty-seven years in the job, I was invited to join the veterinary team there. Brian's successor as senior vet was Peter Thorne, from the Avonvale practice in Ratley, and I learned a great deal from him. In those days, only two vets were required to be on duty at meetings and when I started I was quite nervous about the responsibility, but Peter soon put me at ease and made me feel very much involved. He is such a kind, helpful person and I benefited enormously from his expertise, advice and support. When he, in turn, retired I took over as senior vet and brought Simon into the team.

Our main team at Stratford now consists of Andrew Higgins, from Avonvale, Simon and myself and although we do have back-up, all three of us try to attend as many meetings as possible, simply because we know each other so well and work even better as a team. There are very few incidents or emergencies that one or other of us will not have encountered on the racecourse before.

The on-course care and welfare of racehorses and the facilities for providing routine health checks as well as for dealing with any emergency situations that may arise have changed out of all recognition over the last twenty-five years or so. In the old days and right up until the late eighties the veterinary care available on many racecourses was still, to say the least, a bit hit-and-miss and in some cases appallingly inadequate by today's standards. At some of the smaller, out-of-the-way courses and especially at point-to-points older resident vets who had been doing the job for years and had come to regard it as a bit of a sinecure might not always be up to scratch, while facilities were quite likely to be extremely basic. Where there was a fatality, the recovery vehicle – or 'knacker wagon' as it was commonly known – would all too often be no more than a flatbed truck or tractor and trailer onto which the dead animal would be winched before being driven away in full view of the grandstand. Routine pre-race checks on the general health, fitness and medical records of runners were rare and vets were on hand primarily to deal with emergencies.

It was largely thanks to the efforts of Dr Peter Webbon during his ten years as Chief Veterinary Advisor and then Director of Veterinary Welfare and Science at the Jockey Club in the 1990's that things started to improve significantly. Dr Webbon, who went on to become Chief Executive of the Horseracing Regulatory Authority when it took over from the Jockey Club as the sport's governing body and who now runs the Animal Health Trust, is widely recognised as having been the most influential figure in raising veterinary standards on racecourses throughout the country. Another ruling he introduced was that every course should have enough stables to house each of the day's intended runners – no longer would horses have to wait in their transport before running.

A fantastic character, dedicated and dynamic, he also proved to be a superb leader and most of us on-course vets became his disciples. It was his initiatives that led to the formation in 1993 of the Association of Racecourse Veterinary Surgeons, of which I was to become Secretary in 2003 and Chairman two years after that. The founder members were Simon Knapp, Chris Hammond and Peter Scott-Dunn and the aims of the Association, which held its first meeting at Leicester racecourse under Peter's chairmanship, were to provide a forum for the discussion and development of ideas that would promote the health, safety and welfare of horses at racecourses; to establish a qualifying standard for racecourse vets and to be responsible for the training of new intake; to liaise with racecourse managements over the provision of better treatment facilities; and to investigate and standardise the quality of horse ambulances and recovery vehicles.

One of the first things Peter Webbon did when he took over at the Jockey Club was to bring in a regulation barring anyone over the age of sixty-five from working as an on-course vet, the idea here being to get rid of the 'dead wood', the old guard, some of whom had become complacent, more interested in enjoying a good lunch and a few ports afterwards than in doing a proper job. The rule had to be modified later to avoid accusations of 'ageism', but not before the culture had effectively been changed for the better. He also introduced the rule that at National Hunt meetings there should be at least three vets on duty (at the bigger events such as the Grand National at Aintree and the Cheltenham Festival, there will actually be a lot more). And there are now strict guidelines covering those who can and can't work as racecourse vets, with the requirement that they must have been qualified and working mainly in an equine practice for a minimum of five years and must also have attended at least one of the two-day Casualty Management Seminars run by the Association every year.

The senior vet at each course is responsible for organising and supervising the veterinary team, putting them through emergency drills to ensure that they know exactly what to do in any situation that might develop in any part of the course and checking that horse ambulances and recovery vehicles conform to the set standards and are fully equipped. In this latter respect, there are three or four specialist firms who, between them, cover most of the courses in the country and they are all extremely good and co-operate closely with the on-course vets.

We, in turn, work in conjunction with the Regulatory Veterinary Officers, who are employed by the British Horseracing Authority and are responsible for inspecting passports, supervising dope tests, checking to find out why any particular horse has run below expectations and generally looking at welfare issues.

Thanks, once again, to the tireless efforts of Peter Webbon, they have access to a large database containing the racing records of all horses – including any past injuries, positive dope tests, epistaxis (bleeding from the nose) and other reasons for under-par performances – to which they can refer before racing starts to check out every horse on the card.

They also have the authority to carry out an on-the-spot inspection of any horse that they suspect might have an under-lying health or fitness problem of some sort. In the old days we used to get people who would deliberately race an unfit horse that they no longer had any use for in the hope that it would break down irretrievably on the track and would have to be put down, enabling them to claim the insurance. Once you have a horse with serious tendon injury or other soft tissue problems it usually requires a year off before it is properly fit to resume racing and in most cases it will never be quite the same again. Unscrupulous owners and trainers would patch it up and send it out too early and if, as was highly likely, it then broke down they would encourage us to put it down. You would ask if it had had the problem before and they would swear it had never had a lame day in its life, despite there being obvious signs that it had been fired. And if you did have to put it down, then, sure enough, the insurance claim form would arrive a fortnight later. That's all been stopped now that there are so many more safe-guards in place.

The welfare of the horses is obviously of paramount impor-tance. Sadly, it has to be accepted that accidents do occur during racing, sometimes with fatal results, but at least these days we are working with the most modern equipment, enabling us to treat any problems that arise quickly, efficiently and humanely. That doesn't make it any less distressing for everyone involved – for the owners, trainers, jockeys and stable staff for whom each horse is an individual personality who will have become very much like a member of the family; for the spectators in the grandstand and the enclosures, who invariably fall silent when the screens go up and it becomes clear that there has been a serious injury; and for the vet on duty, who has to make a quick, on-the-spot assessment of the situation, often in very difficult and harrowing circumstances, and who then, in the worst case scenario, has to do what is necessary as sympathetically and painlessly as possible.

You can speak to any number of racecourse vets and they will all tell you the same thing – that if they had to put a horse down every day for the rest of their careers they would never get used to it. It is always extremely upsetting and the only tiny consolation you can take from those situations is that you are putting an animal that is irretrievably broken out of its misery.

As is now the case with the veterinary teams at courses up and down the country, Simon, Andrew and I have established a well-rehearsed routine. We arrive early to go through all our regular checks and to deal with any pre-race problems that may have arisen. Then, once racing gets under way, one of us will take up a position in the stands as an overall observer while the other two follow the horses around, keeping pace with the runners at either end of the field. Each race is tracked on the inside of the course by a convoy of motor vehicles headed by the doctor, the head groundsman, an ambulance and one of us vets, with a second ambulance, vet and groundsman trailing along just behind the back markers. This ensures that if there is a faller or an incident of any kind anywhere on the circuit we will be on the scene within seconds.

Falls are by no means the only cause of serious injuries. Horses can suffer spontaneous fractures even in flat racing and also tendon injuries that cause them to break down lame. Any lame horse is taken off the course in one of the specialist horse ambulances that, at Stratford, are supplied by Leicestershire-based Nick Jones, whose company runs a fleet of state-of-the-art vehicles that come complete with oxygen, padding and hydraulic front and side low loading systems. If necessary, the injured horse will be sent on in the ambulance to the nearest centre of excellence for treatment.

Not all fractures are fatal. Generally speaking, the lower down the limb that the injury is sited, the better the chances that it can be successfully repaired. Damage to the pastern, condyle or hairline fractures of the cannon and even knee fractures are treatable; above the knee and it gets tricky. The problem with any serious leg injury is always the difficulty of keeping a horse standing still without it putting too much weight on the affected leg.

It is always worrying when a horse falls heavily during a race and then doesn't immediately get up. But quite often it turns out that it is only winded. If, when you get to the scene, it is lying there quietly, breathing deeply, and its heart and reflexes are OK you know that nine times out of ten it will eventually get up, even if it sometimes takes as long as ten minutes for it to get its breath back. On those occasions there is that wonderful moment when the horse scrambles to its feet and the crowd starts clapping and cheering like mad out of sheer relief.

Sometimes, however, you will think that everything is going to be OK, only to discover when you decide that it's time to get the horse up that it has been lying on a broken limb or that there is some other hidden complication. There was a particularly distressing situation like that at Stratford when a horse fell at the last fence. It eventually got up but was a little bit wobbly and looked as if it might be concussed. Andrew Higgins, who had got to it first, gave it an injection to help it recover, but it then started to deteriorate and collapsed. Further examination revealed that it must have suffered a haemorrhage in the spinal cord and we had to put it down right in front of the grandstand.

In the very sad circumstances where a horse has to be put down, the preferred method these days involves administering an injection rather than using a gun – the old-fashioned 'humane killer' – and for obvious reasons this is invariably the case in a situation where the public are in close proximity. And yet, wherever possible, I personally still prefer to use a gun. I'm very confident and accurate with it and although it may seem like a more brutal option to an outsider, I know that it's absolutely instant and therefore, as its name suggests, humane. Although drugs are effective they have to be very slowly and precisely injected and that is not always an easy thing to do in a stressful situation in which an animal is in distress and maybe moving around and you're trying to pinpoint the vein. Either way, it is a duty that we all hope to avoid and one to which no vet ever becomes hardened.

During my two-year spell as Secretary of the Association of Racecourse Veterinary Surgeons an increasing number of members based in the north of England and Scotland were starting to complain that the Association was in danger of becoming an exclusive club catering only for vets working in the south of the country. They pointed out that nearly all our meetings were held south of Birmingham, despite the fact that there were just as many racecourses in the north. They were also concerned that, partly as a result of this apparent bias, meetings tended to be dominated by the same vocal minority.

As Secretary, I set about remedying this by making sure that meetings were held at venues spread far and wide all over the country, including Doncaster, Haydock, Newcastle and Carlisle. It proved a highly popular move and the meetings were all packed to overflowing. So, when I became Chairman in 2005 I decided to make a point of visiting every single one of the fifty-seven licensed courses then in existence throughout England, Scotland and Wales (Great Leighs at Chelmsford and Ffos Las in Dyfed had yet to open at the time) with the aim of speaking to as many vets as I could.

I started at Worcester in September 2005 and finished at Epsom in June 2007, writing to the Senior Veterinary Surgeon at each course to arrange a day when it would be convenient for me to visit and making it clear that I was happy to discuss any problems or concerns they might have over a whole range of issues, including welfare, health and safety, the role of the Association and the relationship between the racecourse and the veterinary team. There was a slight suspicion at first among some course managements that I was on a spying mission, but I soon dispelled those doubts. We were honest and open with each other and if I felt that they could address certain areas better or more efficiently then I would say so. Afterwards I would write a letter thanking them for their hospitality and highlighting any concerns we had discussed. The feedback was positive and when my term of office ended I put all my findings into a report that was sent to each of the fifty-seven courses.

Being able to visit all these courses, some of which I'd never been to before, proved to be both an educational and, in most cases, an extremely enjoyable experience. The fact that at the age of fifty-nine I was starting to reduce my workload at the practice meant I had the time to undertake this nationwide tour, during which I also made a point of looking around each local area, seeing the sights and visiting places of special interest, such as the magnificent Minster at Southwell, the renowned misericords in the convent at East Grinstead, just down the road from Lingfield Park, and the castle at Pontefract, the town also famed as the home of liquorice.

When it came to some of the more distant courses I would try to arrange to visit them in clusters over a two or three day period – Ripon, Sedgefield and Beverley in Yorkshire, for instance. Also in Yorkshire, Pontefract is a lovely, very well-run course. I have to confess that one of the reasons why it stands out in my memory could be that on the day of my visit the programme of events included the added attraction of a parade by local West Indian girls, who were going to be competing in the annual Miss Yorkshire contest. Here were these eight gorgeous girls, all wearing elaborate headdresses but otherwise parading around virtually naked, despite the weather being decidedly chilly. The show was being stage-managed by a large and very colourful West Indian chap, who must have weighed about twenty-five stone and who cut a pretty impressive figure himself, with a huge cigar clamped between his teeth. One of the girls complained to him that she didn't want to take part in the parade because it was too cold, only to be told in no uncertain terms: "You get out there and shake that ass, honey, before I *smack* that ass!"

Among the most scenically beautiful courses I visited were Cartmel, a delightful little circuit in a wonderfully picturesque, out-of-the-way setting up in the Lake District; Thirsk, which is in the heart of Herriott country; and Ludlow, with its splendid views over the surrounding Shropshire countryside. The set-up at Hamilton, just south of Glasgow, is very smart indeed and Kelso, up in Roxburghshire, more than lived up to its reputation as the friendliest course in the UK. I had a lot of fun at Redcar, where they were also very hospitable, and Perth, where I went to a night meeting and didn't get back to my hotel until three o'clock in the morning!

They say that you should never try to mix business and pleasure, but at the end of my grand tour I felt that I had managed to do so rather successfully. It had certainly been a very pleasurable experience for me and at the same time it had been extremely useful in helping to promote the Association, through which vets working at every course in the country are able to share expertise and experience and keep up-to-date with best practice in terms of improving all aspects of health and safety in racing.

Back at the practice, our partnership agreement stipulates that one can no longer continue as a partner after reaching the age of sixty, the idea being to ensure that the practice will be rejuvenated over time rather than being allowed to stagnate. I was very happy with this arrangement, which allowed one to continue working on a part-time basis. In July 2006, as the date of my 60th birthday and my enforced semi-retirement approached, I was still only midway through my term of office as chairman of the Association and busily involved in visiting all the racecourses. One Friday morning, as I set off to drive north for a visit to Catterick and York, I noticed to my surprise that a marquee was being erected in the paddock behind the surgery and that there seemed to be a lot more activity than was normal at the practice on a Friday. When I asked Steve what was going on he explained that he was hosting a lunch for members of the XL Veterinary Group, of which we were members.

My curiosity satisfied, I headed off to Yorkshire. Following my visit to Catterick I stayed overnight at Richmond with the intention of getting up early and popping in to have a look at York Minster on my way to the racecourse at York. However, a combination of getting involved with a wedding party at the hotel and having a very late night as a result, plus heavy traffic on the roads the next morning, meant that I had to give the Minster a miss and drive straight to the racecourse. I called home and told Di that I had decided to stay on for another night so that I could visit the Minster the next morning. Cool as a cucumber, Di told me that the children had rung to say they were coming over to see me and that we were then supposed to be going out for Sunday lunch with friends, so I had better come straight back home as originally planned.

I got back quite late on the Saturday evening and on the Sunday morning there was a strange atmosphere in the house – nothing I could really put my finger on but something that was not quite normal. As we were changing to go out I was told to wear something tidy as the place we were going for lunch was quite smart. Then, as we were driving there, Di suddenly announced that we needed to drop in at the surgery to pick up something for our dogs and when we arrived I noticed that there were a lot more cars than usual parked in the vicinity. And the marquee was still up. Di drove round to the front of the marquee and at that point Steve emerged with a big red book in his hands and, as I got out of the car, still wondering what on earth was going on, announced in true Eamonn Andrews style: "Alan Walker – this is your veterinary life"! Spontaneous applause erupted from within the marquee and just for once I was lost for words.

Steve, Simon, Lucy and Di had organized a wonderful farewell party for me with around three hundred guests, including clients past and present, members of staff and others who had been closely involved with my working life as well as many of my friends. Rather appropriately, it turned out that on that very morning a German Shepherd belonging to Mrs Tustian, the lady who had been my very first client, had had to undergo an emergency operation for a gastric torsion.

Several of the guests had been invited to get up and say a few words and, of course, many of the stories that were recounted were heavily embellished. I was completely overwhelmed at first, but once I had got over the initial shock I loved every moment of it. I often look back through the book and watch the video that was taken of the proceedings and when I do it is with mixed feelings of both great pride and yet some sadness when I see again the faces of old friends who are no longer with us. As well as those who spoke at the party there were others who had responded to a request from Steve and Lucy to set down their recollections of me on paper. One of my most treasured possessions is the generous tribute written by Anne Gibbs, who worked for us for two years immediately after qualifying and who went on twenty years later to become one of my successors as Chairman of the Association of Racecourse Veterinary Surgeons. This is what she wrote:

"I started working for Alan in 1991 as a new graduate. Simon Richards started at the same time. Mags ran the smoke-filled office. Tall Sarah managed the Farm Shop. Anna (Jan) and Janet were receptionists and Fran, Sue and Alison were nurses. Morag was at Charlbury and the vets themselves did all the reception and paperwork at the Shipston Portakabin!

"Alan was the best boss in the world and I am so grateful that I started my career with him. He expected hard work but was fully supportive at all times and never appeared frustrated by my inexperienced disasters! I didn't think any idiot would confuse laminitis and colic – until my first night on call. Alan was my back-up and patiently talked me through it – after I had emptied a barn full of hay bales in order to stable the horse! He was more likely to chastise the difficult client for being awkward or unfair than to belittle an assistant and his support was invaluable.

"Trying to follow in Alan's footsteps was always difficult and clients' faces were ashen if I turned up in his place!

"I think Alan hated my dog, called Minty, as she occasionally defecated in the exact spot down the side of the large animal building where he used to sneak for a quiet cigarette. Nothing worse than stepping in it! And then there was the whisky bottle in the filing cabinet, but I guess that is old hat!

"We once had a full scale search for a miniature donkey that had gone missing from a house nearby. CCTV cameras and a distraught owner eventually located it under the cover of a swimming pool in their garden – deceased, of course.

"My worst moment ever was being entrusted with a bottle of a new horse sedative that we were trialling. Alan told me to look after it and be very careful – we needed to document every use of it for a big meeting in Droitwich. I put it on the top of the car and drove out of the yard. Alan never knew and I had to grovel a lot to the rep for a secret supply.

"Alan told me that my future husband was not right for me and ten years later his opinion was confirmed. Always right! Alan is one of life's great men."

It was now time for me to step back and let Simon and Steve get on with doing things their way, the two of them being more than capable of running the practice without me. I had no intention of interfering, remembering only too well how much I had appreciated the way in which my father had relinquished the reins when I took over the business, letting me get on with things while always remaining available to give advice if required and to offer a few words of wisdom – or criticism!

At the same time, I really enjoyed being involved and able to help out. Every time I drove through the avenue of maturing lime trees leading up to the surgery I got – and still get to this day – a warm glow of satisfaction, knowing that I had been largely responsible for creating what remains a superb facility.

I don't know everybody who works there now, although quite a few of them are people whose families I have known for years.

The practice was built on trust; wherever possible we always tried to employ local people and use local suppliers, doing our best to become an integral part of the local community, contributing to it as much as possible. And I like to think that in that way we have helped to develop a long-standing mutual respect.

I can't stress enough how much satisfaction I got from my work. I may have been a slow starter, but I ended up having a wonderful career and thoroughly enjoyed knowing that I was good at what I did. I was also blessed with having a wonderful family, not only at home but at the surgery, too. Because that is how I thought of the practice. I saw myself as head of a family there, too, and while being very noisy I was never dictatorial. Someone once said to me: "When you were cross, Alan, we all knew about it and we just kept out of your way. But you were always fair to us and you were a great communicator."

So, I had much to be pleased and proud about as I set about winding down into semi-retirement. At the same time, I became uneasily aware that some storm clouds were unexpectedly gathering on the horizon. Even so, I never anticipated just how violently my life was about to be blown off course.

12

Conduct Unbecoming

A bombshell dropped through my letterbox in January 2006 in the form of a letter from the Professional Conduct Department of the Royal College of Veterinary Surgeons (RCVS), outlining a complaint about the quality of my veterinary work.

I had been asked to carry out a pre-purchase veterinary examination by a longstanding client. The horse had failed to reach its reserve at the Doncaster Spring Sales and had been taken back home by his owner for a summer holiday. However, the client liked the horse and maintained interest in trying to purchase it. Whilst the horse was still at home with its original owner it sustained an injury that required veterinary treatment. The injury responded to rest and treatment, the horse recovered well and was ready to be examined. Before making the journey I contacted the Veterinary Surgeon who had been treating the horse in the meantime and he reassured me that it had now fully recovered.

Arrangements were then made to go and examine the horse, which, as is often the case with National Hunt horses in the summer when they are 'on holiday', had been 'let down', meaning it had no shoes and wasn't being ridden, so for the exercise element of the examination it was lunged. Over the years I had carried out several 'close season' purchase examinations in exactly the same way.

The prospective purchaser and I travelled together and during the examination I found out exactly where the injury had been sustained. The horse was exercised and then rested before further flexion tests were carried out to determine if it was still sound after exercise. I was very happy with what I had found and passed on my comments. The condition of the horse was further discussed on our return journey, during which I advised that it would be sensible to keep the horse in light work throughout the summer and to make sure that it was exercised on a regular basis to enable the previous injury to heal fully and strengthen. I warned that there might be times when the horse would feel sore, but that this would be due to freshly healed fibrous tissue being less elastic and that it would need to be stretched. As we parted company I said I felt that it was a very nice horse and would be well worth purchasing. Although I completed a Purchase Examination Certificate, which I gave to the purchaser, I did not put my suggestions for the summer exercise programme in writing; nor did I make a formal note emphasising the possible problems that the horse could experience.

I saw the horse a few months later in September, the purpose of my visit being to give the horse his annual flu vaccination. Jockey Club regulations require all racehorses to have a primary course of three influenza injections, with an interval of 21-90 days between the first and second, and then the third one a further 150-215 days later. This horse's injection had lapsed by sixteen days and I agreed to backdate the certificate in order to avoid the major complication of having to start him off from scratch with another full primary course. I was completely wrong to do this, of course, even though the vaccination was only a few days overdue

I saw the horse again in December as he was being prepared for the season's hunter chasing. He looked well and the previous injury, sustained earlier in the year, appeared to have settled well. However, when the horse ran in January it pulled up lame, aggravating the old injury. There was, of course, great disappointment, but I was taken aback to find myself being blamed for the horse's stuttering performance. I was accused of not providing enough information about the nature of the injury and about the risks of buying the horse, and also of negligence in failing to give full written instruction as to how it should be prepared for racing. I was completely taken by surprise and was shocked. I was also very concerned that the horse had become lame and was in discomfort. I wanted to investigate further, but was told that my veterinary services were no longer required.

The horse did not respond quickly to treatment and it became obvious that it would miss that forthcoming racing season. It also became clear that the complaint against me would be pursued, through the courts if necessary, until a satisfactory solution had been found. I was very worried and completely out of my depth in dealing with a situation that I had never faced before and sought professional advice. By now I was starting to have sleepless nights and couldn't get the case out of my mind. I tried to put on a brave face, but underneath it was beginning to take its toll, especially at home. And this was only the start.

I had several meetings with both my legal and professional advisors, and we all felt that I had a very strong case against the allegations, especially as the horse went on to race successfully, which seemed to bear out my original prediction that the injury would have no long term adverse effects.

The wheels of the legal system grind very slowly indeed. There seems to be an initial flurry of activity after which things go quiet for a while before there is another round of letters, phone calls and meetings. It was during one of the quiet periods that I received another letter from the RCVS raising not only the issue of negligence with regard to my veterinary examination, but also the issue of back-dating two other horses' vaccination certificates in previous years. I now found myself facing not only a negligence case in the Civil Court but also a professional misconduct charge in front of the Disciplinary Committee of the RCVS, an extremely serious matter since it carried the ultimate threat of being struck off, something that was potentially career ending at the age of sixty. The pressure was mounting. I was not easy to live with, became increasingly anxious and depressed and probably drank more heavily than was wise.

Then, one evening in June 2006, I received an unexpected telephone call offering me the chance to meet the complainant to discuss sorting out the negligence case before formal statements were made to the RCVS's solicitors. I politely declined the offer, a decision I have never regretted.

The fuse was now well and truly lit and the hearing was set for Monday 29th January, 2007. I had several constructive and informative meetings with both my professional and legal advisors, all of whom had a great deal of experience in dealing with the RCVS Disciplinary Committee. They were extremely honest and warned me that the Committee regarded false certification as very serious and that it was very likely that I would either be suspended or struck off. I felt, however, that although what I had done was wrong, the circumstances were such that I wouldn't be hit with the ultimate sanction. How wrong I was.

In order to be in good time for the hearing , Di and I travelled to London on Sunday 28th January in sombre mood, continually worrying about all the possibilities of the outcome. We stayed in a hotel near Belgravia House, the home of the RCVS. Having endured a mainly sleepless night, we were glad when morning came, resolving to face the day with the attitude of "let's get on with it and learn my fate as quickly as possible". The day then got off to an unsettling start when we sat down to breakfast only for the very people who we would be confronting later on at the hearing, and who we had no idea would be staying at the same hotel, arrived unexpectedly in the dining room. We hurriedly got up and left.

We walked down the road to Belgravia House on Horseferry Road, home of the Royal College of Veterinary Surgeons, and were directed up to the courtroom on the top floor. At the front was a raised area on which stood a large desk. Above the desk, a microphone was suspended in mid-air, attached to a wire that disappeared into the ceiling. Six chairs were placed in front of the desk at a lower level. Facing this was another desk, with tables either side. Behind this to the left and right were eight rows of chairs.

I sat with my legal representatives on the left side while the RCVS representatives sat on the right. Also sitting with them was John Parker, in his role as Veterinary Advisor. We all stood in unison as the robed Committee members filed in: Nigel Swayne, MRCVS; Christine Shield, MRCVS; Alison Bruce; Gill Nute, MRCVS; Caroline Friedman; and Roger Eddy, MRCVS. Sitting as Chairman was Bryan Jennings, and next to him was the Legal Assessor, Mr G. Flather.

The charges were read, the complainant was cross-examined and the Committee asked questions. My barrister had to work hard to get the witness to admit that a telephone call had been made to me in June 2006 offering to withdraw their complaints regarding certification if I would agree an out-of-court settlement of the civil action. It was all very polite and civilised. Then it was my turn. I felt nervous and intimidated by the whole process. I was looking down the barrel of a gun and fighting to preserve my professional career. I answered the questions honestly and accurately. Jenny Pitman then delivered an eloquent testimony and character reference and implored the Committee to look at the bigger picture

Diana and I did not spend a second night in the hotel. We checked out and stayed instead with Andrea and Jim Kiernan in Notting Hill – good, old friends who had been a great comfort and support to us both throughout.

On the afternoon of the second day of the hearing the Committee eventually retired to discuss their findings and I was told to wait in a small room adjoining the courtroom until they were ready to announce their decision. At approximately 4.30pm on January 30th, 2007 Bryan Jennings formally delivered judgement: that the Committee recommended that my name should be removed from the Register. Or in layman's terms – struck off. We were totally devastated. Words cannot express the depths of despair we felt as we adjourned once more to the small waiting room in silence. What little conversation there was between us was forced and hesitant. We were advised to go home, as there was nothing more to be done for the time being. So, with the words of sympathy and support from Jenny Pitman, her husband David Stait and our legal and professional advisors echoing in our ears, Di and I walked slowly and in numbed silence from Belgravia House, down Horseferry Road to the River Thames, along Millbank and on past Westminster Abbey and the Houses of Parliament.

I felt a mixture of emotions. I was both bewildered and angry. I felt that the whole world already knew what had transpired and that people were looking at me, pointing their fingers, accusing me of being a disgrace. And then it seemed that my whole life was unfolding before my eyes in a series of flashbacks – my childhood, the rich and varied Walker family history of involvement with animals for over 300 years, my immediate family. How was I going to tell the children? The frustration of having to wait and study for fifteen years before at last realising my lifelong ambition of qualifying as a Veterinary Surgeon; the building of a modern and highly successful veterinary practice with state-of-the-art facilities and fourteen full-time Veterinary Surgeons, plus support staff; the interest I had developed in horse racing from a very early age, eventually going on to work professionally with some of the country's most successful trainers and to become actively involved in promoting the safety and welfare of racehorses through the Association of Racecourse Vets. All this had been reduced to nothing by those stinging words that still echo in my ears: "Remove Dr Walker's name from the Register."

My wife, always my rock, was at my side, a strong, calm, reassuring presence. "We'll get through this," she insisted. "We *will* get through this!" The journey back to Oxfordshire was long and painful. And yet I was about to discover, in the most extraordinary circumstances, the truth of the old saying that it is only in times of adversity that you find out who your true friends are.

On the way home I contacted all the most important people

in my life – firstly, my partners, Steve Glanvill and Simon Richards, then my children, Lucy and George; and also my long-
standing clients, among them Paul Webber, George Baker, Jane
Starkey, Martin Bosley and Carl Llewellyn. I was still Chairman
of the Racecourse Veterinary Association at the time so I spoke
to the Committee members and to Peter Webbon, who was the
Senior Veterinary Officer for the Jockey Club. I also contacted
Stephen Lambert, who ran Stratford racecourse where I was
Senior Veterinary Surgeon. I told them all what had happened
and that I had a month in which to appeal. I explained that I
could carry on working during that period but said that if they
felt that I would, in any way, be an embarrassment to them then
I would withdraw and stand down immediately. It was heart-
ening to hear the positive chorus of support and endorsement
from every single one of them.

Equally encouraging was the letter I received from John
Parker, the past President of both the RCVS and the British
Equine Veterinary Association, also with thirty-two years experience as a Magistrate, who had sat through my hearing as Veterinary Advisor to the Disciplinary Committee. He wrote to say
that he was dismayed by the attitude of the Committee and their
apparent lack of understanding of the legal process and felt that
I had been treated appallingly, mainly by their lack of propor-
tionality in the sentence. He ended by offering to help me in any
way he could.

Initially, my feeling was that I would have to take it on the
chin, because how often is the Establishment successfully chal-
lenged? However, the more I thought about what had happened
during the hearing, the angrier I became about the way I had
been treated. And yet, if I were to appeal it would be a costly
exercise, not only financially – the Veterinary Defence Society
paid the costs of the original Disciplinary Hearing but I was not
covered for an Appeal – but also in terms of the amount of legal
preparation work that would be involved and the strain of having to relive the entire episode while being subjected to an even

more microscopic examination. I leaned first one way and then the other, finding myself in a total dilemma.

Then, out of the blue, came a totally unexpected intervention. The Saturday after the hearing I called in at the practice to be met by Vicky McGregor, one of our assistant vets, who asked if I had seen an open letter to veterinary colleagues that was being circulated by Richard Stephenson, a vet from Uttoxeter. I had met Richard only once and that was during my tour of the country's racecourses. However, he had always taken a close interest in RCVS matters and he had been dismayed and deeply concerned by the outcome of my hearing and, in particular, the extreme severity of the punishment that been meted out, to the extent that he had drafted a letter to the then President of the RCVS, Professor Sheila Crispin, calling on her to refer the case to a new Disciplinary Committee for re-consideration as a matter of urgency.

In his strongly-worded but very concise two-page letter he highlighted aspects of the case that he said "should give all members of the College great cause for concern", mostly to do with mitigating factors in my favour that had apparently been ignored by the Disciplinary Committee in judging that I should pay the ultimate penalty of being struck off. The mitigating factors he listed included the fact that I had a previously unblemished record; that I had contributed greatly to the profession through my voluntary role as Chairman of the Association of Racecourse Veterinary Surgeons; that I had made a frank statement to the College, admitting the facts of the case; and that there had been no evidence of dishonest intent in what I had done – "in fact, it would have been to Doctor Walker's financial advantage to insist on complete re-vaccination".

He concluded with the comment that "the impression has been indelibly created that the Committee had made up its mind before hearing the evidence." And he went on: "Whilst accepting that the College has a duty to maintain the good standing of the profession, there must be some balance and humanity in its actions. Destroying a fellow veterinary surgeon's life was not in our view justified in the above circumstances (and let us be in no doubt that that is the effect of this decision). A warning might have been appropriate."

He emailed draft copies of the letter to various colleagues in the hope of being able to add further signatories, they passed it on and within forty-eight hours Richard was amazed to be deluged with messages from vets all over the country, and even from overseas, asking for their names to be added as co-signatories. In the end, the list of signatories included 303 Members and seven Fellows of the RCVS.

At the same time, letters of support for me, personally, began to pour in. Altogether, I received well over a thousand letters, faxes, emails and messages of goodwill – some of them from people I hardly knew – all offering sympathy and support. It was an overwhelming and humbling experience. I decided that, apart from anything else, I owed it to them to go ahead with an appeal.

I discussed it with my legal team and asked my solicitor to prepare the necessary papers. I was warned that if I lost the case – if I didn't get the verdict changed in any way, that is – I would be liable not only for my own costs but those of the RCVS as well. My costs were estimated to be around £40,000 and, as we assumed that the College's would be similar, that meant I was looking at a total of £80,000 if things didn't go my way. That was obviously a serious amount of money and although I did have some savings I could not cover it all and could still be left in severely reduced circumstances, given that I had already retired from the partnership and would no longer be able to work even part-time if I remained struck off, leaving me with no earned income at all. It was a daunting prospect – no job, no money.

Here again, Richard Stephenson came to my aid. Having decided on his own initiative that I needed to be able to compete on a level playing field, he went ahead and, without me knowing anything about it, launched the Alan Walker Appeal Fund.

An Appeal Committee was set up, Chaired by Richard Jones, with David Green, one of the racecourse vets from Keighly in Yorkshire, as Treasurer and Richard himself as Secretary. Also on the Committee were Mark Collins, Johnny Pycock and Geoff Lane from Bristol University, all of them very well-known and respected equine vets. The response to the appeal was again overwhelming, with over £23,000 raised in a very short time. This meant that I would be able to afford to employ a QC.

The date for the Appeal hearing was set for 30th October, 2007, but in April of that year the Civil case brought against me for negligence was heard by a Judge at the Oxford County Court. Things did not go my way, and although no judgement was made in court, the Judge directed both sides to retire and agree a settlement in the complainants' favour.

I was very upset to have effectively lost the case, but I had nobody else to blame. I had not written down my advice and findings or details of the suggested rehabilitation programme. It had all been verbal – rather naively, I suppose, I have always believed that my word is my bond. Frustrating though it was, there was nothing more I could do about it. I simply had to get over it, put it behind me and focus on the RCVS Appeal.

My solicitor had engaged the services of a QC who had made a name for himself in the media and sporting world. It seemed fairly unbelievable that my name was to be added to his impressive portfolio of clients.

The night before the Appeal we once again travelled down to London and stayed with Jim and Andrea, to whom we shall remain forever grateful for their unequivocal support and warm friendship.

An Appeal involving the RCVS Disciplinary Committee has to be heard by the Privy Council, which is the highest court in the land, answerable only to the Queen. At the time, the offices were situated in Downing Street. Queuing at the gates to the entrance waiting to be cleared for admission heightened the importance of the occasion. My Appeal was heard by three

Law Lords sitting as the Privy Council – Lord Walker (no relation of course!), Lord Mance and Lord Neuberger. Only my Counsel and the Counsel of the RCVS were permitted to speak, although they could refer to their junior counsels. As Chairman of the Board of Judges, Lord Walker reminded us that two-and-a-half hours had been allowed for the Appeal. Each side was allowed to state their case, and then question time from the Law Lords would take place at precisely 12.15pm.

I was represented by my QC, and supported by my legal and professional advisors and members of my Appeal Committee, together with my wife and daughter. My case was presented first, followed by the RCVS's barrister. As the evidence was reviewed it was obvious that the Law Lords were very perceptive and well informed and it wasn't long before they started to ask the RCVS's legal representative some very pertinent questions that appeared to undermine his confidence. By the time he had finished and sat down, I allowed myself the small luxury of thinking it had all gone well for us. When we retired to the little ante-room next to the main Chamber it was with a feeling of quiet confidence. I thanked my QC for his time and effort on my behalf, but was not going to assume anything.

Three weeks later, at 10am on 21st November, 2007, the barristers and junior counsel were summoned back to Downing Street to hear the reading of the Judgement. The rest of us were told we did not need to be there, but that my solicitors would be allowed to go in thirty minutes in advance of the reading to find out the result, and they could then pass it on to me by phone. However, I would not be allowed to say anything to anyone for another hour, at which point the news would be made public.

My solicitor duly rang me at 9.30am with the news that my punishment had been reduced to a six-month suspension. In announcing their decision, the Privy Council had drawn attention to my "long and otherwise unblemished and excellent career", the fact that my actions had created "no risk to animal or human health" and that I had been "frank and remorseful".

My legal team considered it a massive victory, but I was actually very disappointed. Given the way that almost everything seemed to have gone in my favour during the course of the Appeal Hearing, I felt that a six-month suspension was still very harsh and that I could reasonably have expected to be let off with no more than a slap on the wrist.

My resentment and lingering sense of injustice was further compounded by initial confusion over the precise terms of my suspension. It was assumed that it came into force with immediate effect and that I had to down tools and stop work that very day. I therefore made a point of straightaway emptying my car of what had been the tools of my trade for the previous twenty-five years – the many items of equipment that I carried with me at all times, such as my wolf tooth kit, my twitch, my stethoscope and a variety of other bits and pieces that had accumulated in the boot. However, no sooner had I finished doing this than it turned out that this was incorrect.

Everything that goes through the Privy Council has to be ratified by the Queen and as Her Majesty was abroad at the time there was going to be some delay before that happened. Meanwhile I was entitled to carry on working until the papers were signed. That still wasn't the end of it. I was advised that the papers would be signed on the evening of Friday, 14th December and that I could continue working up until that time, which I did. Imagine my horror when, on the Friday morning, I received a panic call from Di while I was actually out on a job, telling me that the solicitors had contacted her to say that the papers had been signed and the judgement ratified on the evening of Wednesday 12th! So I had been working for two days when I shouldn't have done. At the time of Di's call I was actually in the middle of treating a distressed horse that was suffering from colic and was in considerable pain. What was I supposed to do? Walk away and leave it? Of course not! I carried on and finished the job.

I then immediately wrote to the RCVS, explaining what had

happened and backing it up with emails from my solicitor and the official letter from the Privy Council office that had arrived on Saturday 15th December. I then had to wait six weeks before I got a reply from them saying that they would not be taking any action over the matter. The wait seemed to last a lifetime – you become very sensitive to the possibility of one thing after another going wrong and fate being against you in such situations. I had visions of being hauled up in front of the Disciplinary Committee and having to go through it all again!

Following the success of my Appeal, I was eventually awarded costs by the Privy Council on April 3rd, 2008. I assumed that if costs were awarded then they should be paid in full, but, in fact, that is not the case, and a percentage deduction is always made. After their initial offer was rejected, a subsequent offer was accepted and the episode concluded on Friday 19th December, 2008, a year after the whole process had started. Unfortunately, the delays added £4,000 to my costs, in addition to which there was also an amount of VAT for which I was liable. Thanks to the considerable generosity not only of those who contributed to my Appeal Fund, but also those who organised and administered it, I was not personally out of pocket. However, by the time all the outstanding bills had been settled, only £2,450 remained to be donated to the Veterinary Benevolent Fund.

The RCVS is the regulatory body for all veterinary surgeons working in the United Kingdom. We have to be members in order to practice and are obliged to comply with their rules which quite rightly are aimed at maintaining the integrity of the profession ensuring that high standards of care and conduct are adhered to, and maintaining the confidence of the public – all of which I fully endorse. At the same time I have to say that little things, like getting my initials wrong on letters and documents – after I had been a member since 1981 – were simply irritating.

More serious was the inaccuracy in the transcript of the Disciplinary Hearing submitted to the Privy Council and signed by the Registrar as an accurate record. There were seven people on the Disciplinary Committee yet the transcript only displayed five names. When I wrote to question this I was informed that it made no difference to which I replied, "With due respect, it is not your opinion I am seeking, I want to know the reason why you signed an inaccurate document". The rather dismissive response I received to that was that "Mistakes made in good faith are usually accepted by fellow professionals". What sort of an answer is that?

I was also angered by the lack of respect shown by a member of the Committee who revealed that it was a majority decision of 4-3 in favour of me being removed from the Register, with all the lay members plus one veterinary surgeon voting in favour. This privileged information should have remained behind the closed doors of the Committee's deliberations.

Since my Hearing several major changes to the disciplinary procedures at the RCVS have been instituted to make the process independent, fairer and more transparent. I hope my case may have helped in some way to highlight the inadequacies of the old system, and that by doing so it may have accelerated the need for a much more modern approach to dealing with disciplinary issues. All one can ask for and expect is fair and respectful treatment.

13

Picking Up The Pieces

The strain of the previous two years had taken a terrible toll both mentally and physically. I suffered bouts of deep depression, to the point where my GP and good friend Dr Martin Harris became so concerned about my mental state that he took it upon himself to write to Gordon Hockey, the Assistant Registrar of the RCVS, to inquire whether the College was able to provide experienced professional counsellors to help members in my position. A rather dismissive response came back, saying that no such support was available. Martin was appalled, knowing that in the medical profession counselling was available for anyone who had been subject to a disciplinary investigation and knowing also that, with the exception of dentists, vets had the highest rate of suicide of any professional body.

By this time the heavy drinking that I had resorted to in an attempt to drown my sorrows in the months leading up to the disciplinary hearing had also started to have severe knock-on effects. I didn't drink spirits or beers, just good old red wine, which I thought was supposed to be quite good for you – although obviously not in the quantities that I was now consuming it! After a while I began to notice that I was becoming increasingly breathless, tired and lethargic and in the May of 2006 my legs started to swell and my weight spiralled upwards. I consulted Martin Harris, who rapidly diagnosed a heart problem. The drugs he initially prescribed brought about an immediate improvement, but blood tests confirmed that excess alcohol had already caused liver damage. I was warned that if I didn't stop drinking both my liver and my heart would soon fail. Cardiologist Dr Ian Arnold's findings had an even more sobering effect. An echocardiogram revealed a weak, flabby heart in atrial flutter and other signs of impending heart failure, including a grossly enlarged left ventricle with a thin wall!

More medication and more lectures followed, with the warning that if I did not respond to treatment I would be lucky to survive for more than three years. Despite the pressure I was under I was determined to take their advice and stick rigidly to the rules, having seen what had happened to several friends and acquaintances who, in similar circumstances, had failed to take heed and had either died or suffered the debilitating after-effects of strokes and heart attacks as a result.

I had previously suffered from a heart problem back in February 1998. One Sunday evening when Di was out taking George back to school in Cheltenham I developed some very serious chest pains that eased off when I stood up, but returned with a vengeance as soon as I sat or lay down. When Di got back she was alarmed by the fact that my colour was ashen and told me I should see a doctor straightaway. I decided instead to go to bed and try to sleep through it, but I was soon back downstairs and was then rushed to the doctor's surgery in Bloxham, from where I was referred immediately to the Horton Hospital A&E in Banbury.

The pain was unbearable. I have little recollection of any conversations that took place – apart from admitting that I was still smoking the occasional cigarette. I also assured Di that if anything happened to me she wouldn't have to sell the house! When she got back home later that night the realisation of what I had actually said suddenly dawned on her and she thought: "Oh, my God, he thinks he is going to die! And if he thinks he is going to die then he probably is going to die!!" She sat up for the rest of the night working out a plan of how she would manage. She then rang Simon at 7.00am to tell him what had happened and he lent a sympathetic ear.

I was in the Critical Care Unit, having been diagnosed with Pericarditis. My heart rhythm was all over the place, but the consultant reassured us that I would make a full recovery. Gradually, with the help of medication, my heart returned to normal. It turned out that the cause of the problem was Psittacosis, a disease associated with birds that normally causes respiratory problems in humans, but which, in my case, was one of the less common strains that affects the heart. I had recently attended a conference in the USA and while there had visited a bird sanctuary. It seems that I may have contracted the disease there.

I went back home to recuperate, having been told that it would be at least six months before I fully recovered. I couldn't believe how tired I got. I had a continual stream of visitors and, whilst it was great to see everyone, Di eventually had to ask people not to stay too long – and in some cases not to come at all – because it was taking too much out of me and slowing down my recovery. As my health began to improve I started to get itchy feet, impatient to get back to work. It was springtime, which is a really busy time, and I felt guilty about sitting at home whilst the others were working flat out. I did venture out to see a lame horse in Whatcote and part of the diagnosis involved removing the horse's shoe, something I had done many times before. I managed to do it and sort out the problem, but felt completely exhausted and returned home with my tail well and truly between my legs. I knew I would have to be patient.

My dedication to diet and exercise gradually started to pay off, regular check-ups and blood tests showing a steady but consistent improvement. I lost weight, became less breathless, had more energy and generally felt much better. Then, just as I seemed to be getting out of the woods, I woke up one morning with an excruciating pain in the big toe of my right foot. The hot, angry joint was agonisingly sensitive to the slightest touch of even a sheet or a thin sock and walking was a real challenge. Once again I found myself beating what had become an increasingly well-worn path to the door of Martin Harris's surgery, where he instantly diagnosed gout.

Gout is something I would not wish on my worst enemy. It is unbelievably painful, much more so than could ever be imagined by those who have never suffered from it. And yet people seem to think it a rather comical complaint. The ignorance and lack of sympathy expressed when you reluctantly reveal the reason for your awkward gait is quite amazing – reactions ranging from raised eyebrows and gentle sniggers to hearty, full-throated guffaws. Far from overdosing on port – traditionally, but mistakenly, thought to be the cause of gout – I was off alcohol altogether. Thankfully, medication gradually brought some relief, but a major challenge to my teetotal resolve lay ahead.

Along with horseracing and cricket, my other great sporting passion has always been rugby. The Rugby World Cup was held in France in the autumn of 2007 and I had decided months in advance, long before the Disciplinary Hearing took place and all my troubles really began to pile up, that it would be fun to arrange an extended camping holiday in Provence, Di's favourite region of France, while the rugby was on. So I went ahead and booked tickets for two Pool A matches that were being played in Montpelier during September and started making plans for a month-long stay in the area, never imagining that by then I would have been warned off drinking, almost literally on pain of death! With so much quality red wine on offer I knew that I would have to hold on very tight if I was to avoid falling off the wagon. It took a mammoth effort of will to resist temptation, but I somehow managed it, determined to get myself back to full health. My preferred tipple for the whole month was Perrier with sirop de grenadine. And whenever I got bored with that I would substitute sirop de citron or sirop de vanille. At the same time, I did take great vicarious pleasure in perusing the wine lists in the restaurants we visited in order to choose wines for Di. The fact that my non-alcoholic tipple was more expensive than her wine didn't make it any easier!

With our trailer tent hitched to the car, we had taken our time driving down from Calais to Montpelier, stopping off en route at Chalons-en-Champagne, Dijon, Macon and Beaune. Our son, George, and his girlfriend joined us in Montpelier, and we all went to watch Tonga v Samoa, a superb, close-fought match made even more entertaining by the noisy, colourful supporters of both sides, Tonga eventually winning 19-15. George stayed with us for five days, after which Di and I moved camp to Salon de Provence and toured around Nimes, Arles and Avignon. We then rented a gite near Beziers, with the Canal du Midi at the bottom of the garden, where we were joined by our friends Russell and Janet Collins and my sister-in-law Penny and her partner Jeremy. Russell and Jeremy both had big birthdays to celebrate – Russell's 65th and Jeremy's 50th – so we were in party mood as we went along to watch the Springboks beat the USA 64-15 in a predictably one-sided match during which we had fun cheering on the underdogs. Di and I then headed inland to the Auvergne, where we spent a long afternoon in a crowded bar, watching on television as England beat Australia 12-10 before France then caused an upset with a 20-18 victory over the mighty All Blacks that sent the locals delirious with joy. The level of noise and excitement was incredible as convoys of cars came charging through Issoire with klaxons blaring.

For us, of course, the rugby ended on a disappointing note when South Africa beat England 15-6 in the final at the Stade de France. But at least we gave the Springboks a bit more of a run for their money than we did when we played them in the earlier group stage and got stuffed 36-0! Di and I watched that game on television in a café, lone Brits surrounded by hoards of gloating French who took great delight in taking the mickey out of 'les rosbifs'.

Despite my enforced abstinence, the trip was a wonderfully intoxicating experience in all sorts of other ways. Provence in the autumn was superb, the carnival atmosphere of the rugby was exhilarating and the healthy combination of the outdoor camping life and a liquid intake of nothing stronger than the various sirops had the desired therapeutic effect. I felt much better and made sure I enjoyed every moment of this welcome break away from all my troubles, while doing my best not to dwell on the prospect of my Appeal before the Privy Council that awaited me on my return and which had been hanging over my head for so many months like the proverbial sword of Damocles.

I still had a few more weeks to wait following our return from France before the Appeal was heard; and a further three weeks after that before the threat of being struck off was finally lifted with the announcement that the Appeal had been allowed and my 'sentence' reduced to suspension for six months, to take effect from December 12th 2007.

So, no longer part of the practice; name removed from the headed notepaper, certificates taken off the wall and small stainless steel nameplate outside the surgery taken down, exposing a telltale patch of bare wood surrounded by a varnished border. I was still allowed to visit the premises – I could not be barred from entering what was my own property – but any discussion of veterinary matters was strictly forbidden and I was not permitted to offer advice or help of any kind to clients, staff or grooms. The rule was: you can come in by all means, but keep quiet.

By and large I kept away from the surgery, anxious not to be seen hanging around like a spare part. Mostly, I just called in to collect my post and to see if there had been any calls that I needed to pass on to the other vets. Occasionally, I would sit and have coffee with them or with other members of the staff, catching up on all the latest happenings. I also continued to drop in socially on my regular clients at their yards, watching the horses out on the gallops and generally seeing how things were progressing. Everyone was very supportive and understanding, never once asking me to do anything that would compromise my position. Even on the one or two occasions that emergencies arose in the yard just when I happened to be there, the surgery was always contacted and someone else asked to come and deal with the situation. And, without exception, all those regular, long-standing clients made a point of telling me that as soon as I was ready to go back to work they wanted me to carry on where I'd left off – although one or two of them said that they would understand if I decided that I'd had enough, given the way I'd been treated.

People expressed their sympathy in different ways. Shortly after my suspension came into effect I bumped into a young lad who lived in the same village as me. He always seemed to be in some sort of trouble, but had a heart of gold. I liked him and had tried to help him out on one or two occasions. He was obviously delighted to see me – probably because he knew I would buy him a pint! He proceeded to tell me how sorry he was to hear what had happened to me and then, after a slight pause, added: "Never mind, Al, you're one of us now!" I wasn't quite sure whether I should feel flattered or alarmed to be welcomed as a member of his particular fraternity!

I preferred to think of my suspension as 'gardening leave', which is exactly what it turned into. I had always been interested in gardening, but because of my busy working life I never seemed to have enough time to do things properly and it became a chore rather than a pleasure. Now, all of a sudden, I had more than enough time on my hands in which to exercise my green fingers. The family bought me a propagator and a small greenhouse and whereas, previously, I used to go out and buy all our bedding plants, I now took great pride in growing things from seed – simple things like marigolds, alyssium, lobelia, nasturtiums, sunflowers, sweet peas and 'Sweet Williams'. I gained a lot of basic knowledge from various books and manuals, but it was the old, experienced gardeners among my friends and clients whose know-how and tips proved most valuable.

Taking cuttings from fuchsias, geraniums, sage and rosemary – it was all new and fascinating to me and I got the same glow of pride from watching things that I had nurtured blossom into mature plants as I had done from packaging father's drenches and powders as a small boy fifty years earlier. We had a few fruit trees in our garden, including Conference pears and Bramley and Cox's Orange apples and there is nothing better than picking the fruit to eat and share with friends, especially when you have carefully nurtured the trees throughout the year.

Freed from the relentless work schedule that had previously dominated my life, I also found myself getting involved in the sort of domestic shopping chores that I am rather ashamed to say I had largely managed to avoid over the years, rather belatedly learning to navigate my way around the crowded aisles of Tesco's, Sainsbury's, Morrison's and Asda and to endure the misery of the checkout queue. There were also visits to John Lewis and – a real eye-opener, this – Ikea! A whole new world was being opened up to me, reminding me of what a colleague had previously told me – that there is a life outside veterinary practice!

For so long, nearly all my time had been devoted to building up the practice and providing a round-the-clock service to our clients while simultaneously keeping up-to-date with the latest treatments and methods, ensuring that the veterinary standards within the practice were of the highest order, listening to the concerns of clients and staff alike and making sure that any issues, however minor, were sorted out. In addition to all that, I felt that it was important to give time freely to local organisations and institutions, contributing to the good of the community and helping to educate the public about animal welfare wherever possible. The rewards were high and satisfying but, as in all walks of life, you don't get 'owt for nowt', as they say, and somewhere a price had to be paid.

I know that I must have let the family down on occasions, all too often being late home, too tired for social engagements and missing out on Lucy's netball matches and George's singing and rugby. This kind of thing could well have threatened some relationships, but, fortunately, I have a very strong marriage and Di was always right behind me if not, as in the early days, right there at my side, actively helping out. And as far as Lucy and George are concerned, the fact that my relentlessly heavy workload prevented me from seeing as much of them as I would have liked during their formative years does not seem to have left any kind of emotional scar. We get on well and always have done. I also have the consolation of knowing that all that overtime I poured into creating a successful business meant that I could afford to give them both the best education as well as various little treats – such as their own cars as soon as soon as they learned to drive. For Lucy it was a dark blue Daihatsu Sirion and for George a red Nissan Micra, both recommended by my friend Dean Woods from the Firs Garage in Hook Norton. Watching them drive off for the first time gave me a great feeling of satisfaction.

I had already been preparing the way for retirement for some months before my suspension took effect, introducing new vets to long-established clients, many of whom I had been dealing with for years, working relationships that in some cases stretched back over two generations of the same farming, horse-owning or racehorse training families. The handovers were not always easy because there were clients who had got so used to me that they found it hard to trust anyone else – much as some of my father's clients had at first been reluctant to accept me as anything but second best, a lad who knew nothing! In this respect, my suspension, coming into force at a time when I was already in the process of winding down, helped to facilitate the transition process, the period of my enforced unavailability allowing my successors to establish themselves with my long-standing clients without my shadow looming over them.

When the suspension was lifted on June 12th, 2008, I held a 'Return to the Register' party in the courtyard of our lovely old house in Hook Norton as a thank you to all those who had supported me and stood by me. I was fortunate to have perfect weather – it was dry and warm all night, and we enjoyed a tremendous evening. Two things about that night stand out vividly in my memory. I had abstained from all alcohol during the previous year and was looking forward to raising a glass of red wine to toast everyone (knowing that my doctor, Martin Harris, would be present to pick up the pieces if necessary), but to my great disappointment I found that I didn't enjoy the wine at all – and actually still don't. But the white wine – ah well, that's different! The other vivid and more poignant memory, is of the moment when my son, George, sought out Richard Stephenson and shook his hand, saying simply: "Thank you for all that you have done to help my Dad".

Free to return to work, I did so on a completely different basis. My old partners, now my bosses, were extremely generous in giving their blessing to a very loose arrangement whereby I am basically employed as a part-time consultant. I go into the surgery most mornings and continue to visit two or three of the clients with whom I have worked most closely over the years, keeping an eye on their horses and calling in one of the other vets at the practice to provide treatment whenever necessary. I cover for partner Simon Richards if he is away for any reason and I am also there to offer advice to the younger vets if required. And I still work as the on-course vet at Stratford-upon-Avon and occasionally at Warwick. It is an arrangement that suits all of us involved very well, reflecting the degree of trust that has been forged over many years.

As far as I am concerned, it has been the perfect way in which to ease into retirement. It has enabled me to stay in close touch with favourite clients, whom I count as some of my best and oldest friends, to keep up with all the latest horseracing gossip and to go on enjoying visits to yards with which I have been associated for so many years and in which I continue to take a keen interest. It is also good to know that I can still put my professional experience to good use and that I have not entirely been put out to grass!

These days I am lucky enough to have the best of both worlds. I am still able to do a bit of the work that has always given me such great satisfaction, although at a much gentler pace, while I also have the time and opportunity to relax and enjoy the pleasures of life, including regular trips abroad and to our cottage in Devon. I went to Australia in 2013 and Di and I together recently visited Cuba and have other big holiday adventures planned. And yet, in many ways, it is the simpler pleasures that can be enjoyed closer to home that I find most relaxing and rewarding.

Although I am a countryman, born and bred, and despite the fact that my entire working life has been spent at the very heart of the rural community, it is only since retiring that I have fully come to appreciate the true beauty of the countryside that in the past I had tended to take for granted. Too much time had previously been spent breaking the speed limit on country lanes as I raced from job to job, largely oblivious of my surroundings. That has all changed now. Not only am I no longer a slave to an over-crowded appointments book, but, in the interests of maintaining a healthier lifestyle following the heart problems brought on by the stress of dealing with the RCVS Hearing and Appeal, I have also been encouraged to get out of my car and onto Shanks' pony as much as possible and cross-country walking has become a favourite pastime. As a result I have been able to take great pleasure in becoming more closely familiar than I ever had been before with both the flora and fauna and also the local history and geography of what is an especially attractive neck of the woods here on the borders of Oxfordshire, Warwickshire and Gloucestershire.

On my walks I have always had an equally enthusiastic dog or two for company. First there was Lolly, a Black Labrador bitch who lived to eat. A lovely, calm, good-natured animal, she walked at her own pace and was never afraid to trespass if there was a morsel from a stranger's bowl to be had. Unfortunately, she also took particular delight in sniffing out and rolling in fox poo, which gives off the most disgusting stink, a lingering stench that seems to resist the most powerful deodorising medications on the market.

Scampi is a very different character. A brown Lakeland/Border-cross terrier bitch, she is small in stature, with long legs and a distinctive tail, but big in attitude. She knows no fear and never backs off anything. She is independent, stubborn, yaps incessantly to get attention and can be a complete pain at times. It took me a while to train her not to chase virtually anything that moves. She still thinks she can out-run a hare, despite repeated evidence to the contrary. The hare always leaves her trailing, running her ragged and round and round in circles until she is exhausted, after which she remains mercifully quiet for the rest of the day. Perhaps because they were such complete opposites, she and Lolly got on well and were great company for me as we roamed the countryside together. Sadly, Lolly suffered a fatal stroke in 2010 at the age of twelve, so now it is just me and Scampi who set out on one or other of our well-worn circular itineraries, Scampi's excitement mounting as she sees me donning my wellies and reaching for her lead.

Walking the ancient footpaths, bridleways and farm tracks that lead over the hills and valleys, through the fields, woodlands and heaths and along the hedgerows and brooks of the extended rural area that has been familiar to me since my earliest childhood, stopping to chat with the farmers and fellow countrymen I often bump into along the way – many of them former clients – serves to bring back vivid memories of people and places where, following in my father's footsteps and those of his father and grandfather before him, I was first taught the basics of veterinary care.

Heading over towards Sutton-under-Brailes, I regularly find myself walking past Arthur Taylor's farm, where, at the age of twelve, I had the unforgettable experience of lambing my first ewe. And skirting around the Warriner estate at Weston Park, just a few miles down the road, I am reminded of the time, just a few months later, when, following careful instructions from my father, I first put my hand into a calving cow.

Less than five miles up the road from Weston Park is Chinslade, where, about twenty years later, when I was still a student at Cambridge, I was taught another salutary lesson by my father when he was called out by dairy farmer Bill Gilkes to calve a cow. He took me along with him and decided that it would be an ideal opportunity for me to do the job, while he stood by to help out if I got into difficulty. After carrying out an internal examination, feeling around inside the womb to check that everything was as it should be, I announced in a loud voice that it was a live calf, adding confidently: "This is going to be easy!"

All went well, the calf duly arrived and I was feeling rather pleased with myself. Ominously, however, there was no comment from father and I could sense that he was unhappy about something. With the calf up and sucking, we said our goodbyes to Bill Gilkes, climbed back into the car and drove off. No sooner had we got out of the farm gate than father turned to me and gave me the most almighty rollicking. "Never tell clients it is going to be easy because they will then think they could have done it themselves," he growled. "And never ever predict that it is a live calf until it is actually delivered." I never made that mistake again.

Walking up the main street in the middle of Burmington village, you pass a farm owned and run by John Thame. His father, Roland, kept a small herd of dairy cows and one Christmas morning when I was twelve or thirteen there was an emergency situation involving one of the cows that was having difficulty calving. It turned out that there were complications that not even father was equipped to deal with. Mr Thame was determined to do everything possible to save the calf so Peter Moody, a Veterinary Surgeon from Stratford-upon-Avon who specialised in cattle, was summoned to perform a Caesarian. I was allowed to watch the proceedings, with strict instructions to do anything I was asked to do, but not to get in the way.

Mr Moody was a man who, even at the best of times, tended to live up to his name and he was certainly not in the happiest frame of mind when he arrived, hardly surprising given that he had been dragged from the bosom of his family on Christmas Day. He didn't waste any time. The cow was sedated and tied up and an area on its left flank was then clipped and cleaned several times, after which a local anaesthetic was administered. The area was cleaned again and covered with a big, green sterile piece of material into which a hole had been cut. I could not see too much of what went on after that, but there was a good deal of cutting and swabbing until eventually a large calf was delivered 'via the side door', as they say. At this point I was thrilled to be given the job of looking after the new arrival. I already knew exactly what to do – rubbing it down, clearing mucous from its airways and dipping its navel in iodine before making it comfortable. Mr Moody, meanwhile, stitched up the cow, packed up his kit and cleaned up. The adults then retired to the farmhouse for a wee festive dram or two while I was left outside with the cow and calf, still in awe and wonder at what I had just observed.

Farmers Jack and Harry Randall lived at Sharpers Lodge on the road between Whichford and Stourton and were good friends as well as clients. They kept a variety of animals, including an enormous and notoriously bad-tempered sow. She often had trouble farrowing and when father was called to assist he would instruct them to feed her a gallon of ale to quieten her down. I was about fourteen when he decided it was time for me to play midwife and, to be on the safe side, instructed the Randalls to make sure the expectant mum had an extra pint or two!

On the way over, the lecture started. Pigs, sows especially, can be quite nasty, I was warned. They are the only domestic animal with a full set of teeth – forty-four to be exact – and they can easily bite right through your arm. In pregnancy, the piglets lie in both horns of the womb and what often happens when the sow goes into labour is that two will arrive in the middle bit together and will then get stuck. That's what you have to watch out for.

When we got there I went into the pigsty a little nervously to be confronted by the sight of this huge black pig, lying on her side in fresh straw, seemingly out for the count. The Randalls assured us that she had had more than enough to drink!

As they looked on, father started giving me detailed instructions. He told me first to get myself washed and then to clean the sow before putting my hand in to feel around and find out what was going on. Sure enough, I could feel that two of the piglets were jammed together, unable to pass through the narrow neck of the womb. I was told to try and push one back very gently to see if that would free things up. It didn't. I was then told to try pushing the other one back and this did the trick. It moved back and the other one came through. Very excited, I shouted triumphantly: "It's here, it's coming!"

I was straightway ordered to stay calm and make sure not to squeeze the piglet's ribs as it came out because that might make it squeal and wake mum up! Very gently I lifted it out and laid it near the sow's head so that she could clean it. The second one arrived very quickly after that and I was told not to be in any rush because the rest would come when they were ready now that the obstacle had been cleared.

At this point refreshments were brought out – "something with which to wet the babies' heads" – and father sat on a bale of straw, with a whisky in one hand, overseeing the rest of the birthing process while generally putting the world to rights. I cannot now recall whether the bottle was emptied before the sow had finished farrowing, but he drove me home in high spirits, very pleased with the safe delivery of fourteen live, healthy piglets. The Randalls would certainly not be short of bacon the following year, he observed with a satisfied chuckle. And I basked in his approval, proud to have passed this test with flying colours.

Another memorable landmark in my early education came when father received an emergency call from Roland Pritchard's stables at Whatcote, where a mare was about to give birth and appeared to be in difficulties. "You have never seen a mare being foaled so you must come with me," said father, adding: "I don't know what we will find when we get there. Horses are delicate and, in this case, valuable. We will be lucky if we can save both the mare and the foal."

On arrival, we found the mare lying on her side in the barn, straining and clearly in some distress. A halter was put around her neck and she was coaxed to her feet. Father then stripped to the waist and washed himself thoroughly before examining her internally. In those days there were no sedative drugs or antibiotics. I was handed the halter and told: "Keep her walking around in a large circle if you can, while I walk behind her, working away at her rear end. Every time I ask you to stop she will strain and try to lie down. Let her. Then, when I tell you, we will need to get her up again."

I followed his instructions, watching in silence and slightly nervous fascination as the process unfolded – walk, walk, stop, lie down, get up, walk on. A rope was called for, then another and then a third. I remember thinking rather stupidly: "This one must have three legs, no wonder she can't foal!" In fact, the first two ropes were for the foal's front legs, while the third was for its head, placed gently behind the ears with the end of the loop in its mouth.

Once everything was in position the mare soon ejected the foal. Sadly, however, it was found to be stillborn, despite all father's valiant efforts. A great feeling of sadness and deflation descended, along with sorrow for the mare that had lost her baby. "I'm afraid you left her a bit too long, Ro," said father, with a shake of his head, adding: "Have you got another foal to put on her?" Roland bred a lot of horses, but had no other foals at the time. "We'll just have to leave her to let her milk dry up," he said.

Father gave him some chloral hydrate to put in her water to keep her calm. The afterbirth was not yet ready to come so he tied what was showing in a knot and said he would be back the next day to check on her. Meanwhile, he flushed out her womb with antiseptic wash and generally cleaned her up. "Take the foal away and leave her quiet. Don't touch her udder, she will then dry up more quickly." Over the inevitable drink in the house he explained that the afterbirth would need to be completely removed within twenty-four hours or there would be a risk that she could become toxic and get laminitis. Happily, when we returned the next morning there was great relief all round as the mare had discharged the afterbirth on her own and she went on to make a full recovery.

Dorothy Holder, nicknamed 'Bun', was an unmarried lady who farmed at Wyton's Piece, Ascot, which lies along the route of one of my favourite walks. Whenever I pass it, my mind goes back to the time when father put me in charge of castrating and tailing about fifty of her lambs, the first time I had been allowed to do this particular job. The ewes and lambs were penned and the catcher handed each lamb to father over the fence. Father would be the holder and I the operator – a reversal of what had been our usual roles up until that day.

As ever, I was given precise instructions – cut there, expose the testicles, clamp the cords and cut through them with the sharp end of the iron. Cauterise the ends to stop any bleeding and then take a dollop of green antiseptic cream on the end of a small stick and use the heat of the iron to melt it gently into the scrotum. Now stand up off the bench, the tail in the left hand, the iron in the right, and push down to cut through the tail – not to near the lamb's bottom or it will always get fly strike. These days, tailing is done differently, using rubber rings.

Walking along past the historic Rollright Stones and the King Stone you reach a point where you can look down on Long Compton in the valley below, and beyond that to Shipston-on-Stour. From here you can also see the farm known as Kings Brake. Part of the Warriner estate, it was once the home of my uncle, Alf Walker, but I remember it when Bill Yells used to farm there. Father used to describe him as a neat, tidy farmer and respected him as a good stockman. He reared calves from a young age and when they were well established they would need castrating and disbudding. The reason for castrating the

male calves was that, as bullocks, they would be less dangerous and easier to handle than bulls, of which only very few are
needed for breeding purposes. Just as with the lambs and pigs,
the operation involves removing the testicles using a sharp knife.
And although perhaps not something to be comfortably con-
templated by the squeamish, it is actually a routine veterinary
procedure that is fairly painless for the animal and causes surprisingly little distress.

Disbudding is done to stop the horns developing, a necessary
procedure because if the horns are allowed to grow the cattle will become more aggressive and fight each other. It is very
simply and easily done, using a local anaesthetic and a hot gas
disbudder, a solid cylinder with a hollowed out end that fits over
the horn bud. By pressing down and twisting it you burn the bud
loose and remove it. It is a quick, easy and painless operation
and, with father's guidance, I became proficient at an early age.

Just north of Kings Brake lies Little Wolford, and as you come
into the village you pass Pepperwell Farm, where Rad Cox used
to keep horses. Rad and his wife Edna were good friends with
my parents and used to come up to the house every now and
again to play card games such as whist, gin rummy and half-
penny nap. There was an occasion when Rad asked father to
examine one of his horses that had gone lame and I was taken
along to look, listen and learn.

Father took me through the process of examination and diagnosis step by step. I was told that, first of all, it was important to
have the horse trotted up on a smooth, firm surface so that you
could make up your own mind about which leg was affected,
because the owner would often have got it wrong. "Imagine having a stone in your right shoe," he explained. "You will always
put more weight on your left foot. Likewise, a horse, when it is
lame in the front, will always 'nod' towards the sound side."

I was then invited to carry out the initial examination and
correctly established that the problem was in the left front leg.
Father instructed me to get the hoof testers, which are like

pinchers with flat ends, and to squeeze around the foot in a slow, methodical way to establish exactly where the sensitive spot was. Having done this, I then had to take the shoe off. Horse shoes are attached to the hoof by a series of nails, the heads of which are turned over on themselves to make clenches that are then smoothed over by the farrier using a rasp. To get the shoe off, the clenches need to be knocked up and pulled off using a buffer and hammer. The sharpened end of the buffer is placed under the clench and then tapped with the hammer until the clench is lifted up and freed, quite a tricky job for a novice, especially when dealing with a fidgety horse!

Once I had removed the shoe I was told to clean the foot properly and then to use the hoof tester again to identify the sensitive areas. With a searching knife, which has a blade that curves round in a semi-circle, I was instructed to pare away any black areas, one of which duly released a pocket of puss. Once this was cleaned out father told Rad to put a bran poultice on the wound for three days in order to draw out all the remaining poison before putting in a bit of cotton wool to prevent anything else getting back in. "Get your farrier to dress the site with Stockholm Tar and then re-shoe the horse next week," he added.

Also located in Little Wolford was a farm once owned by Sid Dyer. It is still there, although most of the farm buildings have since been converted into residential homes. I liked going there because Sid had two sons, Peter and Trevor, who were contemporaries and friends of mine. With father around, however, there was no time for play; there was always work to be done and on one particular occasion it involved dehorning six cows. They were mature milking cows with thick horns and Sid had heard that they would be better off without them.

Father and I arrived to find them standing quietly in their stalls in the cowshed, each one tethered to a sturdy post by means of a chain around the neck.

"Right, Sid, we will do them in here," said father, adding as he approached the first cow: "Get a halter on her and then put your fingers in her nose to keep her still."

As with the calves, 5cc of local anaesthetic was first injected. To prevent any bleeding a piece of baler twine was tied tightly around the base of each horn to act as a tourniquet. The horns were then sawn off using a Tenon saw, which I was told had to be kept razor sharp. However, these old horns were tough and hard and there was soon a lot of huffing and puffing and swearing from father, especially when the cows refused to stand still. Eventually the job was done and all twelve horns succumbed to the saw, father noting proudly after each one: "Look! Not a drop of blood!" I was amazed to see that the horns were hollow and that the hollows extended right down into the cows' heads.

It had been a long tedious business, hard work that inevitably worked up the sort of powerful thirst that could only be slaked by copious quantities of Sid's home-brewed cider. "Now, Sid, put all the hay on the floor rather than in the manger for the next three days so that the seeds don't get shaken down and find their way into the wounds, " advised father. "Keep them clean and I will come back in four days to remove the tourniquets and make sure that everything is OK. If, in the meantime, any of the stumps get knocked and start to bleed then get a handful of cobwebs and push them into the holes."

It is a blessing that this job is rarely performed in this way any more, mainly because most cattle are disbudded when only a few months old. If for any reason de-horning has to done later, a large metal guillotine is used, which is heavy but effective. If the horns are too tough for the guillotine then a length of cheese wire is often preferred.

Dehorning cows was straightforward compared with performing the same operation on strong young wild steers weighing around six hundredweight each. Arthur Coles lived at Park Farm, Bloxham and was another of father's great friends among his clients. He was also one of the few who could make more noise than father when things weren't going quite as planned.

Arthur had about ten unruly steers shut in a barn, corralled behind five-bar gates that were arranged to form a funnel at one end, leading into a metal crush. This was supposed to make handling them easier and less dangerous. The crush was like a cage, about three foot wide and six foot high, with gates at both ends. The front gate had an adjustable yoke that could be clamped around the animal's neck to hold it steady while the gate behind it was slammed shut. So, in theory at least, no escapees!

Arthur's son, Geoffrey, was the same age as me, and a good friend. "I tell you what, Arthur, " said father. "These two strong young lads can do the hard work today."

Turning to me, he said: "Alan, when their heads are in the yoke you can put the halter on. Make sure you get it well behind their ears. Then pull their heads to one side so that I can inject the anaesthetic before removing the horns."

On this occasion he was using a long-handled guillotine. He reckoned that in order to speed things up we would get each steer in the crush, inject it, wait until the anaesthetic took effect and then remove the horns before releasing it out of the crush rather than doing it in two stages – first anaesthetising them all and then sending them through the system again to have the horns removed.

All was going well until halfway through the job, when we found ourselves dealing with an especially hyperactive steer that refused to stand still. One horn was removed and then, to everyone's horror, the steer managed to throw off the yoke, burst through the gate and went charging out of the barn into the adjoining field, with me still hanging on to the halter as if my life depended on it. I was dragged around through the muck and mud and all I could hear ringing in my ears was the sound of father shouting: "Don't let the bloody thing go because we'll never catch it again!"

I stuck to my task until the crazed animal eventually tired and between us we managed to get it under control. Plastered from head to toe and sore from being bumped across the yard and all around the field I was nevertheless feeling rather proud of myself for not letting go and was expecting congratulations. But no! Instead I was greeted with comments like: "If you had shut the gate properly in the first place it wouldn't have happened!" And: "Good job you are strong and stupid, otherwise you would never have hung on!" Somehow I rarely, if ever, seemed to get it right as far as father was concerned.

One day when I was with father in the outhouse surgery at Burmington, mother came over from the house with a message: "Jack, Will Honor at High Furze needs you urgently. He's got a cow with bloat."

We set off straightaway because this sounded like a real emergency. High Furze is a farm just outside Tidmington, a hamlet consisting of five or six cottages, a small church and a large manor house that was the home of Thomas Beecham, a son of the famous conductor of the same name who owned much of the surrounding land. A bridge takes the main road that runs through the little community over the River Stour and there is then a turn off signposted to Ditchford that is actually a dead end. High Furze lies along this lane. The area here is one of Scampi's favourite walks, with plenty of open space, wide verges, hedgerows, ditches, arable fields, meadows and lots of rabbit burrows – a veritable doggy Paradise.

Arriving at the farm, father and I were greeted by an anxious Will Honor, who reported that the animal had started showing signs of distress shortly after being turned out in a field close to the house the day before. Father shook his head and told him: "You know, Will, that lush spring grass is very tasty and young cattle will gorge on it, often leading to bloat."

We found the stricken animal lying on its right side, groaning and frothing at the mouth. A halter was quickly put round its neck and then father reached into his bag and produced a carved piece of wood that he placed between the stricken animal's teeth and secured with a leather strap around its head in order to keep its mouth open. "That will prevent it from choking," he explained, adding: "It's a good job it is lying on its right side because this procedure can only be done from the left."

Out from the bag came something wrapped in cloth – a rather fearsome looking syringe-type piece of stainless steel equipment that featured a handle and a metal prong with a sharp diamond-shaped tip encased in a hollow tube, around the end of which was a flat, circular plate with two small holes in it (the trochar and canular, as I later discovered). Father pummelled the cow's side for a few seconds before announcing: "I'll do it here". Then, with great force, he plunged the whole thing into the poor animal's side. When it was in right up to the hilt, the inner bit with the handle was very slowly and gently withdrawn.

Turning to me with a look of satisfaction on his face, father said quietly: "Listen and learn. You mustn't let the gas out all at once because the beast will faint due to the pressure being released too quickly." He proceeded to withdraw the plunger very gradually, bit by bit, and the smell of escaping methane gas pervaded the air. As the bloated stomach slowly subsided, father explained: "I'm in the rumen. A cow has four stomachs but it is the rumen that does all the fermenting of the cellulose in the grass. Once all the gas has been released we will put a gallon of liquid paraffin in through the hole to stop more gas forming. And, as a further precaution I will stitch in the canular using the two holes in the flat circular surface and we will leave that in overnight."

He then told Will to get some Vaseline and smear it below the line of the tube. "That will stop the stuff that bubbles out of the hole from burning and scalding the hide." He also told him to get the rest of the cattle out of the field and to keep them in overnight. "After that, you can make sure the same thing doesn't happen to the others by restricting their time on the fresh grass until they adjust to it."

Not far from High Furze, on the back road towards Shipston-on-Stour, again a prime dog walking area, lies a farm known as Shoulderways. I remember it from my youth as consist-ing of little more than a whitewashed farm cottage and some rather ramshackle outbuildings, surrounded by just a few acres of pastureland. Scraping a living there, mostly from a small dairy herd, was a young couple named Hopkins, who had only moved in relatively recently and who, although hardworking, were 'townies', without a great deal of farming experience. My mother nevertheless took to them and encouraged father to help them out as much as possible.

Another fairly common problem with cattle in the springtime, especially milking cows, is what is known as "grass staggers". Father did not know the whys and wherefores of the condition, but he did know how to deal with it effectively, as long as he got to the victims quickly enough. Answering an emergency call from Mr. Hopkins, he rushed straight over to find the best milking cow in the herd collapsed in the field. Her legs were twitching and every time she tried to get up she would stagger drunkenly for a few steps before falling down again. It would be a potential disaster for the young farmers if they lost her.

Father wasted no time in getting to work, while also providing a running commentary mainly for my benefit. He started off by warning: "Cows with the staggers can be wild and unpredictable because they don't know what they're doing, so watch points and be prepared to move quickly."

He had brought with him a selection of dark bottles from his medicine cabinet, including some labelled Magnesium in heavy black writing and another labelled Calcium in red and blue lettering.

"I will catch her and then try to pump the full bottle of magnesium under the skin, using the same apparatus as for milk fever," he continued. After what seemed like an age the entire contents of the bottle disappeared, causing a big bulge under the skin that he would flatten out every now and again with the palm of his hand, clearly causing the animal some discomfort.

After waiting a while, he announced: "Now that she is calmer I can risk putting some calcium mixed with a bit more magnesium straight into a vein, but I must do it very slowly so as not to overdo it as that might possibly kill her."

He proceeded to empty out about a quarter of the contents of the bottle of calcium, approximately 100cc, and then replaced it with magnesium before injecting the mixture bit by bit. Of course, he knew exactly what he was doing and the effect seemed almost miraculous. Within fifteen minutes the cow was back up on her feet and behaving quite normally as if nothing had happened. To prevent a recurrence, father advised getting some feed supplements that included Magnesium and suggested that the same field should not be used for a while. These days the treatment is much less dramatic, magnesium bullets being drenched into the animal and left to lie in the bottom of the rumen, releasing the content slowly as a preventative measure.

Honington, just north of Shipston-on-Stour, is a picture postcard village approached on one side by an ornate stone bridge over the River Stour and featuring sixty or so beautiful Cotswold stone houses and thatched cottages, separated from the road by wide grass verges that are lovingly looked after by the residents. Voted Britain's Best Kept Village on several occasions, it was the home of Alf Goodwin, a large, red-faced man who was a local farmer/butcher and one of father's regular racing companions.

Alf kept quite a few pigs, which have a habit of routing whereby they use their snouts to burrow into the soil looking for treats like acorns – all very natural but also very destructive, making an awful mess of whatever field they are in and turning it into a quagmire in wet weather. One way of trying to prevent this happening is to put a ring in the pig's nose, but they are not easy animals to handle and this procedure can be quite a performance. On one occasion Alf called father in to carry out a ringing and suggested that he bring me along to help out.

We arrived to find this large snow-white pig eyeing us expectantly from its sty. A regular pigsty has doors about four feet tall and when you approach pigs will often stand and rest their front trotters on the door, grunting loudly in anticipation of being fed. This one was no exception. Father marched boldly into the sty carrying a rope with a noose on the end of it in one hand and a flat board about three foot square in the other.

Prior to this, there had been much discussion about the size and type of ring that was to be used. Generally speaking, there are two main types, the simplest of which is a thin, plain split ring with pointed ends that you fitted into an instrument like a pair of pliers that squeezed the two open ends together through the fleshy part on the top of the snout, which sounds rather drastic but is actually no more painful than having your ears pierced. However, Alf decided he didn't want this type. He felt that they came out too easily and he was after something more substantial. So father rootled around in the boot of the car and produced a box labelled Ketchum Large Pig Ring! This comprised a sturdy, copper-coloured ring that was hinged on one side so that it could be opened up and the two ends, one sharply pointed, then closed and clamped together through the cartilage between the nostrils of the snout.

Alf having decided that this would be perfect, it was then time to catch the pig and get the ring inserted. Using the board both to protect himself and to manoeuvre the pig, father finally got it cornered. The rope with the noose was then dangled over its nose in the hope that it would open its mouth, which it eventually did. The noose was then swiftly pulled into the mouth, past the tusks and secured tightly. This was when the squealing started in earnest! Alf and I were instructed to take the end of the rope and pull it over the top of the sty door and under no circumstances to let go. With the pig hog-tied, as it were, father took the bright shiny ring out of his pocket and opened it. At the front of a pig's snout the two nostrils are separated by flesh and cartilage. Father took the sharp end of the ring and pushed it through the fleshy middle bit of the nostril. Not surprisingly, all hell was let loose at this point, the squealing reaching fever pitch and father shouting at us to hang on to the rope. He assured us that the animal would soon settle and indeed it did, allowing him to close up the ring by tightening the retaining screw.

All that remained to be done was to remove the noose. Taking the board in his right hand again to protect himself against an attack from the understandably angry porker, he advanced warily back into the sty. Alf and I were then ordered to let go of the rope and with a quick jerk the noose was loosened and dropped out of the pig's mouth, whereupon the animal scampered to the back of the sty, shaking its head, while father made good his escape. "Job well done, Alf – time for a drink," he said, rubbing his hands. With that, the pair of them retired to the house, while I went and sat in the car and fell asleep waiting for father to drive us both home.

Before I fell asleep I thought back to another occasion when Alf Goodwin really annoyed me. He was due to go to Worcester races with father and two other friends, Michael Gaden and Joe Oughton, but had then announced a couple of days before that he would be unable to go. I was excited because that meant I could go in his place. I was already changed when Alf suddenly turned up at Burmington to say he was able to go after all. I was furious. Father told me to stay at home and pick up the stones in the front paddock, saying it was high time I did it as he had already asked me many times before. The car had not been gone long when two boy scouts appeared looking for work as part of 'Bob-a-Job' week. What luck! I eagerly told them the job that needed doing and they worked all afternoon clearing the paddock and putting the stones in neat piles. I gave them their money and felt quite smug. Much later, I heard father saying to mother: "Our Alan has done a good job in the paddock and I've had a good day at the races, so I think he deserves a reward." He gave me a crisp pound note and, most unusually, was fulsome with praise. I accepted it all and said nothing. I also forgave Alf Goodwin.

Another of father's great friends was Mervyn Griffin, a sheep farmer who lived at the crossroads between Fifield and Milton under Wychwood, Mervyn had about two hundred pedigree Suffolk ewes, all beautifully bred, and his ram lambs were much in demand by other breeders. He treated his sheep like family and referred to his ewes as his gals. During the lambing season in January and February he would convert his barn into a large maternity unit, using straw bales with individual pens for about sixty of the 'gals'. He would never bring them to the surgery to lamb them, we always had to visit him, whatever time of day or night. You would always get the same lecture – be gentle, be careful and don't stress them. Mostly the lambings were success-ful, but on those occasions when it wasn't he would obviously be very disappointed, but would always say: " You tried your best, you can do no more."

Outside the barn was his shepherd's hut, a large shed on wheels that could be towed around the farm when needed. It contained a bed, an area for his sheepdogs to rest and a stove that was kept going continuously, providing much needed heat for the new-born lambs as well as for the shepherd, and also a means of cooking. A stewpot resided permanently on the top of the stove and various culinary additions were made all the time. He also had a generous supply of drinks and always enjoyed "wetting the baby's head" when lambs were born.

Mervyn was a great man and taught me a very good lesson early on in my career. He hated injecting his 'gals' – he didn't want them to think he might be hurting them – so I inherited the job from father of vaccinating his ewes for the varying clostridial diseases. It was a routine job, but very enjoyable provided it was dry – he had good handling facilities. The drug manufacturers had been developing a vaccine against Pasturella to be com-bined with that for Clostridial, but they were late in pricing up the product, so when Mervyn rang to order his vaccines and arrange a time to do the job, the price had not been finalised. I told him this and asked him to trust me, adding that I would do my best to get a good price for him. The quick reply was "Boy, if I didn't trust you, I wouldn't be dealing with you". Enough said.

Beyond the Rollright Stones, heading towards Stow-on-the-Wold, is a narrow road known as Golden Lane. This makes for another good walk, with splendid views out over Chipping Norton and on towards Stow. At the bottom of the lane lies the village of Salford, which was home to one of father's most important and influential clients, Sir Andrew Horsburgh-Porter. A true gentleman of the old school, Sir Andrew was highly respected, a former cavalry officer with the 9th/12th Lancers who had been awarded the Military Cross during the Second World War. A great horseman, he was also an international polo player with an 8 goal handicap who went on to become the Polo Correspondent for *The Times* and Hunting Editor of *The Field*.

He and father got on very well and both enjoyed a drop of the amber liquid. Father would often be instructed to take me along to see him – Sir Andrew always seemed to take quite an interest in me and what I was up to and would regularly make a point of urging me to carry on the family business and not to let the old traditional veterinary secrets die. It was for him that I injected a horse in the jugular vein for the very first time. Having become very lethargic, the horse had been diagnosed with anaemia and needed intravenous multivitamins and iron. "You're a lucky young man to be allowed to do it," Sir Andrew told me. "But your father has assured me that you are perfectly capable." What a responsibility – and thank goodness I didn't mess it up.

At the other end of the social scale from Sir Andrew among father's clients was Tom Smith, Senior, the head of the family who ran the Smiths of Bloxham scrap metal empire. Although a rough diamond, he was a wonderful character in many ways, highly regarded by those who knew him well, including father. As well as running the scrap metal business he also owned a farm, where he kept a herd of prized Jersey cows, and it was his son Pete who reminded me of the time when one of the cows was having difficulty calving and Tom announced: "We must send for Jack Walker – right now!"

The phone call came through and father set off straightaway. When he arrived at the farm Pete was told to take him to the pen where the cow had been isolated. Father took one glance and then turned to Pete and instructed him to go and tell his father that this cow would not calve until a bottle of whisky had been sent down. Pete couldn't quite understand how this would help but did as he was told and soon returned with a full bottle and a glass. Still confused, he asked how it would help. "You'll see," said father, filling his glass, adding some water from a nearly tap and then seating himself on a bale to keep a close watch on the cow's behaviour. He refilled and drained the glass two or three times before suddenly announcing: "I think she is now about ready, boy." And with that he rolled up his sleeves, washed his hands, examined the cow and duly delivered a live calf.

Venturing further afield in the opposite direction to Bloxham, through Chipping Norton and Stow-on-the-Wold and on towards Tewkesbury, you pass the village of Ford before going down Stanway Hill, a long winding descent, heavily wooded on the right hand side. In the spring, when the laburnum trees are in full flower, the cascades of bright yellow flowers hanging down are a magnificent sight. At the bottom of the hill a side road leads off to Paper Mill, which used to be farmed by a real character named Joe Sadler. Father loved visiting him and when the job was done they would retire to the kitchen where they could always be found with a bottle of Joe's favourite VAT69 open between them.

In the spring of every year, colt cutting – castration – would usually be high on father's agenda. As already mentioned, he was widely renowned for his skill in carrying out this far from delicate but very necessary procedure in the days before modern emasculators made the job a lot easier and more straightforward. I was still only about fifteen when he decided that the time had come to initiate me by letting me give him some hands-on assistance. On the appointed day he was booked to do about ten castrations for Joe Sadler. "We'll see how we go and wait until we get a quiet one for you to help with – no point in ruining your confidence," he said.

When a suitable candidate was identified, my job was to put

one of the pegs on the cord of the exteriorised testicle. With the colt haltered, twitched and blindfolded, this involved opening up the peg into a V shape and getting it into position before closing the V and slipping on a leather washer to tighten it. I was naturally a little bit nervous at first but managed it OK and ended up putting the pegs on two or three more that morning. However, it was some time before I was allowed to complete the whole operation myself.

A suitable patient had been brought to the stables at Burmington Manor for gelding and father decided that this would be an ideal opportunity for me to be put to the test, especially as nobody else would be around. Dave Winchcombe, a lad from the village, was summoned and asked to hold the colt while I received full, step-by-step instructions. "First, clean the scrotum with cotton wool soaked in disinfectant. Feel around both sides to make sure there are no abnormalities, like a rupture or thickening of the cord. Then position yourself facing the colt's left hind leg and remember that it can cow kick – kick to the side, that is – so you need to make sure that your right leg is out of the firing line. Take the far testicle in your left hand, squeezing it gently down between your forefinger and thumb. With the open knife make a bold cut to expose the testicle, then get a peg and put it around the cord and tighten it up with the washer, just as you did at Joe Sadler's. Now repeat with the other testicle."

Having successfully completed the job I was feeling very pleased with myself and had a big smile on my face. "Well, they won't all stand as quiet as that," commented father drily. He was superb at the job, earning a reputation that spread far and wide for his expertise in castrating colts standing up, and he taught me well. I did several more castrations with him after that and altogether over the years I must have done over a hundred, but I will never forget that first one. By the time I qualified and joined him in practice even fewer people were castrating colts standing up and as a result I was almost as much in demand as he had been.

In cutting colts standing, one was exposed to some physical hazards, of which the risk of being kicked was obviously one. I had long arms and could usually stand outside the arc of the 'cow kick', but being tall and therefore unable to bend my head down far enough to get a clear view of exactly what I was having to do presented another problem altogether, especially with smaller and less well-endowed colts. Unable to visualise the area of operation completely, part of the procedure had to be carried out by feel. With a sharp scalpel in my right hand and the said testicle held in my left hand, one swift action would cut into and expose the testicle. Every so often the animal would move just at the vital moment and a part of my left hand would experience first a numb feeling followed by a sharp, cold, stinging sensation and profuse bleeding. On one such occasion, with blood pouring from the ball of my thumb, I completed the job only to be taken severely to task for creating such a bloody mess! I received very little sympathy when I pointed out that it was me that was bleeding and not the fidgety ex-colt! Fortunately my stitch kit and local anaesthetic were available for me to carry out running repairs.

The risk of physical injury is not the only occupational hazard of caring for animals. There is also the chance of catching an animal disease, the main examples of zoonoses (the process whereby diseases are transmitted between humans and animals) are Weils disease, caused by leptospira, Brucellosis and Psittacosis. A few years ago, during a routine visit to Jem Hayward, my optician in Banbury, he scanned my retinas and found a plaque in the left side that had been caused by the larvae of *Toxacara canis*, a roundworm found in dogs. If the larvae are accidentally ingested they can migrate via the optic nerve and cause blindness, especially in young children. One of the reasons dogs are not allowed on playing fields or in playgrounds is that infected eggs are present in faeces. However, humans can also get toxocariasis just by stroking an infected dog's fur and accidentally ingesting the eggs – hence the importance of regularly worming all your pets. Fortunately, in my case I had no signs of a problem and the offending plaque was sited outside my main field of vision. So, being a vet is not without its dangers – not that I would ever want to put any one off!

I have so many vivid memories from those early years and although father and most of the farmers and other characters he worked for have now passed on, their faces and voices are as clear today as they were fifty-odd years ago. I hear them in my head and see them in my mind's eye as I walk through the familiar countryside, passing the farms that figured so prominently throughout my formative years, recalling so many key moments in my life and career and reflecting with quiet satisfaction on how I got to where I am today and how happy I am to be there. My one sadness is that I seem destined to be the last in the long line of Walkers who have looked after the animals of our local farming and horse-owning community continuously through five different centuries. But at precisely 1.22pm on June 14th, 2014, my first grandson Jack Lindsay arrived, so who knows? Maybe there will only be a gap of one generation!

14

Olympic Games Maker

I have always been a huge sports fan and I particularly look forward every four years to the Olympic Games. I take a keen interest in just about all the events – with the possible exception of synchronized swimming! – and I keep a patriotic eye on the medals table, hoping that our final haul will put us up there at the head of the also-rans who inevitably trail behind the USA and China. I was as thrilled as anyone when, in 2005, London was chosen as the venue for the 2012 Games – especially satisfying as we had ultimately found ourselves competing head-to-head with Paris for the honour. I made multiple applications for tickets as soon as they went on sale, but ended up being allotted only two – for the men's hockey. That was far from being at the top of my list of preferences, but given that so many people who applied were left empty-handed I felt fortunate to have got anything at all. At that stage it never crossed my mind that I was destined to become more than just a spectator.

It was not until June 2010 that I happened to read that the body set up under the chairmanship of Lord Coe to oversee the planning and development of the Games – the London Organising Committee of the Olympic Games and Paralympic Games (LOCOG) – was looking for unpaid volunteers to become Games Makers, helping with the day-to-day running of the Olympic Village and all the various events. In particular, quite a large number of qualified vets were required to provide cover for the equestrian events, including the Cross Country section of the Three Day Event. For this, there was to be a medical and veterinary team on standby at every one of the twenty-eight fences throughout the course, ready to provide on-the-spot treatment for any fallers and to stabilise any seriously injured horses, supervising their sedation and loading them into an ambulance if necessary.

My long experience as a racecourse vet meant that I was well qualified to be a member of the Cross Country Veterinary Team but, even so, having sent off an application form and had it accepted, I was then summoned to Cardiff to be 'vetted', along with the other applicants, as the first stage in what proved to be a lengthy and very thorough process of selection, preparation and training. Arriving at the Coal Exchange, a lovely old building right in the heart of Cardiff's regenerated docklands, I was asked for proof of identity and qualifications before being registered and issued with a badge. After viewing a display that included pictures and exhibits relating to the proposed layout in Greenwich Park, where the equestrian events were to be held, along with detailed information about the aims and objectives of the veterinary team, we were then shown a short introductory film explaining other aspects of the planned operation before being subjected to a searching 20-minute interview. I was asked a whole range of questions aimed at establishing my suitability for the job: What did I think were my leadership qualities? What was I like in a crisis? When did I last go the extra mile to help someone? I then had to wait a few weeks before receiving an email congratulating me on having been selected as a Games Maker and advising me that further communications would follow.

Starting with what was described as a 'Venue Familiarisation' visit to Greenwich in June 2011, there followed a series of briefings, training sessions, dummy runs and full rehearsals spread over the thirteen months before our big day finally arrived on July 30th 2012 – all part of the 'London Prepares' programme that saw similar planning procedures organized at various Olympic venues throughout the capital.

The main purpose of that first visit to Greenwich Park in June 2011 was, as the title suggested, to ensure that we were properly acquainted with the venue site and its facilities, the proposed layout of the course and the surrounding area. I had never been to that part of London before and I found it a pleasantly surprising eye-opener. For instance, anyone who, like me, thought that there were no hills to speak of in London and who imagined that the park would be flat should try walking up the steep slope to the Royal Observatory! From this unexpectedly high vantage point the view out across the Thames and over to the City of London is truly magnificent. I am told that the Games organisers took two coachloads of Olympic officials and media representatives on a guided tour of alternative sites, including Windsor Great Park, Gatcombe Park, Badminton and Burghley, but it was the panoramic view from the Observatory that clinched it for Greenwich. Even at night, with the surrounding buildings illuminated and the lights of the City twinkling in the distance, the vista was impressive.

Apart from its convenient location and stunning views, Greenwich Park also has a fascinating history. Extending to 180 acres, it is the oldest enclosed Royal Park in London, dating back to 1433. A royal residence since the 14th century, Greenwich Palace was the birthplace of Henry VIII, who introduced deer to the Park and whose daughters, Mary I and Elizabeth I, were also born there. It was demolished in the 17th century and the Old Royal Naval College now stands on the site.

The Park was formally re-designed in the French style and laid out in the early 1600s on the orders of James I, who enclosed it with a twelve-foot-high brick wall, parts of which still survive, and who then gave it as a gift to his wife, Anne of Denmark. She, in turn, brought in architect Inigo Jones to design what was known as the Queen's House and which now houses the National Maritime Museum. Later, Charles II, who had a great interest in science and founded the Royal Society, commissioned Sir Christopher Wren to build the Royal Observatory, originally named Flamsteed House after the first Royal Astronomer, John Flamsteed.

With so many very special historic and truly British associations, it seemed there could be no more appropriate venue at which to stage such a prestigious event as the equestrian Olympics. There were, nevertheless, strong objections from people who were alarmed by the prospect of huge crowds, let alone horses, trampling all over what is a World Heritage Site. However, assurances were given that everything possible would be done to ensure the protection of the natural environment. This included putting down layers of woodchip coverings to preserve the delicate superficial root systems of the 400-year-old Spanish Sweet Chestnut trees planted when James I had the Park laid out.

The overall veterinary operation for the Cross Country Eventing was masterminded by Veterinary Services Manager Jenny Hall, who worked tirelessly to assemble her team and all the back-up services, ably assisted by Simon Knapp in his capacity as Field of Play Services Team Leader. I knew them both well. Jenny, who had previously been team vet for the British Three Day Event team at the Sydney, Athens and Beijing Olympics was also a racecourse vet at Epsom, Sandown and Kempton and went on to succeed Peter Webbon as Chief Veterinary Officer for the British Horseracing Association. Simon, Clinical Director at the Scott Dunn Equine Clinic in Wokingham, was also an experienced racecourse vet and an old friend.

Once we had got our bearings in the Greenwich Park site on that first visit, we were briefed on exactly what would be expected of us before then taking part in a dummy run. Instead of horses, a series of golf buggies drove around the course, displaying different placards as they passed each fence – horse fallen; horse refused; horse looking tired; rider injured; spectator blocking course – and the team would react accordingly. At each fence there was a veterinary surgeon – I was allocated Fence 5, Chestnut Logs – plus an assistant vet, a medic, two fence judges and a timekeeper, all of us equipped with a radio for instant communication. The course was divided into sectors, each of which had a Sector Manager responsible for coordinating the various emergency services, which included an ambulance, a horse ambulance, a rehydration team, an emergency veterinary team and an anaesthetics team for each sector. The dry run went very well and everything worked smoothly.

A month later, in July 2011, there was a second trial run, this time with forty horses taking part over eighteen fences – not the full quota since only half the Park was being used. On this occasion there were also some two thousand spectators walking around the course, to give us a better feel for what it would be like on the day. The procedure in the event of an incident was that any injured horse was to be assessed on the course and then taken by ambulance to the on-site equine clinic for further assessment. If specialist treatment was then required, ambulances would be on standby to transport the animal to one of three Centres of Excellence in Newmarket, London and Ashford, Kent. Any horse that fell would be automatically withdrawn and could not be remounted, but would have to be led back to the stables by a mounted chaperone.

I was impressed by the fact that every eventuality had been catered for and no stone left unturned in making sure that everything possible was done to ensure the safety and wellbeing of the equestrians and their horses. As it happened, the course rode well and jumped well during the trial and the event finished without incident. As soon as the last horse had completed the course the jumps were dismantled and everything returned to normal as quickly as possible in order to cause as little interference as possible to the delicate ecosystems. By now, my appetite for the real thing had been well and truly whetted, but that was still some way off.

There was an interlude of more than six moths before the next stage in the Games Makers' preparation. Entitled 'Orientation Training', this took place on February 4th, 2012 at Wembley Park Arena. Altogether, 70,000 Games Makers had been recruited and so each of the seven four-hour-long 'Orientation Training' sessions was attended by around 10,000 people. Given that every single one of us had to be screened before we could get in, this made it a logistically difficult and frustratingly slow process. Things weren't helped by the fact that it turned out to be one of the coldest days of the year.

The training was led by triple jumper Jonathan Edwards and Lord Seb Coe, together with various personalities ranging from BBC newsreader Huw Edwards to comedian Eddie Izzard, the overall purpose being to review the glorious history of the Olympic and Paralympic Games and to provide a pep talk underlining the importance of our role in helping to deliver a safe, secure and sustainable Games. Views were mixed as to the value of this particular module, but it was delivered with tub-thumping enthusiasm, designed to make sure that we volunteers fully embraced the Olympic dream.

Two weeks later we were summoned to Hackney Community College for 'Common Role Training' and 'Role Specific Training'. The former again provided a general overview of the Games and guidance on how we should conduct ourselves, stressing the need to think of ourselves as ambassadors and to do our best to make spectators and competitors from around the world feel at home. This message clearly got through to everyone involved because so many visitors to the Games made a point of commenting on how wonderfully welcome they had been made to feel by the friendly, smiling volunteers who were always on hand to offer help and assistance, often without being asked.

Our 'Role Specific Training' session was conducted by Jenny Hall, who once again explained the role of the Veterinary Services Team and the structure of the organisation in detail. She reminded us that although some of us would only be present for the Cross Country event, there were many other equestrian events – show jumping, dressage, modern pentathlon and all the same disciplines for the Paralympics at all of which a veterinary presence would also be required.

Three months later on June 8th, 2012 we collected our uniforms and accreditation badges from a warehouse in West Ham. Once again, the security was very strict and the checks rigorous. My driving licence happened to have been renewed since I had submitted my original Games Maker application and included one letter that was different to the previous one. This led to me being double-checked and treble-checked before I was eventually given my accreditation.

When it came to picking up my uniform, I felt a bit like a raw National Service recruit being issued with his kit. After filling in a size chart I went along with my accreditation badge to the distribution centre, where I was given a pair of shoes, two pairs of trousers and an anorak, all packed into a bag together with an umbrella, water bottle, watch, socks and a cap. I was also given an Oyster card for use on the days that I was working.

A week later it was back to Greenwich for another briefing session before walking the course and touring the various facilities. A huge amount of work had been carried out in the Park since our last visit and it was barely recognisable now that grandstands had been constructed, along with show jumping and dressage arenas, practice areas and an all-weather canter up the hill. There were also stables, an equine clinic complete with x-ray and scanning facilities and an operating theatre.

On July 26th, 2012 there was a final rehearsal over the full course of twenty-eight fences, but again using golf buggies and placards instead of actual horses. I went up to London the night before and stayed in a flat near Blackheath that had been loaned to me by Ed Kiernan, son of our great friends Jim and Andrea, the couple who had been so kind to us during the Disciplinary Hearing. Ed had got a job with the top Mexican television company Televisa, who were in London to cover the Olympics. He was working as a production manager and was required to stay in the hotel where the company had set up its headquarters. This meant he didn't need the flat himself and was delighted to let me borrow it. As it happened, the tenancy was due to expire the day after the Cross Country event and Ed was not planning to renew it, so the timing was absolutely perfect for me.

I arrived at the flat on what was a hot and humid evening, dumped my kit and set out to find somewhere to eat. After a

45-minute walk into Blackheath Village I found that every res-taurant seemed to be fully booked. In the end I found a really nice-looking place called Chapters that was again packed, but just as the manager was apologetically turning me away a party of people sitting at a long table in the middle of the restaurant invited me to join them. The table was for ten, but one of their friends hadn't turned up. It soon turned out they, too, were all Olympic volunteers and I ended up having a great fun evening and didn't get back to the flat until quite late!

The next morning, I was pleased to discover that I was only ten minutes' walk from the Blackheath Gate entrance to the Park, from where there was a regular shuttle service down to St Mary's Gate, close to the Devonport House hotel and con-ference centre, where the entire Equine Veterinary Services Team were to assemble for a briefing before moving out onto the course for the final run-through.

Jenny Hall and Simon Knapp went through both the routine and the various emergency procedures again in detail, making sure that everybody knew exactly what their role was and what was expected of them. One thing that was stressed was that in no circumstances was a horse to be put down on the course. In the event of an injury being considered terminal, the horse was to be sedated and then taken away in an ambulance.

I had been telling Simon for ages, with a nudge and a wink, that as the oldest vet on duty I should be allocated a fence that was relatively less testing for the horses and riders, not too far out on the course and, preferably, with a nice tree nearby to pro-vide some shade if it turned out to be a hot, sunny day! Simon duly came up trumps and put me down for Fence No 3, The Bandstand Rails, which was conveniently close to the Control Centre. With me, as my assistant, was a student vet named Sam, along with a medic, two fence judges and an Australian time-keeper, Peter, who was a veteran of no less than six Olympics.

The final test run went like clockwork, although we were warned that things might not be quite so easy on the day, when there would be upwards of 50,000 spectators milling around the course, making quite a lot of noise, obscuring lines of vision, possibly getting in the way of emergency vehicles and generally adding a distraction. But by now there was a mounting sense of excitement and anticipation among the veterinary teams.

After an early night at Ed's flat on the eve of the event itself I awoke to a bright, sunny morning, with a pleasant, cooling breeze. Dressed in my uniform, I walked along Charlton Way towards the Park and although it was still only 8.00am one could sense an atmosphere building. The footbridge over the road at Charlton Way was full and there was already a long queue stretching back towards Blackheath. Fortunately, I didn't need to queue as my accreditation badge ensured that I was fast-tracked through, along with several colleagues from the Veterinary Services Team, whom I had met up with en route.

Inside the Park, we could again feel the tension growing. Around the stables there were horses and riders everywhere, people of all nationalities chatting and calling out to each other in different languages. Up on the all-weather canter we could see the British team riders exercising their horses.

After registering at Devonport House, we collected our water and meal vouchers before going on to the Control Centre to pick up our radios. Then it was up to the Athlete's Tent in the cooling area next to the Cross Country finish, where huge fans were blowing out an ice-cold mist. There I was issued with a medical kit, which my young assistant, Sam, carried up to Fence No 3. Final checks were made under the supervision of our Sector Manager and by 11.00 am we'd got everything sorted out.

By then the crowds were already building. Well-wishers, friends and clients stopped by to have a chat with us. As it happened, we were located at a very busy part of the course where two pedestrian walkways crossed the course and intersected. One of the special features of Cross Country Eventing is that spectators are allowed to walk right around – though not actually on – the course, enabling them to get close up views of the fences and the competitors. If you imagine a circular walkway, there was a pedestrian crossing over the course in the outward direction between Fences 2 and 3 and on the way back between Fences 21 and 3, with a joining intersection. Every time a competitor was about to come through, a whistle would be blown very loudly and enthusiastically by one of the fence judges, whereupon the crossings would be closed. The crowd was very orderly and well behaved and there were no incidents, but the sheer volume of people did tend to make things slightly more difficult. By the time the first competitor was due to go off people were lining the course four or five deep and I could not see Fence 2 from my original position and had to move around in order to get a clear view.

Fence 3 was set at right angles. In keeping with its title, Bandstand Rails, the design featured artificial topiaries in the shape of musical notes – quavers, treble clefs and minims – plus seats on which were perched various wind instruments. There were two options as to how the riders tackled it. Either they could go the long way round, which meant jumping through the middle section and then continuing on past the assembled topiary notes before turning at right angles to jump the second element – or you could risk taking a short cut.

The general consensus was that none of the fences were too formidable, the biggest challenge being the tricky, undulating nature of the overall terrain and the time constraint. The full course distance was 5,728 metres, the optimum time was ten minutes and three seconds and the time limit exactly double that. So, any short cuts were well worth taking.

At Fence 3, however, this was not an easy option. It meant jumping the right hand corner of the first element before then negotiating a narrow gap with a mature tree on the left hand side. This created a problem because the approach from Fence 2 now involved a left curve with a slightly adverse camber that unbalanced some of the horses. In order to take the short cut successfully the horse needed to be presented accurately and well-balanced and although most of the riders managed this, some found that they were going a little too fast and overshot the point at which they needed to turn into the jump. Of the fifteen horses that failed to complete the course, five came to grief at Fence 3 and, sadly, one of the female Canadian riders suffered a broken pelvis. So much for me requesting one of the easier fences! Thankfully, none of the horses was injured as a result of the falls.

Needless to say, the noise level of support from the supporters rose appreciably every time a British team member came through. First of the team to go was Number 9, Nicola Wilson. As the first one out, she had the added responsibility of reporting back to the rest of the team on how the course was riding and jumping. She jumped an immaculate and highly professional clear round and nobody should underestimate her immense contribution to what turned out to be a great team effort. Next to go was the popular and evergreen 51-year-old Mary King at Number 24. The volume pumped up even more as she completed another superb round, but even so that was nothing compared to the roar that greeted Zara Phillips as she went out, Number 40 of the seventy-four riders taking part. Given the deafening cacophony of noise that followed her all the way round I was amazed that she and her mount, High Kingdom, were able to maintain their concentration to complete another clear round. The decibel level was raised once again as Tina Cook contributed a third clear round at Number 56 and by the time William Fox-Pitt went out at Number 72 the team had moved into the silver medal position overall that they held onto in glorious style in the final day's Show Jumping section.

The last competitor of all to go out was veteran New Zealander Mark Todd, the great five-time Olympic gold medal winner – and then it was over for me. Nobody wanted to leave – the atmosphere was still buzzing. And yet the fence builders were already moving in to dismantle and remove the fences from the hallowed Greenwich Park ground.

In some ways, I suppose it was a bit of anti-climax. Our instructions were to wait until we were told to stand down by Vet

Control and then to return the medical kitbags and radios to the Athlete's Tent next to the cooling area, where the later horses were still being cooled off. And that was it. There was no de-briefing, no post-event party. A few of the vet team had a chat on the way out, all of us delighted with the way things had gone.

As I rather reluctantly headed off towards the main exit I found myself, quite by chance, walking behind the British team's four lady members, carrying their saddles. As they passed a group of cheering, flag-waving, camera-toting young fans, a smiling Mary King walked over to them and asked: "Would you like to have your picture taken with us?" You can imagine the response! What followed will remain my enduring memory of London 2012 – the four ladies from Team GB so generously vol-unteering to pose for pictures that will have made the day for those kids and probably served as an inspiration. What wonder-ful role models! I thought it was a magnificent gesture. After a good twenty minutes of snapping from all angles by an ever increasing crowd, Mary announced: "Just time for one more and then, as I am sure you will appreciate, we need to go and see to our horses." The happy youngsters thanked her profusely and dispersed very happily. I walked over to Mary and told her: "That was as good as a gold medal for those fans."

I, too, then joined the exodus from the Park and walked with the crowd towards Blackheath in search of liquid refreshment and the chance to sit down with a pint and reflect on the whole experience before heading back home to Oxfordshire with mixed feelings – happy that everything had gone so well, sad that it was all over.

I enjoyed it so much that I have already made tentative inquir-ies about the possibility of joining the Vet Team again at the next Olympics in Rio in 2016. I'll be seventy by then, so I guess they might think I'm a bit too old! But I'm working on it. As Jenny Hall agreed, experience will count for a lot. And on top of that, there can't be many specialist equine vets with a profes-sional pedigree going back more than 300 years!

Epilogue

I have been fortunate in so many ways. I was a late starter in the veterinary world, but armed with a respected surname and local knowledge going back many years, I was able to make up for that lost time. I have been brilliantly supported by my wife, Diana, and also by my two working partners, Steve and Simon. Together, with hard work and a large helping of luck, we were able to transform an old fashioned one-man veterinary practice into a modern day hospital, with up to seventeen full-time vets supported by part-timers, a skilled nursing staff, great receptionists, office, accounts and general staff. It is a team effort, covering equine, farm and small animals.

There have been plenty of ups and downs along the way, but it is during the down periods that the support of staff and colleagues can never be overstated. Even when the going got tough, I still thoroughly enjoyed the whole world of veterinary medicine – it was a privilege to work for, and with, so many loyal people.

Horse racing has smiled on me. I have had the opportunity to work with many magnificent horses and some very talented top-class trainers, but it is the jockeys for whom I have always had the greatest admiration. They are a tough, resilient fraternity, hard as nails, continually travelling the length and breadth of the country to ply their demanding trade. It is thanks to the Injured Jockeys Fund that they are able to receive the best of treatment and rehabilitation in times of need and can also be given valuable assistance in pursuing other careers when their racing days are finally over. I am therefore proud to donate a percentage of the proceeds from sales of this book towards improving the lot, in some small way, of these brave and often unsung heroes of the racing world.

As time marches on I did not want to stand in the way of new ideas and new developments, and wanted people to ask WHY and not WHEN I would be retiring. I still get a warm glow of satisfaction whenever I drive through the avenue of maturing lime trees to Whitehills Surgery, seeing how busy it is and how well organised things are. I am also certain that Jack Walker, glass in hand, will be looking down with approval from above – and maybe thinking that one day his great grandson Jack Lindsay might join the team!

Appendix

After my father died in 1988 I sorted through his veterinary books and catalogues and also his collection of medicinal recipes, some of them hand-written in old English copperplate. I was fascinated to read about the various concoctions he used, some referred to simply as 'Walker's Specials'. I was also struck by how painstaking and time-consuming the collection and preparation of all the different ingredients would have been.

My ancestors had no formal training and had learned their trade from their families and friends, and whilst they did not always know what had caused many of the diseases and conditions they had to deal with, they certainly knew how to cure presenting symptoms. Their powers of observation and the meticulous recording of animal behaviour that they encountered were quite outstanding. And now, sixty years later, I fully understand the pride and precision as well as the care and attention that went into the preparation of my father's unique range of cures.

I can see myself in the old white Surgery at Burmington, doing exactly as he told me, and listening as he stressed the importance of presentation. During his lifetime he kept all his old traditional remedies secret and I feel a bit guilty about revealing the precise measurements and mixing procedures involved, but technology in the drug manufacturing industry has obviously advanced rapidly in recent years and a lot of his old methods have long been superceded.

Apart from finding some of the handwriting illegible (not in his case – he had a precise, clear hand), I hadn't got a clue what some of the ingredients were. What on earth is Conosise Sublimate (mercuric chloride) or Hartshorn (ammonia solution) or White Vitriol (zinc sulphate)? However, with the considerable help of the MERCX Index, which lists most chemicals known, together with their alternative names, and after much research I eventually produced a booklet entitled "Walker's Wonder Cures" and I have selected a few of the recipes it contained to share with you.

Cough Powders

½ oz ginger
½ oz fenugreek
½ oz liquorice
½ oz arrowroot
½ oz lobelia powder
½ oz camphor

Mix up thoroughly and feed 1 tablespoonful twice daily.

Windy Colic Drink

1 oz spirits of turpentine
1 oz dulcified spirit of nitre
1 oz powdered bay berries
1 oz powdered ginger
½ oz oil of juniper
½ oz tincture of opium

Mix with a pint of warm beer and drench horse. Repeat twice daily until settled.

To Catch a Horse

1 oz oil of cumin
1 oz oil of cinnamon

Mix and put a few drops on the palm of your hand, and on your handkerchief.

Back Lotion

¼ oz sulphate of zinc
¼ oz sugar of lead
3 tablespoons brown vinegar
1 dessert spoonful of Epsom Salts

Put powder and vinegar into a 2 pint bottle and fill up with rain water.
Apply lotion when the back is warm. Give it a good soaking and leave for 12
hours. Keep the back warm with a sheet.

Leg Lotion

Take a 2-3 gallon wooden bucket (not metal). Put in a large lump of rock salt,
cover with 2 gallons of rain water. Add 8 oz saltpetre and 6 oz strong iodine and
mix well. Use 2 cotton bandages or material that doesn't tighten when water is
well salted. Soak the loosely rolled bandages in the solution so that it penetrates
them (stand bucket outside stable). Put bandages on the legs and change as often as
possible during the day. Don't leave on at night, use an ordinary bandage. You can
work the horse normally if there is no heat in the leg. Continue treatment through
the season if needed.

Curbs, Splints and Spavins

1 oz croton seeds steeped in 4 oz spirits of wine
3 oz euthorlium steeped in 4 oz methylated spirits

Leave for 3 weeks, strain and mix together.
Add ½ oz sulphuric acid very carefully and ½ oz chloroform.

Shake well and leave to stand for 12 hours until well cooked.
Clip the hair around the affected are and paint with a camel hair brush.

White Linament

2 oz acetic acid
1 oz spirits of turpentine
1 oz spirit of camphor
1 oz olive oil

Mix together well and rub into the affected area using the palm of your hand.

To Mouth a Horse

1 oz oil of cloves
Bind the bit with hemp and soak.

For Thrush in Feet

1 lb honey
1 oz iodoform
1 oz white vitriol (zinc sulphate)
Mix well and put on a piece of tow (coarse cotton wool). Dress daily.

Setfast Powders

Equal parts of:
  Aniseed powder
  Potassium nitrate
  Sulphur
  Colophony powder
Mix up well using a pestle and mortar to smooth the mixture.
Feed 1 dessertspoonful twice a week.

For a Bad Feeder

One gallon of urine
One handful of wormwood (absinth dried leaves and tops)
One handful of pine (pine oleo resin)
One handful of rosemary (dried leaves and tops)
1 oz tobacco

From the chamber pot collect one gallon of urine in a wooden bucket. With a spatula mix in all the other ingredients and let it stand covered for 3 days. Give one pint in its water first thing in the morning. Continue for 8 days.

Writing out these recipes brings back the atmosphere of the old white wooden shed, the smells, the aromas and the precision of his preparations. The memories remain so vivid, it could have been just yesterday.

Acknowledgements

I can't remember exactly when I started to think about writing this book, but it certainly seems like a long time ago. There have been many false dawns followed by the pledge that I will never put pen to paper again.

Thanks must go to my great friends Jenny Pitman, for writing the Foreword, Russell Collins, for coming up with the title, and Diana Webber for generously allowing me to use photographs from her family albums. Thanks also to Caroline Palmer for the cover photograph of me and the photograph of me with grandson Jack; to John Grossick for the cover photograph of Flying Instructor; and to cranhamphoto.com for the delightful photographs of Jenny Pitman with Royal Athlete and Garrison Savannah.

In addition, I would like to express my gratitude to Steve Glanvill and the staff at the Hook Norton Veterinary Surgery, who have been so supportive, not only with the marketing of this book, but in the way that they have been mainly responsible for dragging me into the modern world of technology.

Finally, I am indebted to my publisher, Mike Cable from Live Wire Books, who has listened to my ramblings patiently, and then polished and restructured my prose – and has done a magnificent job of making sense of it all. Also to my wife, Di, who has been a great encourager and an astute critic – and who had the unenviable task of transferring my handwritten chapters onto the computer. Without these two the book would not have been possible.

To all of you, a big thank you.